听力 阶梯

（第4版）

秦蕾 徐志敏 刘涓涓　主编

苗天幸 张志芳 刘长城 王越　副主编

Listening

Step by Step

人民邮电出版社

北　京

图书在版编目（ＣＩＰ）数据

听力阶梯 / 秦蕾，徐志敏，刘涓涓主编. -- 4版
-- 北京 : 人民邮电出版社，2020.9
ISBN 978-7-115-54398-1

Ⅰ. ①听… Ⅱ. ①秦… ②徐… ③刘… Ⅲ. ①英语—
听说教学—高等学校—习题集 Ⅳ. ①H319.9-44

中国版本图书馆CIP数据核字(2020)第116166号

内 容 提 要

　　本书分为基础篇、提高篇和强化篇。其中，基础篇为单词和短语的听写练习，帮助读者有效记忆核心词汇；提高篇讲解大学英语四、六级听力考试中的短对话、长对话、短文听力和复合式听写等各种具体题型的答题技巧，并为读者精心设计训练长对话和复合式听写的"过渡练习"；强化篇选择 10 套全真模拟题，帮助读者有计划地提高自己的听力水平。

　　本书内容多、容量大，可作为广大读者准备大学英语四、六级考试的首选教材。

◆ 主　编　秦　蕾　徐志敏　刘涓涓
　　副主编　苗天幸　张志芳　刘长城　王　越
　　责任编辑　刘向荣
　　责任印制　周昇亮

◆ 人民邮电出版社出版发行　　北京市丰台区成寿寺路 11 号
　　邮编　100164　　电子邮件　315@ptpress.com.cn
　　网址　https://www.ptpress.com.cn
　　北京天宇星印刷厂印刷

◆ 开本：787×1092　1/16
　　印张：15.5　　　　　　　2020 年 9 月第 4 版
　　字数：409 千字　　　　　2020 年 9 月北京第 1 次印刷

定价：49.80 元

读者服务热线：(010)81055256　印装质量热线：(010)81055316
反盗版热线：(010)81055315
广告经营许可证：京东市监广登字 20170147 号

前　言

学而不舍，循序渐进，日有所获，是为阶梯。《听力阶梯》取材广泛，为处于不同学习阶段，听力水平参差不齐的读者有计划、分步骤地提供阶梯式系统训练与答题解析。本书简明实用，强化词汇与听力的实训，非常有利于读者的词汇量与听力水平的稳步提升，对读者的英语学习可起到循序渐进的促进作用。本书是南京邮电大学从事大学英语教学的众多优秀教师多年教学经验的总结与集体智慧的结晶，也是为准备大学英语四、六级考试的同学量身定制的一本非常实用的听力与词汇教材。

本书分为以下三部分。

基础篇（Listen & Learn）

本书在基础篇独具匠心地设计了单词和短语的听写练习，听写的词汇和短语都是大学英语四级大纲的核心词汇与常用短语，并通过链接、词族和一词多义列举和解析了与核心词汇密切相关的词和词组。掌握这些词汇不仅对听力考试甚为必要，对英语基础能力的提高也非常有益。词汇按照从词到词组，再到句子的顺序循序渐进，帮助读者有效记忆核心词汇。同时，听写的句子大多是英语中的经典句子，可供读者赏析。

提高篇（Skill & Practice）

考试技巧是大学英语四、六级听力考试成功的重要一环。提高篇讲解大学英语四、六级听力考试中的短对话、长对话、短文听力和复合式听写的各种具体题型的答题技巧，并为读者设计了训练长对话和复合式听写的"过渡练习"。长对话通过分析语境、预判问题，让读者在听对话之前可以做到心中有数，胸有成竹；复合式听写大多选用了涉及热点问题的文章，帮助读者了解英语世界的新变化。提高篇是为了解决读者基本功薄弱，针对这两个方面的训练较少、方法不多等情况而精心设计的，也是本书区别于其他听力教材的特色和优势所在。

强化篇（Test Yourself）

强化篇精心选择了 10 套全真模拟题，帮助读者有计划地提高自己的听力测试水平。正所谓"工欲善其事，必先利其器"，读者在掌握了基本的答题技巧和答题方法后，准备听力考试最重要的一环莫过于不断地进行实战练习，因此找到好的听力材料进行真题练习，才是听力考试跨越巅峰的关键。本书中的全真模拟题在语音、语速和难度上与真题相仿，听力的题目类型、长度、难度完全按照大学英语四、六级考试大纲的要求设计，极其适合读者在大学英语四、六级考试复习的基础阶段使用，训练效果甚佳，对读者听力水平的提高非常有帮助。

感谢南京邮电大学外国语学院谢忠明老师对本书长期以来的关心和支持，并为本书的改版提供了大量的宝贵建议和素材。

编　者

目 录

基础篇

Listen & Learn

听录音，背单词，学句子，这是本书的独到之处。句子中所缺的单词多为大学英语四、六级核心高频词汇。题目的设计绝不局限于复合式听写中的单词听写训练，更是为了帮助同学们掌握这些核心词汇，从而为学习的进步打好坚实的基础。通过单词的听写，既可以锻炼同学们的听力，又可以帮助同学们记住这些核心的词汇。更为重要的是，这些句子中有许多是英语的经典句式，记住它们对于同学们的写作以及今后的英语学习大有裨益！同时，许多核心词汇都包含与该词有密切联系的词族、多义或链接，可帮助同学们非常有效地扩展词汇量，取得事半功倍的良好效果。

Part I   Word Dictation

Unit 1

1. Will it _____ you if I turn on the radio?
2. I do _____ about his real purpose.
3. The house is _____; even the nearest shore would be 20 miles away.
4. The tops of some mountains in this area are completely _____.
5. Dr. King _____ defended the civil right of black people.
6. When people become unemployed, it is _____ which is often worse than lack of wages.
7. Some people like doing shopping on Sundays so as to pick up some wonderful _____ in the market.
8. A goal is a dream with a _____.
9. The Great Wall is a wonderful tourist _____ to people both in and out of China.
10. The hopes and fears _____ significantly between the rich and the poor.
11. Corn _____ in American continent.
12. The organization is to _____ in people a love of art.
13. This kind of glasses _____ by experienced craftsman wears comfortably.
14. Some diseases are _____ by wild animals.
15. He is _____ about his chances of winning a gold medal in the game.
16. His old car _____ much gasoline.
17. The computer revolution may well change society as _____ as did the Industrial Revolution.

18. As we can no longer wait for the delivery of our order, we have to _____ it.
19. Young people are not _____ to stand and look at works of art; they want to _____ in.
20. People _____ on the square to celebrate the new birth of the nation.
21. Decoration of house would _____ a lot of work.
22. By living a thrift life he soon _____ a considerable amount of wealth.
23. Cancellation of the flight _____ many passengers to spend the night at the airport.
24. On New Year's Eve, New York City would hold an outdoor _____ which could attract a crowd of thousands of people.
25. If this kind of fish becomes _____, future generations may never taste it at all.
26. Speech _____ man from the animals.
27. The _____ pass mark in the examination is 60 out of 100.
28. Operations which left patients _____ and in need of long periods of recovery now leave them feeling relaxed and comfortable.
29. He _____ his wife and went away with all their money.
30. Almost everybody was moved by his _____ sorrow.

解析

1. bother
bother 表示打扰。
译文：我开收音机会不会打扰你？
链接：disturb 表示打扰。例，Please don't disturb：请勿打扰！ disturbing 表示烦人的。例，the disturbing noise：烦人的噪声。

2. wonder
wonder 表示怀疑、想知道、奇怪。
译文：我真怀疑他的真实目的。
一词多义：wonder 名词表示奇迹。
常用词组：work wonder：创造奇迹。
例，So long as you persist to your dream, your endeavor would at last work wonders. 只要你坚持自己的梦想，你的努力最终一定会创造奇迹。
链接：work magic; move the mountain 都表示创造奇迹、取得美妙的结果之意。

3. isolated
isolate 表示使隔绝。
译文：房子比较偏远，即使最近的海滩也在20英里之外。
常用词组：isolate oneself from：把自己与……隔绝起来。例，He often isolated himself from society. 他经常将自己和社会隔绝开来。

4. bare
bare 表示裸露的、光秃的。例，bare land 不毛之地；bare foot 赤脚。
译文：这个地区有些山顶光秃秃的。
链接：bald 表示秃顶，例，Nowadays more and more young people become bald under the pressure from life and work. 今天越来越多的年轻人在生活和工作的压力下开始谢顶了。naked 表示裸露的（身体）：a naked child。barely 表示几乎没、几乎不，例，I can barely understand her. 我几乎不能理解她。barely nothing：几乎没有。

友情提醒：与 bare 发音相同的词 bear 表示①熊，②忍受。例，I cannot bear your bad manners. 我无法忍受你粗鲁的举止。

5．vigorously

vigorously 表示强有力的、精力充沛的。

译文：金博士（指马丁·路德·金——famous civil rights movement leader in American history 美国历史上著名的民权运动领袖）奋力保护黑人的民权。

词族：vigor 表示精力、活力。例，He is a man full of passion and vigor. 他是一个充满激情和活力的人。

6．idleness

idleness 表示无聊、赋闲无事。

译文：当人们失业时，赋闲无事比没有工资更为糟糕。

词族：idle（1）形容词：①无聊的、游手好闲的。例，When the machine break down, all workers were left idle. 机器一坏，工人们都无事可做。②无聊的。例，Don't talk about those idle words anymore.（2）动词：①不做事、游手好闲。例，He was idling on the street the whole day. 他一整天都在街上闲逛。② idle away 消磨时间，同 kill time。例，He just watches television to idle away time.

7．bargains

bargain（1）名词：契约、便宜货。例，It's a real bargain. 这买卖真是不错。（2）动词：讨价还价、议价。例，If you **bargain with** them they might reduce the price. 你如果还价，他们可能会把价钱降低。

译文：有些人喜欢在周日买东西，以便在市场上挑到一些便宜货。

8．deadline

deadline 表示最后期限。

译文：人的目标就是有期限的梦。

9．attraction

attraction 表示吸引。

译文：长城是吸引中外游客的旅游胜地。

词族：（1）动词：attract 表示吸引。

（2）形容词：attractive 表示吸引人的。例，She has a pleasant personality as well as an attractive appearance.

10．vary

vary 表示变化、存在不同。

译文：富人和穷人的希望与恐惧截然不同。

词族：（1）形容词：various 表示各种各样的、不同的。例，for various reasons：各种各样的原因。（2）名词：variety 表示多样性、变化，固定搭配 a variety of 与 various 意思相同。例，a variety of goods：各种各样的商品。

链接：（1）diverse 表示不同的、多样化的。例，diverse interests：不同的兴趣。（2）diversity 表示差异、多样性，例，a diversity of culture：文化的多样性。

11．originated

originate 表示起源于，originate in 是固定搭配，与另一常用词组 stem from 意思相同。

译文：玉米的原产地是美洲大陆。

词族：（1）形容词：original 表示原始的、最初的、原创的。（2）名词：origin 表示起源、血统。例，origin of man：人类的起源。例，Many Americans were African by origin. 许多美

国人是非洲血统。

12．cultivate

cultivate 表示培养、开垦。uncultivated 表示未经开垦的，例，uncultivated land：未经开垦的土地、处女地。

译文：该组织的目的是培养人们对艺术的爱好（兴趣）。

13．manufactured

manufacture 表示生产。

译文：这种由有经验的工匠制作的眼镜戴起来很舒适。

友情提醒：当 wear 表示穿起来、戴起来的意思时，不可以使用被动语态，如：It wears comfortable。同类的词还有 smell、taste 等。

14．transmitted

transmit 表示传输、传播。

译文：有些疾病是通过野生动物传播的。

词族：transmission，常用表达：data transmission: 数据传输。

15．optimistic

optimistic 表示乐观的，常用表达：be optimistic about。

译文：他对在运动会上获得金牌非常乐观。

16．consumes

consume 表示消耗、消费。

译文：他的老款车耗油量很大。

词族：（1）consumption 表示消费。例，The nation's consumption of coal decreased continuously last year. 去年全国耗煤量持续下降。（2）consumer 表示消费者。常用表达：cost-consuming：耗钱的；energy-consuming：消耗精力；time-consuming：耗时的。例，The project is both cost-consuming and time-consuming. 该工程既耗钱又耗时间。

17．fundamentally

fundamentally 表示根本地、基础地。

译文：计算机革命将如同工业革命那样使社会发生根本改变。

18．cancel

cancel 表示取消。

译文：因为我们不能继续等我们订购的货物了，于是决定取消订单。

词族：名词：cancellation。

链接：call off 与 cancel 都表示取消。例，The meeting has been cancelled (called off). 会议被取消了；postpone 与 put off 则表示推迟。

19．content；participate

（1）content 表示满意的，be content to 是固定搭配；（2）participate 表示参与、参加，participate in 是固定搭配。

译文：年轻人不满足于成为艺术作品的旁观者，他们想参与其中。

一词多义：content 作为名词表示内容、目录（常用复数形式）。例，contents of a book：书的目录（或内容）。

20．assembled

assemble 表示聚集。

译文：人们聚集在广场庆祝这个国家的新生。

一词多义：assemble 作动词表示装配。例，assemble a machine：装配机器。

21. involve

involve 表示涉及、包括、使陷入。常用词组：get involved in (with) 卷入（为……所缠）

译文：房屋的装修涉及很多工作。

22. accumulates

accumulate 表示积累、集聚。

译文：通过节俭的生活，他很快积累了大量的财富。

23. obliged

oblige 表示迫使，常用表达：oblige somebody to do，也可以表达为 force somebody to do。

译文：航班的取消迫使乘客们在机场过夜。

24. event

event 表示活动。

译文：在新年前夜，纽约市都会举行室外盛会，吸引成千上万的市民到场。

一词多义：event 作名词，表示事件。例，historical event：历史事件。

25. scarce

scarce 表示缺乏的、不足的、稀有的。

译文：如果这种鱼变得越来越稀有，我们的后代可能永远也品尝不到了。

链接：表示动物稀有的词类还有（1）rare animal 表示稀有动物。（2）endangered animal 表示濒危动物。（3）extinct animal 表示灭绝的动物。

26. distinguishes

distinguish 表示区别、区分，tell ... from ... 也表示区分。例，I cannot tell Rose from Mary as they are so similar in style. Rose 和 Mary 风格如此相似，我无法区分她们。

译文：言语使人区别于动物。

27. minimum

minimum 表示最小值。例，minimum wage：最低工资。

译文：考试的最低及格分数是 60 分，总分 100 分。

词族：minimize 将……降到最低。例，The company tries every means to minimize the loss. 公司想尽一切办法将损失降到最低。

链接：maximum 表示最大值；maximize 表示将……最大化。例，Almost all merchants are prone to maximize their profit. 几乎所有的商人都倾向于将他们的利润最大化。

28. exhausted

exhausted 表示筋疲力尽的、疲惫不堪的。

译文：曾经使病人疲惫不堪、需要很长恢复期的手术现在让他们感到轻松而舒适。

29. abandoned

abandon 表示抛弃、离弃。

译文：他抛弃了妻子还带走了两人所有的钱。

一词多义：（1）放弃。例，They abandoned their plan in the midway. 他们中途放弃了他们的计划。（2）放纵、放任。例，He abandoned himself to despair. 他彻底自暴自弃了。

链接：（1）desert 表示遗弃、放弃。例，He deserted his wife and child and ran away. 他抛妻弃子离家出走了。（2）discard 动词表示丢弃、抛弃。例，discard old beliefs：抛弃陈旧的观念；作为名词表示废品、废料。例，the discards of society：为社会所抛弃的人。

30. intense

intense 表示剧烈的、强烈的、热情的（即程度深的）。例，intense heat：酷热；intense pain：剧痛。

译文：几乎所有人都为他极度的悲伤所触动。

链接：（1）tense 表示紧张的，拉紧的。例，The players were tense at the start of the game. 队员们在比赛开始时很紧张。tense muscles：绷紧的肌肉。（2）dense 表示密集的。例，This area is densely populated. 这个地区人口密集。

Unit 2

1. According to the American federal government, residents of Hawaii have the longest average life _____: 77.2 years.
2. The millions of calculations _____, had they been done by hand, would have lost all _____ value by the time they were finished.
3. Before they could start a storm _____.
4. With the development of science and technology, man can make various flowers _____ before their time.
5. A season ticket _____ the holder to make as many journeys as he wishes within the stated period of time.
6. _____ the new production line will be a _____ deal for the company.
7. Calvin is _____ to get a seat for the concert even if it means standing in a queue all night.
8. The car club could _____ to meet the demands of all its members.
9. I can _____ you of the reliability of the news.
10. Extensive reporting on television has helped to _____ interest in a wide _____ of sports and activities.
11. The president promised to keep all the board members _____ of the proceeding of the negotiation.
12. Eating too much fat can _____ to high blood pressure and cause heart disease.
13. Petrol is _____ from the _____ oil we take out of the ground.
14. He is quite sure it's _____ impossible for him to _____ the task within two days.
15. In the Chinese _____, grandparents and other relatives play _____ roles in raising children.
16. Eye contact is important because wrong contact may create a communication _____.
17. There is no _____ to the house from the main road.
18. _____ energy under the earth must be _____ in one form or another, for example, an earthquake.
19. He wasn't _____ chairman of the committee.
20. Attractive _____ is very necessary.
21. This can has a _____ of four liters.
22. They are _____ although they are poor.
23. The government of that nation tends to adopt an _____ foreign policy.
24. The statistical _____ in that survey are not _____.
25. He _____ to his customers and halved the price.
26. The author of the report is well _____ with the problems in that nation.
27. The ship's generator _____, and the pumps had to be operated _____ instead of mechanically.

28. This brand of tinned beans contains no _____ coloring.
29. There has been a _____ increase in _____ sales.
30. We'd like to _____ a table for five for dinner this evening.

解析

1. span

span（1）**名词**表示跨度、间距。例，a span of 1 000 meters：跨度为一千米。life span 为固定表达，表示寿命。（2）**动词**表示持续、延续。例，a memory that spans 30 years：持续 30 年的记忆。

译文：根据美国联邦政府的报告，夏威夷居民的平均寿命最长，为 77.2 岁。

2. involved；practical

involve 表示涉及，involved 在本句中是过去分词后置作定语。had they been done by hand 是虚拟语气，即 if they had been done by hand。

practical 表示实际的、实用的。

译文：涉及数以百万计的计算，倘若以人工完成，到完成时将失去其所有的实用价值。

3. arose

arise 表示引起、发生。

译文：在他们出发前一场风暴已经发生了。

链接：常用词组 give rise to 表示引起。例，His smoking has given rise to a fire. 他抽烟引起了火灾。

4. bloom

bloom 表示开花、使繁荣。例，A variety of ideas became bloomed during the period. 各种各样的观点在那个时期繁荣起来。

译文：伴随着科技的发展，人类可以让各种各样的花提前开放。

5. entitles

entitle 表示授权、赋予……的权利，一般表达为 entitle somebody to do。

译文：季票持有者在规定的时间内可以自由旅行。

6. Purchasing；profitable

（1）purchase 表示购买。常用表达，purchasing power：购买力。（2）profitable 表示可盈利的。

译文：购买新的生产线对公司来说将是赚钱的买卖。

7. determined

determine 表示决定、使下定决心，既可以用主动语态的 determine to do 表示决定做……，又可以用被动形式的 be determined to do 表示下定决心做……。

译文：凯文决心弄到一张演唱会的门票，哪怕这意味着要通宵排队。

词族：（1）determined 表示坚决的。例，a strongly determined man：一个坚定的人。（2）determination 表示决心、果敢。例，That girl has great determination, I am sure she will do well. 那女孩子决心很大，我肯定她会做好的。

8. guarantee

guarantee 表示担保、保证、承诺。例，Many shopkeepers guarantee satisfaction to customers. 许多店主对顾客承诺保证让他们满意。

译文：该汽车俱乐部保证满足会员的需要。

9. <u>assure</u>

assure 表示断然地说、保证，带有很强的主观性。

译文：我可以向你保证这消息的可靠性。

链接：（1）ensure 表示确保、保证，往往指采取客观的保障来确保达到一定的结果。例，I fitted a new lock to ensure that the bicycle would not be stolen. 我装了一把新锁以确保自行车不致失窃。（2）assured 表示确定的、有保证的。例，you may rest assured that... ：对……您尽可放心。

10. <u>generate</u>；<u>variety</u>

（1）generate 表示产生、发生、引起。（2）variety 表示品种、种类、多样性。a variety of 为固定表达，表示各种各样的。

译文：电视的广泛报道激起了人们对各种体育活动的兴趣。

词族：vary；various；varied。

（1）vary 表示变化、不同、改变。例，The weather varies distinctly from season to season in areas other than in equatorial region. 除了在赤道地区，天气会随着四季明显发生变化。（2）various 表示不同的、各种各样的，与 a variety of 意思相同（强调多样）。（3）varied 表示各式各样的、不同的。例，varied opinions 不同的观点（强调不同）。

11. <u>informed</u>

inform 表示通知、告知。固定搭配：inform somebody of，告知某人……

译文：董事长承诺让每一名董事随时知悉谈判的进行情况。

词族：informed 表示见多识广的，例，a well-informed man：一个见多识广的人。

12. <u>contribute</u>

contribute 表示捐助、捐赠。contribute to 为固定表达，表示有助于、促进。例，Plenty of fresh air contributes to good health. 大量的新鲜空气有助于身体健康。

译文：摄入过量的脂肪会导致高血压，进一步导致心脏病。

13. <u>refined</u>；<u>crude</u>

（1）refine 表示提炼、使……更精致。（2）crude 表示天然的、粗糙的。例，crude salt：粗制盐。

译文：汽油是从地下开采的石油提炼而成的。

14. <u>absolutely</u>；<u>fulfill</u>

（1）absolutely 表示绝对地。（2）fulfill 表示实现、完成。例，fulfill his long dream (desire)：实现他的梦想（愿望）。fulfill the task：完成任务。

译文：他非常肯定要他在两天内完成任务是绝对不可能的。

15. <u>household</u>；<u>indispensable</u>

（1）household 表示一家人、家庭或家庭的、家用的。例，household affairs：家务事。（2）indispensable 表示不可缺少的、绝对必要的。

译文：中国家庭的祖父母和其他一些亲戚在抚养孩子方面起着不可或缺的作用。

16. <u>barrier</u>

barrier 表示障碍、屏障、壁垒。例，trade barrier：贸易壁垒。

译文：视线交流很重要，因为错误的交流可能产生交流的障碍。

17. <u>access</u>

access 表示通道、入门。have an access to something 表示可以接触、获得某样东西。

译文：主干道不能直达房子。

词族：accessible 表示可接近的、可获得的、可到达的。例，The books in this library is also accessible to students. 这个图书馆的书同样对学生开放。反义词：inaccessible 表示不可获得的。

注意：不论是名词access还是形容词accessible往往都与介词to搭配。

18. Accumulated; released
（1）accumulated 表示累积的、积聚的。（2）release 表示释放。release somebody from：把某人从……解脱出来。
译文：地下积聚的能量必须以某种形式释放出来，例如地震。

19. appointed
appoint 表示任命、制定。
译文：他没有被任命为委员会主席。
一词多义：appoint 表示指定、约定。例，to appoint a time for the meeting：指定开会时间。
词族：appointment（1）表示约会。例，I made an appointment to see the doctor. 我约定了看医生的时间。（2）表示任命。例，The appointment of the chairman made many people disappointed. 主席的任命让很多人感到失望。

20. label
label 表示标签，商标；也可以用作动词表示贴上标签，标示。例，The bottle is labeled poison. 瓶上标明有毒。
译文：具有吸引力的标签非常必要。

21. capacity
capacity 表示容量、容积。
译文：这个罐的容量有四升。

22. ambitious
ambitious 表示有雄心的、野心勃勃的。
译文：他们虽穷却很有志气。
词族：名词 ambition 表示野心、雄心。例，He is a man full of ambition. 他是个野心勃勃的人。

23. aggressive
aggressive 表示好斗的、咄咄逼人的、侵略性的。
译文：那个国家的政府往往采取强硬的外交政策。

24. figures; accurate
（1）figure 表示数字。（2）accurate 表示精确的。
译文：调查中的统计数字不精确。
一词多义：figure（1）作名词表示外形、轮廓。例，do exercises to improve one's figure：锻炼改善身材。表示人物，例，a great figure in history：历史上的伟大人物。（2）作动词表示演算、考虑。常用词组，figure out：计算出、领会、想出。例，I couldn't figure out who the lady with the sunglasses was. 我想不出戴太阳镜的那位夫人是谁。

25. yielded
yield (to) 表示屈服、让步。
译文：他向客户做出让步，将价格减半。
一词多义：（1）作动词表示生产、结果。例，The tree yields fruits in autumn. 这种树在秋天结果。（2）作名词表示产量、收益。例，This year's yield from the coal mine was

very large. 这个煤矿今年产量颇丰。

26．acquainted

acquaint 表示使熟知。常用搭配：be acquainted with 表示知道、了解。

词族：acquaintance 表示相识、熟人。

译文：报告的作者对那个国家的问题了如指掌。

27．broke down；manually

（1）break down 表示毁坏、瘫痪。（2）manually 表示手工的。

译文：船的发动机发生故障，只好用人工代替机械操作水泵。

28．artificial

artificial 表示人造的、假的。常用表达，artificial intelligence：人工智能。

译文：这种品牌的罐装青豆不含人造色素。

29．considerable；retail

（1）considerable 表示客观的、大量的。（2）retail 表示零售的。

译文：零售增长相当可观。

链接：形近词 considerate 表示体贴的。例，It's very considerate of you to bring the coat for me. 你给我带了衣服来真是太体贴了。retail 的对应词是 wholesale，表示批发。

30．reserve

reserve 表示预定、保留。

译文：我们想预订一张今晚晚餐的五人桌。

Unit 3

1．The drug may _____ you of the pain to some extent.

2．The unexpected rainstorm caused the _____ of the roof.

3．Gas was _____ out of the pipe.

4．He cannot _____ an apartment.

5．She could hardly _____ the temptation of delicious food.

6．The team leader _____ everyone to follow his example.

7．Their products are frequently overpriced and _____ in quality.

8．To our _____, his illness proved not to be as serious as we feared.

9．Many African people like white color as it is a _____ of purity.

10．If you are _____ you will study for another year.

11．He couldn't _____ for his foolish mistake.

12．Some people go back for their education to _____ another degree or _____ to impress the society.

13．The shop assistant was dismissed as she was _____ of cheating customers.

14．How much did he _____ you for repairing the bicycle?

15．Everyone should be _____ to a decent standard of living and an opportunity to be educated.

16．The markings are so blurred that it is difficult to _____.

17．Apart from caring for her children, she has taken on such heavy _____ housework as carrying water and firewood.

18．The police are trying to find out the _____ of the woman killed in the traffic accident.

19. We have planned a publicity _____ with our advertisers.
20. Owing to _____ competition among airlines, travel _____ have been reduced considerably.
21. The hotel _____ our reservations by telegram.
22. A fire engine must have _____ as it usually has to deal with some kind of _____.
23. John doesn't believe in _____ medicine; and he has some _____ of his own.
24. The film gives a deep _____ into a wide range of human souls.
25. We should concentrate on reducing interest rates to pull the economy out of _____.
26. The _____ of finding gold in California attracted a lot of people to _____ down there.
27. I suffered from mental _____ because of stress from my job.
28. The rest of the day was entirely at his _____ for reading or recreation.
29. You will not be _____ about your food in time of hunger.
30. _____ is increasing worldwide, and there is every reason to believe the _____ will continue into the next decade.

解析

1. relieve
relieve 表示减轻、减缓，常用搭配：relieve somebody of the pain 表示缓解某人的痛楚。
译文：药会在某种程度上减轻你的痛楚。
词族：relief 表示（痛楚）减轻、安慰、解脱。例，I felt great relief when I heard I had passed the examination. 听说我已经通过了考试，我感到轻松多了。

2. collapse
collapse 作名词表示倒塌、崩溃，也可以用作动词，意思相同。例，The roof of the old house collapsed. 这座旧房子的房顶坍塌了。
译文：突然来临的暴风雨使屋顶坍塌了。

3. leaking
leak 表示泄漏、渗出。例，The negotiations between the two parties were leaked to the press. 双方的谈判内容泄漏给新闻界了。
译文：煤气正从管子里泄漏出来。

4. afford
afford 表示负担得起。
译文：他负担不起一套住房。

5. resist
resist 表示抗拒。一般用 resist doing something 表示抗拒做某事。
译文：她经受不住美食的诱惑。

6. inspired
inspire 表示激励、启发。
译文：团队的领头人激励每个人向他学习。

7. inferior
inferior 表示劣等的、次品的。常用表达 be inferior to：比……低劣的。
译文：他们的产品往往价高且质次。
链接：反义词 superior 表示上好的、优等的。常用表达，be superior to：比……优的。

8. relief

relief 表示安慰、解脱、松一口气。

译文：让我们宽慰的是他的疾病没有我们担心的那么严重。

9. symbol

symbol 表示象征。

译文：很多非洲人喜欢白色，因为它是纯洁的象征。

10. sensible

sensible 表示明智的。

译文：如果你明智的话，你就再学习一年。

链接：形近词 sensitive 表示敏感的。例，She is sensitive to what people think of her. 她对人们的评价很是敏感。

11. account

account (for) 表示解释、说明。

译文：他无法解释他所犯的愚蠢错误。

词族：名词（1）表示考虑。常用词组 take … into account 意同 take… into consideration，表示把……考虑在内。（2）表示账户。例，My account is empty. 我的账户没钱了。

12. acquire ; diploma

（1）acquire 表示获得。（2）diploma 表示文凭。

译文：有些人回到学校去接受教育，再取得一个学位或一张文凭，以提高自己在社会上的地位。

链接：形近词 enquire 表示问询，也可作 inquire ; require 表示要求、指令。

13. accused

accuse 表示谴责、指控，be accused of 为固定表达，表示被谴责。

译文：这名店员被解雇了，因为她被指控欺骗顾客。

14. charge

charge 表示收费。

译文：他修理自行车收了你多少钱？

一词多义：动词（1）表示指控。例，He was charged with stealing a car. 他被指控偷了一辆汽车。其中 be charged with 为固定搭配，请注意与前面 13 题 be accused of 相区分。（2）表示充电。例，Does your car battery charge easily? 你那辆汽车的蓄电池容易充电吗？

15. justified

justify 表示具有正当理由的、证明……是正当的。

译文：每个人都有权享有体面的生活和受教育的机会。

16. identify

identify 表示识别、辨认出。

译文：标记如此模糊以致难以识别。

17. time-consuming

time-consuming 表示耗时的；consume 表示消耗；-consuming 为固定构词方式，表示消耗……，如 energy-consuming 表示消耗精力。

译文：除了要照顾孩子，她还要承担繁重而耗时的家务活，例如挑水、捡柴。

18. identity

identity 表示身份。

译文：警方正努力调查在交通事故中丧生的女子的身份。

19. <u>campaign</u>

campaign 表示战役、运动、活动,如美国的大选活动叫作 election campaign。

译文:我们已经和我们的广告商策划了一次广告宣传活动。

20. <u>fierce</u>;<u>expenses</u>

(1)fierce 表示激烈的、猛烈的、凶猛的。例,fierce animals:凶猛的野兽。(2)expenses 表示费用、开支、开销。

译文:由于航空公司间的激烈竞争,旅行费用大大地降低了。

21. <u>confirmed</u>

confirm 表示确认、核实。

译文:旅馆来电确认我们的预订。

22. <u>priority</u>;<u>emergency</u>

(1)priority 表示优先权。常用表达 have priority 或 take priority:具有优先权。(2)emergency 表示紧急状况。常用表达 in case of emergency:在紧急状况下。

译文:消防车具有优先(通过)权,因为它通常要处理一些紧急状况。

23. <u>conventional</u>;<u>remedies</u>

(1)conventional 表示传统的、习惯的、常规的。例,conventional weapons:常规武器。(2)remedy 表示治疗方法、救济、补偿。例,Your only remedy is to resort to law. 你唯一的补救方法就是诉诸法律。

译文:约翰不相信传统的药物,他有自己的医疗方法。

24. <u>insight</u>

insight 表示洞察力、深刻的见解。

译文:影片广泛深刻地洞察了人类的心灵。

25. <u>recession</u>

recession 表示衰退、不景气。

译文:我们应极力降低利率,使经济摆脱不景气。

26. <u>prospects</u>;<u>settle</u>

(1)prospect 表示前景。(2)settle 表示解决、定居。settle down 为固定搭配,表示定居下来。

译文:在加州可以找到黄金的前景吸引了很多人到那里定居。

词族: prospective 表示预期的。例,prospective benefits:预期的收益。

27. <u>fatigue</u>

(1)fatigue 表示疲劳、疲乏。例,metal fatigue:金属疲劳。(2)stress 表示压力、重压。

译文:因为工作上的压力,我不得不承受精神上的痛苦。

28. <u>disposal</u>

disposal 表示处理、处置。常用词组 at one's disposal:供某人处理、由某人处置。

译文:那天余下的时间由他自由安排,或看书或娱乐。

29. <u>particular</u>

particular 表示特别的。常用表达 be particular about:对……很挑剔、吹毛求疵。

译文:饥饿的时候你就不会对食物挑三拣四了。

链接: 与 be particular about 意思相近的词组有(1)find fault with 表示对……挑剔。(2)be critical about 表示对……挑剔。

30. <u>Crime</u>;<u>trend</u>

(1)crime 表示犯罪。(2)trend 表示趋势。

译文:犯罪在世界范围内增长,而且我们有充分理由相信这种趋势将延续到下个十年。

Unit 4

1. You shouldn't have written in the _____ since the book belongs to the library.
2. The _____ of airplane engines announced another coming air_____ .
3. The dress _____ when I washed it.
4. He was proud of being chosen to _____ in the games, and he _____ us that he would try as hard as possible.
5. A dark suit is _____ to a light one for evening wear.
6. A culture in which the citizens share similar _____ beliefs and values is more likely to have laws that represent the wishes of its people than is a culture where citizens come from _____ backgrounds.
7. He gave a _____ to handle the issue in a friendly manner.
8. Many people lost their jobs during the business _____ .
9. Mr. Smith was the only _____ who said that the fire was _____ .
10. He was such a _____ speaker that he held our attention every minute of the lecture.
11. Because of a _____ _____ Lora couldn't attend my birthday party last Saturday.
12. Not having a good _____ of English can be a serious _____ preventing you from _____ your goals.
13. It's very _____ of you not to talk aloud while the baby is asleep.
14. All their attempts to _____ the child from the burning building were in _____ .
15. The university has _____ a research center to develop new ways of _____ bacteria which have become _____ to drug treatments.
16. There is no solid _____ that people can control their dreams, at least in _____ situations.
17. So far, _____ winds and currents have kept the thick patch of oil southeast of the Atlantic _____ .
18. Some plants are very _____ to light; and they prefer the _____ .
19. As one of the world's highest paid models, she had her face _____ for five million dollars.
20. Ten days ago the young man informed his boss of his intention to _____ .
21. Only those who can _____ to lose their money should make high-risk _____ .
22. During the lecture, the speaker occasionally _____ his point by relating his own experiences.
23. It is obvious that this new rule is _____ to everyone without _____ .
24. Last night he saw two dark _____ enter the building, and then there was the _____ .
25. This is what you should bear in mind: Don't _____ on a salary increase before you actually get it.
26. Science and technology have _____ in great ways to the improvement of agricultural production.
27. Salaries for _____ positions seem to be higher than for _____ ones.
28. Norman Davis will be remembered by many with _____ not only as a great scholar but also as a most delightful and _____ friend.
29. Can you give me even the slightest _____ as to where her son might be?
30. Tomorrow the mayor is to _____ a group of Canadian businessmen on a tour of the city.

📝 **解析**

1. margin

margin 表示页边的空白、边、缘。例，the margin of river：河边。

译文：你不应该在页边上写字，因为书是图书馆的。

词族：marginal（1）页边的。（2）边际的。例，marginal efficiency：边际效应。marginal cost：边际成本。二者都是经济学的重要概念。

2. roar；raid

（1）roar 表示呼啸、吼叫。（2）raid 表示袭击。

译文：飞机引擎的轰鸣声预示着又一场空袭的到来。

3. shrank

shrank 为 shrink 的过去式，表示收缩。

译文：这件衣服洗后缩水了。

4. participate；assured

（1）participate 表示参与。participate in 为固定搭配，表示参加。（2）assure 表示保证、信誓旦旦地说。

译文：他为被选中参加比赛而感到自豪，并且向我们保证他会竭尽全力。

5. preferable

preferable 表示更可取的、更好的、更适合的。be preferable to 为固定搭配，表示前者比后者更适合。

译文：深色西服比浅色西服更适合做晚装。

6. religious；diverse

（1）religious 表示宗教的。（2）diverse 表示各种各样的、多样化的。

译文：与公民有不同背景的文化相比，公民有相同宗教信仰和价值观的文化更可能产生体现民意的法律。

7. pledge

（1）pledge 表示保证、发誓，也可用作动词，表示担保、发誓。例，pledge one's support：发誓支援。（2）manner 表示礼貌、举止、方式。例，in good manner：有礼貌的。

译文：他发誓要友好地解决这个问题。

8. depression

depression 表示萧条，business depression 表示经济萧条，注意区分 economic recession：经济衰退。

译文：很多人在经济萧条时期失业。

一词多义：depression 更常用的意思是沮丧、消沉。例，A long holiday will certainly help relieve his depression. 长假一定会有助于缓解他的消沉。

9. witness；deliberate

（1）witness 表示目击者，可用作动词表示目睹、目击。例，The first decade of 21st century would continue to witness a fast economic development in China. 21 世纪的第一个十年必将继续目睹中国经济的快速增长。（2）deliberate 表示故意的。

译文：史密斯先生是目击者中唯一认为是有人故意纵火的。

10. dynamic

dynamic 表示精力充沛的、有活力的。

译文：他是个如此富有活力的演讲者，我们的注意力全程被他紧紧抓住。

一词多义：dynamic 还可以表示动力的、动态的、动力学的，同 static（静态的、静力的）相对应。

11. prior；engagement

（1）prior 表示在前的、优先的。常用搭配 be prior to：在……之前、优于……（2）engagement 表示约定，另外还有订婚的意思，请同学们注意。

译文：因为一个先前的约定，劳拉无法参加我上周六的生日聚会。

12. command；obstacle；achieving

（1）command 表示掌握、命令。（2）obstacle 表示障碍。（3）achieve 表示实现、获得。

译文：英语掌握不好，可能会成为你实现目标的严重障碍。

13. considerate

considerate 表示体贴的、周到的。

译文：你真体贴，孩子睡觉时你没有大声讲话。

链接：形近词 considerable 表示大量的、相当可观的。

14. rescue；vain.

（1）rescue 表示拯救。（2）vain 徒然的、无益的、虚荣的。in vain 为固定搭配，表示白费地，徒劳无益地。

译文：从着火的房子中拯救孩子的所有尝试都没有成功。

15. launched；combating；resistant

（1）launch 表示发起、发射。（2）combat 表示战斗、搏斗、抗击。（3）resistant 表示抵抗的、有抵抗力的。例，cold resistant crops：抗寒的庄稼。

译文：学校成立了一个研究中心，以开发抗击对药物治疗已形成抵抗力的细菌的新方法。

链接：resist 及物动词表示抵抗、抗拒。例，resist the temptation of smoking：抗拒吸烟的诱惑。另外，一般用 resist doing 表示抗拒做某事。

16. evidence；experimental

（1）evidence 表示证据，solid evidence 表示确凿的证据。（2）experimental 表示实验的。

译文：没有确凿的证据表明人可以控制自己的梦境，至少在实验的情况下如此。

17. prevailing；coast

（1）prevailing 表示占优势的、盛行的、主导的、主流的。（2）coast 表示海岸。

译文：目前为止，盛行的风和洋流把厚厚的油层淤积在大西洋的东南海岸。

18. sensitive；shade

（1）sensitive 表示敏感的，be sensitive to 为固定搭配，表示过敏、灵敏。（2）shade 表示阴凉处、荫。

译文：有些植物对光很敏感，他们喜阴。

19. insured

insure 表示给……保险。

译文：作为世界上薪酬最高的模特之一，她给自己的脸投保了 500 万美元。

词族：名词 insurance，例，insurance company：保险公司。

20. resign

resign 表示辞职。

译文：十天前，那个年轻人告知了老板自己辞职的想法。

21. afford；investments

（1）afford 表示承担得起，通常表达为 afford to do 或 afford something，表示承担（做）某事。（2）investment 表示投资。

译文：只有能承担得起亏钱的人才能进行高风险投资。

22. illustrated

illustrate 表示阐述、说明。

译文：在演讲过程中，演讲人偶尔会用自己的亲身经历来阐述他的观点。

23. applicable；exception

（1）applicable 表示适用于。（2）exception 表示例外。

译文：很明显，这条新规则适用于每一个人。

词族：（1）apply 表示申请，通常和 for 连用。例，apply for the position of sales manager in your company：申请贵公司销售经理的职位。application 是名词，表示申请。例，a letter of application：一封申请信。（2）exceptional 表示例外的、特别的。例，He is exceptionally smart. 他特别聪明。

一词多义：apply/application 还可以表示应用。例，The principle of diligence and frugality applies to all undertakings. 勤俭节约的原则适用于一切事业。This new invention has little value of practical application. 这项新发明几乎没有什么实用价值。

24. figures；explosion

（1）figure 表示身影。（2）explosion 表示爆炸。

译文：昨夜他看到两个身影潜入大厦，然后爆炸就发生了。

25. count

count 表示数、计算。count on 是固定词组，表示指望、依赖。

译文：你应该记住：在真正得到加薪之前，不要指望它。

26. contributed

contribute 表示贡献，contribute to 是固定搭配，表示捐献、促成。

译文：科学和技术对农业生产做出了巨大贡献。

27. temporary；permanent

（1）temporary 表示暂时的、临时的。（2）permanent 表示永久性的。例，a permanent damage 永久性损伤。

译文：临时性职位的薪水似乎比永久性的要高。

28. affection；faithful

（1）affection 表示爱、友爱、真爱。（2）faithful 表示忠诚的，与 loyal 意思相同。

译文：诺曼·戴维斯将不仅作为一个伟大的学者，而且作为一个令人愉快的、忠诚的朋友为许多人爱戴和牢记。

29. clue

clue 表示线索。

译文：她儿子有可能在哪里，你能告诉我哪怕是一点点的线索吗？

30. accompany

accompany 表示陪同。

译文：明天市长将陪同访问该市的一群加拿大客商。

Unit 5

1. The _____ that exists among nations could certainly be lessened if misunderstanding and mistrust were removed.
2. The writer was so _____ in her work that she didn't notice him enter the room.
3. The most basic reason why _____ should be preserved is that language helps to _____ a culture.
4. Mass advertising helped to _____ the emphasis from the production of goods to their _____.
5. Because of his excellent administration, people lived in peace and _____, and all _____ neglected matters were taken care of.
6. Showing some sense of humor can be an _____ way to deal with some _____ situation.
7. The mayor _____ the police officer a medal of honor for his heroic deed in _____ the earthquake _____.
8. The native Canadians lived in _____ with nature, for they respected nature as a provider of life.
9. All the arrangements should be completed _____ to your _____.
10. We need to create education standards that prepare our next generation who will be _____ with an even more _____ market.
11. In the late seventies, the amount of fixed _____ required to produce one vehicle in Japan was roughly _____ to that in the United States.
12. To speed up the _____ of letters, the Post Office introduced _____ sorting.
13. These _____ students show great _____ for learning a new language.
14. Politically these nations tend to be _____, with very high birth rates but poor education and very low levels of _____.
15. The London Marathon is a difficult race. _____, thousands of runners _____ every year.
16. Being _____ of the law is not accepted as an _____ for breaking the law.
17. Within two days, the army _____ more than two hundred rockets and missiles at military _____ in the coastal city.
18. It is said in some parts of the world, goats, rather than cows, serve as a _____ _____ of milk.
19. In _____ of recent developments we do not think your _____ is practical.
20. Jessica was _____ from the warehouse to the accounting office, which was considered a _____.
21. It's not _____ to _____ the experiment without the instruction from our teacher.
22. During our growth we have to _____ _____ pains and disappointments.
23. You can hire a bicycle in many places. Usually you'll have to pay a _____.
24. The food was bad and the bill was _____ in this restaurant.
25. Dr. Smith was always _____ about the poor and the sick, often providing them with free _____.
26. Thomas Jefferson and John Adams died on July 4, 1826, the fiftieth _____ of American Independence.

27. Nowadays computers often _____ the task of experiment and _____ in some scientific _____ .

28. The _____ at the military academy is so _____ that students can hardly bear it.

29. The test results are beyond _____ ; and they have been repeated in labs all over the world.

30. In order to make things _____ for the people, the department is planning to set up some _____ shops in the residential area.

解析

1. tension
tension 表示紧张（状态）、压力。international tension：国际紧张局势。
译文：如果消除了误解和不信任，国家之间的紧张局势当然可以缓解。

2. absorbed
absorb 表示吸收、吸引。be absorbed in 为常用表达，表示全神贯注于。absorb moisture from the air：从空气中吸收水分。
译文：作家如此全神贯注于她的作品以至于没有注意到他进了房间。

3. dialects ; retain
（1）dialect 表示方言。（2）retain 表示保持、保留。例，to retain one's balance：保持平衡。
译文：方言应该受到保护的最根本的原因在于语言有助于文化传承。

4. shift ; consumption
（1）shift 表示转移、变化。（2）consumption 表示消费。
译文：大量的广告将宣传重心从商品的生产转向商品的消费。

5. content ; previously
（1）content 表示满足。（2）previously 表示之前地、以前的、先前地。
译文：由于他卓越的管理，人们生活得和平而满足，所有之前被忽略的事情都得到了妥善处置。

6. effective ; stressful
（1）effective 表示有效的。（2）stressful 表示紧张的、充满压力的。
译文：幽默感能够成为应付紧张局势的有效途径。

7. awarded ; rescuing ; victims
（1）award 表示授予、颁奖，也可作名词，表示获奖。例，award of Nobel Prize：获得诺贝尔奖。（2）rescue 表示拯救。（3）victims 表示受害者、罹难者。
译文：市长给警官颁发荣誉勋章，嘉奖他拯救地震受害者的英勇行为。

8. harmony
harmony 表示和谐，live in harmony with 是常用词组，表示与……和睦相处。
译文：加拿大人与自然和谐相处，因为他们尊重自然，认为自然是生命之源。
词族：harmonious 表示和谐的，例，harmonious society：和谐社会。harmonize 表示使……和谐、使……协调，例，harmonize one's views with facts：使某人的观点和事实一致。

9. prior ; departure
（1）prior 表示在……之前、在……先，通常和 to 搭配。（2）departure 表示离开、启程。
译文：在你离开之前，所有的安排必须就绪。

10. <u>confronted</u>；<u>competitive</u>

（1）confront 表示使……面对。be confronted with 是常用搭配，表示面对（困境）。
（2）competitive 表示充满竞争的。

译文：我们应该制定教育标准，为下一代做好准备，因为他们将面临竞争更激烈的市场。

11. <u>assets</u>；<u>equivalent</u>

（1）asset 表示资产、财富，例，Good health is a great asset. 健康是巨大的财富。
（2）equivalent 表示相等的、相当的，be equivalent to 是固定搭配，表示相当于，等同于。

译文：在 20 世纪 70 年代后期，在日本生产一辆汽车所需要的固定资产量与美国的大体相当。

12. <u>delivery</u>；<u>automatic</u>

（1）delivery 表示递送、交付。（2）automatic 表示自动的。

译文：为了加快信件的投递，邮局引入了自动分拣法。

一词多义：delivery（1）分娩。例，delivery of a child。（2）交货。例，delivery of goods。

13. <u>overseas</u>；<u>enthusiasm</u>

（1）overseas 表示海外的、国外的。（2）enthusiasm 表示热情。

译文：这些外国的学生对学习一门语言表现出极大的热情。

14. <u>unstable</u>；<u>literacy</u>

（1）unstable 表示不稳定的、不牢固的。（2）literacy 表示（人的）识字能力、文化水平。

一词多义：literacy 表示文学。例，American literacy：美国文学。

译文：出生率高、教育程度差、文化水平低的国家政治上容易不稳定。

15. <u>Nevertheless</u>；<u>participate</u>

（1）nevertheless 表示尽管如此、然而，一般放在句首，也作 nonetheless。（2）participate 表示参加，参与。

译文：伦敦马拉松赛是很有难度的比赛，尽管如此，每年都有很多人参赛。

16. <u>ignorant</u>；<u>excuse</u>

（1）ignorant 表示无知的，常用搭配 be ignorant of，表示不知道。（2）excuse 表示借口、托辞。

译文：对法律无知不能成为违反法律的借口。

17. <u>fired</u>；<u>targets</u>

（1）fire 表示开火。（2）target 表示目标、靶子。

译文：两天内军队向那个海滨城市的军事目标发射了两百多枚火箭和导弹。

一词多义：fire 可以表示解雇的意思。例，You are fired. 你被解雇了。

18. <u>vital</u>；<u>source</u>

（1）vital 表示至关重要的、生死攸关的。（2）source 表示源头、来源。例，energy source：能量源。pollution source：污染源。

译文：据说，在世界的某些地区，重要的奶源是山羊而不是奶牛。

19. <u>view</u>；<u>scheme</u>

（1）view 表示景色、风景、观点、意见。in view of 是固定词组，表示考虑到、鉴于。
（2）scheme 表示计划。

译文：鉴于最近的发展情况，我们认为你的计划不实用。

一词多义：scheme 表示阴谋。例，All the schemes are doomed to fail. 一切阴谋都是注定要失败的。

20. <u>transferred</u>；<u>promotion</u>

（1）transfer 表示调动、转移。（2）promotion 表示晋升、升职。

译文：杰西卡从库房调到了会计室，这被认为是一种晋升。

21. <u>feasible</u>；<u>conduct</u>

（1）feasible 表示可行的。例，His plan sounds feasible. 他的计划听起来可行。（2）conduct 表示处理、实施。

译文：没有老师的指导来做试验是不可行的。

22. <u>undergo</u>；<u>various</u>

（1）undergo 表示承受、经历。（2）various 表示各种各样的。

译文：在成长过程中我们必须经历各种各样的痛苦和失望。

23. <u>deposit</u>

deposit 表示保证金、定金。

译文：你可以在很多地方租到自行车，通常你需要支付一笔保证金。

一词多义：deposit 表示（1）沉淀、沉淀物。（2）存款、存放物。

24. <u>excessive</u>

excessive 表示过量的。例，Excessive eating of fat is very harmful to health. 过量地摄入脂肪对健康非常有害。

译文：这家餐馆饭菜很糟，价钱又很贵。

25. <u>concerned</u>；<u>medical care</u>

（1）concerned 表示关心的。（2）medical care 表示医疗。

译文：史密斯医生一直关心穷人和病人，经常给他们提供免费的医疗。

词族：concern（1）名词表示关注，通常和 over 连用，表示使关心……例，a worldwide concern over the game：全世界对比赛的关注。（2）动词表示关注、与……有关的，通常 be concerned about 表示关心、关注某件事，而 be concerned with 表示与……有关的。例，The book is concerned with economics：这本书是关于经济学的，也可以表达为 The book concerns economics.

26. <u>anniversary</u>

anniversary 表示周年纪念。

译文：托马斯·杰斐逊和约翰·亚当斯卒于 1826 年 7 月 4 日，美国独立 50 周年纪念日。

链接：ceremony 表示典礼、仪式。例，wedding ceremony：结婚典礼。

27. <u>undertake</u>；<u>calculations</u>；<u>research</u>

（1）undertake 表示承担、从事。（2）calculation 表示计算。（3）research 表示研究。

译文：现在，计算机在一些科学研究中经常承担实验和计算的任务。

28. <u>discipline</u>；<u>rigid</u>

（1）discipline 表示纪律。（2）rigid 表示严格的、死板的。

译文：军事院校的纪律如此严格以至于学生们几乎无法承受。

29. <u>dispute</u>

dispute 表示争论、辩论。

译文：实验的结果是无可辩驳的，它们已在世界范围内经过了无数次验证。

> 提示：注意 beyond 的用法，表示超出范围、不可……例，The door was seriously damaged and beyond repair. 门损坏严重，无法修复了。

30. <u>convenient</u> ; <u>mobile</u>

（1）convenient 表示方便的。（2）mobile 表示可移动的、机动的。例，mobile phone：移动电话。

译文：为了方便人们，该部门计划在居民区建立一些可移动的便利店。

Unit 6

1. The _____ are very good at sensing a mood and then _____ it.
2. The board of the company has decided to _____ its _____ to include all aspects of the clothing business.
3. Doctors warned against chewing tobacco as a _____ for smoking.
4. When carbon is added to iron in proper _____ the result is steel.
5. You should try to _____ your _____ and be more realistic.
6. Please _____ dictionaries when you are not sure of word spelling or meaning.
7. At yesterday's party, Elizabeth's boyfriend _____ us by _____ Charlie Chaplin.
8. She keeps a supply of candles in the house in case of _____.
9. The group of technicians are _____ in a study which _____ almost all aspects of urban planning.
10. The lecture which lasted about three hours was so _____ that the audience couldn't help _____.
11. The machine looked like a large, _____, _____ typewriter.
12. Though she began her _____ by singing in a local pop group, she is now a famous Hollywood movie star.
13. Within two weeks of _____, all foreigners had to _____ with the local police.
14. These teachers try to be _____ when they _____ the integrated ability of their students.
15. They wish that prices would_____.
16. There are various kinds of crimes, such as theft, bribery, _____, burglary, robbery, drug trafficking, smuggling, kidnapping, rape and _____.
17. The _____ should enjoy their _____ years in happiness.
18. Having _____ for other cultures can help you avoid unnecessary _____.
19. War is _____ when the _____ is to restore peace.
20. Once you become _____ to smoking, it will be hard for you to _____ the habit.
21. Life is not always what we expect. We are sometimes driven into a helpless or _____ situation.
22. Reality TV is very popular among viewers of all ages because it _____ _____ and companionship, _____ and monetary reward.
23. Non-smokers in many countries are _____ for the _____ of smoking in public places.
24. _____ an _____ view on aging can add years.
25. Lottery（彩票）winners should invest their money in _____ businesses or projects.
26. Remembering birthdays can help us _____ our lives.
27. Eye contact may _____ sincerity and attentiveness in some Oriental cultures but too

much eye contact may _____ people in some western cultures.

28．To be _____ by a friend is most painful.

29．All human beings have the need to eat, to have _____ and to work.

30．What you do today is important because you are _____ a day of your life for it.

解析

1．media ; exaggerating

（1）media 表示媒体、传媒、媒质。（2）exaggerate 表示夸张。

译文：媒体善于捕捉情绪，然后进一步夸大它。

2．expand ; operations

（1）expand 表示扩张。（2）operation 表示运营、业务。

译文：公司的董事会决定扩大公司的业务，以涉及服装业的全部领域。

3．substitute

substitute 表示替代、替代品。

译文：医生警告不要用咀嚼烟草的方式代替抽烟。

4．proportion

proportion 表示比例。

译文：将恰当比例的炭加入铁就可以形成钢。

5．restrain ; ambition

（1）restrain 表示限制、克制。（2）ambition 表示抱负，雄心。

译文：你应该克制你的野心，更现实点。

6．consult

consult 表示查询、咨询。例，consult a doctor：看医生、找医生咨询。

译文：在不确定字的拼写或含义时，请查字典。

7．amused ; imitating

（1）amuse 表示使愉快。（2）imitate 表示模仿。

译文：昨天的晚会上，伊丽莎白的男朋友模仿卓别林，这让我们感到很有趣。

词族：amused 表示开心的、愉快的。例，I feel amused to see the program. 看了这个节目我很开心。amusing 表示令人愉快的、有趣的。例，Everybody couldn't help laughing with his amusing expression. 看到他那有趣的表情，大家都忍不住笑起来了。

8．power failure.

power failure 表示停电。

译文：她在房间里储备着一些蜡烛，以防停电。

9．engaged ; embraces

（1）engaged 表示忙碌中的、忙于。be engaged in 为固定搭配，表示忙于。（2）embrace 表示包含。

译文：那群技术员正忙于一项研究，该研究几乎包含了城市规划的所有方面。

一词多义：engaged 表示（1）订婚的，例，get engaged. 表示订婚。（2）使用中的。例，The washing closet is engaged. 洗手间正在使用中。

10．tedious ; yawning

（1）tedious 表示枯燥的。（2）yawn 表示打哈欠。

译文：那个持续约三小时的讲座真枯燥，观众们都忍不住打哈欠了。

11. clumsy ; old-fashioned

（1）clumsy 表示笨重的、笨拙的。（2）old-fashioned 表示老式的。

译文：那台机器看起来像一台笨重、老式的打字机。

12. career

career 表示职业生涯。

译文：虽然她是作为一个当地流行乐队的歌手开始自己的职业生涯的，她现在却是一个好莱坞的著名影星。

13. arrival ; register

（1）arrival 表示到达。（2）register 表示登记。

译文：在到达的最初两个星期，所有的外国人都必须到当地的警方进行登记。

14. objective ; evaluate

（1）objective 表示客观的。（2）evaluate 表示评估、评价。

译文：这些老师在评价学生们的综合能力时，尽可能地客观。

15. decline

decline 表示下降。

译文：他们希望物价能下降。

一词多义：decline 用作动词（1）表示衰退、衰落。例，The economy has declined significantly. 经济衰退得很严重。（2）表示拒绝（某人或某事），这里是指委婉地拒绝。例，She declined his invitation politely. 她礼貌地拒绝了他的邀请。注意：reject 与 turn down 也都表示拒绝的意思。而 refuse 一般用法为 refuse to do。

16. corruption ; murder

（1）corruption 表示腐败、贪污。（2）murder 表示谋杀。

译文：犯罪种类很多。例如，盗窃、贿赂、贪污、入室行窃、抢劫、毒品交易、走私、绑架、强奸和谋杀等。

17. elderly ; remaining

（1）the elderly 与 the aged 同义，表示老年人群体。（2）remaining 表示剩余的。

译文：老年人应该享受他们的晚年生活。

18. respect ; misunderstanding

（1）respect 表示尊重，通常和 for 搭配。（2）misunderstanding 表示误解、误会。

译文：对其他文化的尊重可以帮助你避免不必要的误解。

19. justified ; motive

（1）justify 表示证明……正当。（2）motive 表示动机。

译文：出于恢复和平的目的而进行的战争是正当的。

20. addicted ; quit

（1）addicted 表示上瘾的、入迷的。（2）quit 表示放弃。

译文：一旦抽烟上瘾，你就很难放弃这个习惯。

21. frustrating

frustrating 表示令人沮丧的；frustrated 则表示沮丧的。

译文：生活并不总是如我们所预期的那样。有时我们会陷入无助或沮丧的境地。

22. combines ; competition ; adventure

（1）combines 表示结合、（使）联合。（2）competition 表示竞争、比赛。（3）adventure 表示冒险、充满冒险的经历。

译文：写实电视节目受到各年龄层次观众的欢迎，因为它结合了竞争与友谊，冒险和褒奖。

23．appealing；prohibition

（1）appealing 表示呼吁。（2）prohibition 表示禁止。

译文：许多国家的非抽烟人群都在呼吁公共场所禁止吸烟。

24．Maintaining；optimistic

（1）maintain 表示维持、保持。（2）optimistic 表示乐观的。

译文：对变老保持乐观的态度可以延长寿命。

25．worthwhile

worthwhile 表示值得的。例，a worthwhile job：一项值得做的工作。

译文：彩票的中奖者应该将他们的钱投在值得投资的生意或项目上。

26．treasure

treasure 作动词表示珍惜，作名词则表示珠宝。

译文：记住生日有助于我们珍爱生命。

27．convey；embarrass

（1）convey 表示传达、搬运。（2）embarrass 表示使尴尬。名词为 embarrassment，embarrassing 表示令人尴尬的。

译文：在东方文化中，目光交流可以传达真诚和关爱，但是太多的目光交流可能让西方文化（背景）的人感到尴尬。

28．betrayed

betray 表示背叛。

译文：被朋友背叛是令人痛苦的事。

29．shelter

shelter 表示藏身之处、掩体、庇护所。

译文：所有人都有衣食住行和工作的需要。

30．exchanging

exchange 表示交换。例，exchange ideas：交流看法。

译文：今天你做什么很重要，因为你在用生命中的一天与它交换。

Part II   Dictation Upgrading

1．There cannot be day without night, spring without winter, nor _____.

2．A well-done poll can provide _____ information about the public's priorities and _____, but _____.

3．If winter comes can _____?

4．I don't mind you _____ as long as it is not too late.

5．_____, the man tore up everything within reach.

6．It didn't _____ that our team had lost the game.

7．Man in the past often _____ that water is a certain limitless natural resource.

8．The fire _____.

9．All tasks _____, they decided to go on holiday for a week.

10．You will be _____ to let your child go to school by himself.

11．The overall goal of the book is to _____.

12．His wife is _____, which almost drives him mad.

13. A culture in which the citizens share _____ is more likely to have laws that represent the wishes of its people than is a culture where citizens come from diverse backgrounds.

14. Money brings you food, _____; medicine, _____.

15. Friendship _____.

16. True friendship is a plant of slow growth, the value of which is seldom known until it can _____.

17. I'd like to make friends with those who are _____.

18. If you tell your joy to your friend, _____. And if you pour your sorrow to your friend, _____.

19. Money can sometimes be _____.

20. Polling topics can be as diverse as public policies, _____, elections, _____ and academic research projects.

21. Old people are more _____.

22. In order to prevent drug abuse, we can _____ drug education programs to teach young people about the risks involved, toughen laws to prevent drug offenses, _____ drug dealings.

23. War is a human _____. Millions of people die and fall apart _____ war.

24. _____ the world is getting smaller and smaller.

25. Human beings can only _____.

26. Economic growth cannot _____ of developing countries.

27. We are inhabitants of the earth only for a short time. We _____.

28. War is _____.

29. To _____ your memory, try to _____.

30. The teacher tries to give a report to _____.

31. Polls give people an _____ that affect their lives.

32. Smoking is known _____.

33. Do not let a stranger in _____.

34. To prepare for war is one of _____.

35. _____ between nations should be _____.

36. A drug addict will _____.

37. People over 65 years old _____.

38. Don't try to _____ all the facts, but _____.

39. Money _____.

40. _____ everywhere.

41. At twenty years of age, the _____ reigns; at thirty, the _____; and at forty, the _____.

42. Genius is _____ in quiet, character _____ life.

43. _____, live for today, and _____.

44. _____.

45. I will love you still till _____.

46. Giving thanks is _____.

47. Live as though _____, and work as though _____.

48. To _____ men, every day is a day of _____.

49. The tragedy of life is not _____.

50. Work is the grand _____ of all the maladies and _____ that ever beset mankind.

51. A man can fail many times, but he isn't a _____ until he begins to _____ somebody else.

52. Better to light one candle than to _____.

53. We must accept finite _____, but we must never lose _____ hope.

54. There is only one success — to be able to _____.

55. Fear not that the life shall _____, but rather fear that it shall _____.

56. Man can only be free _____.

57. The important thing in life is to _____, and _____.

58. A man can succeed at almost anything for which _____.

59. A man is not old _____; and a man is not old until regrets take the place of dreams.

60. Nothing in life is _____. It is only _____.

答案

1. joy without sorrow
   译文：世间没有无黑夜的白天、没有无寒冬的春天、也没有无悲伤的快乐。

2. valuable；viewpoints；poorly conducted poll easily mislead people
   译文：一个好的民意测验可以提供关于民众偏好与观念的有价值的信息，而差的民意测验则容易误导民众。

3. spring be far behind
   译文：如果冬天已经来临，春天还会远吗？

4. delaying making the decision
   译文：我不介意你推迟做决定，只要不太迟即可。

5. In a sudden burst of anger
   译文：一时暴怒，那位男士撕碎了身边的所有东西。

6. occur to him
   译文：他没有意识到我们的球队已经输了。

7. took it for granted
   译文：人们过去会想当然地认为水是无限的自然资源。

8. was finally brought under control
   译文：火势最后被控制下来。

9. having been fulfilled ahead of time
   译文：所有的任务都提前一周完成，他们决定休假一周。

10. running a risk
    译文：让孩子自己去上学，你要冒一定的风险。

11. bridge the gap between teaching and learning
    译文：本书的宗旨在于打通教与学。

12. constantly finding fault with him
    译文：他的妻子总是对他吹毛求疵，这让他抓狂。

13. similar religious beliefs and values
    译文：与公民有不同背景的文化相比，公民有相似宗教信仰与价值观念的文化更可能产生体现民意的法律。

14. but not appetite ; but not health
    译文：金钱给你带来食物，但不是胃口；给你带来药品，但不是健康。

15. involves affection and intimacy
    译文：友谊包含友爱与亲密。

16. stand the test of time
    译文：真正的友谊就像缓慢生长的植被，经受住时间考验以后，它的价值才会为人所了解。

17. honest, sincere, kind-hearted and reliable
    译文：我愿意与那些诚实、真诚、善良与可靠的人交朋友。

18. your joy will double ; your sorrow will be reduced by half
    译文：当你将快乐与朋友分享时，快乐将加倍；当你将忧伤向朋友倾诉时，忧伤将减半。

19. a terrible master as well as an excellent servant
    译文：金钱既可以拙劣地支配你，也可以很好地为你所用。

20. controversial social issues ; consumer preferences
    译文：民意测验的话题多种多样，如公共政策、社会争议问题、大选、消费偏好、学术研究等。

21. experienced and responsible
    译文：老人们更有经验、更负责任。

22. launch ; make great efforts to crack down on
    译文：为了阻止毒品滥用，我们可以开展毒品教育项目，教育年轻人毒品的危害性，强化法律防止毒品犯罪，加大打击毒品交易的力度。

23. tragedy ; as a consequence of
    译文：战争是人类的悲剧，数百万的人因此失去生命，流离失所。

24. With the rapid development of transportation means and the information technology
    译文：随着交通方式与信息技术的迅速发展，世界正变得越来越小。

25. survive by living in harmony with nature
    译文：人类只有与自然和谐共处才能生存。

26. be based on the over-exploitation of the natural resources
    译文：经济发展不能建立在对发展中国家的自然资源过度开采的基础上。

27. ought to protect it for future generations
    译文：我们只是地球的短暂居住者。我们应该为子孙后代保护地球。

28. costly in money, resources and human lives
    译文：战争在金钱、资源与生命上代价昂贵。

29. stimulate ; use your memory to the utmost
    译文：为刺激记忆力，尽量最大强度地使用它。

30. evaluate the students' performance
    译文：老师努力评估学生的表现。

31. opportunity to express their views on issues
    译文：民意测验给予人们机会，以表达他们对影响其生活问题的看法。

32. as a fatal cause of lung cancer
    译文：吸烟被认为是导致肺癌的致命因素。

33. without checking his identity

译文：在没有核查其身份前，不要让陌生人进入。

34. the best ways to preserve peace
译文：为战争做好准备是维护和平的最佳途径。

35. conflicts ; resolved through peaceful means
译文：国家之间的争端应该通过和平途径来解决。

36. resort to crime and violence
译文：瘾君子会采取犯罪与暴力（手段）。

37. are generally considered senior citizens
译文：一般来说，超过65岁即为老年人。

38. memorize ; focus on what you consider more important
译文：不要试图记住所有事情，关注你认为更重要的东西。

39. in itself is neutral
译文：金钱的本质是中性的。

40. Human nature is essentially the same
译文：人类的本质是相同的。

41. will ; wit ; judgment
译文：20岁时主导（一个人）的是意志，30岁时是机智，40岁时是判断。

42. formed ; in the stream of
译文：天才形成于平静，性格来自生活的点点滴滴。

43. Learn from yesterday ; hope for tomorrow
译文：从昨天中学习，为今天而生活，对明天充满希望。

44. Great minds think alike
译文：英雄所见略同。

45. all the seas go dry and the rock melt with the sun
译文：我会依然爱你，直到海枯石烂。

46. a sign of noble race
译文：感恩是高贵者的标志。

47. you intended to live forever ; your strength were limitless
译文：要这样生活，仿佛你寿命永恒；要这样工作，仿佛你精力无穷。

48. sensible ; reckoning
译文：对聪明人来说，每一天的时间都是要精打细算的。reckon表示计算、思考。

49. so much what men suffer but what they miss
译文：人生的悲剧不在于人承受了多少苦难，而在于他们错过了什么。

50. cure ; miseries
译文：工作是医治人间一切病痛和疾苦的万能良药。

51. failure ; blame
译文：一个人可以失败许多次，但是只要他没有开始责怪别人，他还不是一个失败者。

52. curse the darkness
译文：与其诅咒黑暗，不如燃起蜡烛。

53. disappointment ; infinite
译文：我们必须接受失望，因为它是有限的，但千万不可失去希望，因为它是无穷的。

54. spend your life in your own way
译文：只有一种成功，那就是能够用自己的方式度过一生。

55. come to an end ; never have a beginning
    译文：不要害怕你的生活将要结束，应该担心你的生活永远不曾真正开始。

56. through mastery of himself
    译文：只有通过掌握自己，才能使自己得到解放。

57. have a great aim ; the determination to attain it
    译文：人生重要的是确立一个伟大的目标，并决心实现它。

58. he has unlimited enthusiasm
    译文：只要有无限的热情，一个人几乎可以在任何事情上取得成功。

59. as long as he is seeking something
    译文：只要一个人还有追求，他就没有老。直到后悔取代了梦想，一个人才算老。

60. to be feared ; to be understood
    译文：生活中没有什么可怕的东西，只有需要理解的东西。

Part III   Vocabulary Exercises for CET 4

Directions: For each sentence there are four choices marked A), B), C) and D). Choose the ONE answer that best completes the sentence.

Unit 1

1. She _____ her trip to New York because she was ill.
   A) called off   B) closed down   C) put up   D) went off

2. _____ the storm, the ship would have reached its destination on time.
   A) But for   B) In case of   C) In spite of   D) Because of

3. We should concentrate on sharply reducing interest rates to pull the economy out of _____.
   A) rejection   B) restriction   C) retreat   D) recession

4. The _____ of finding gold in California attracted a lot of people to settle down there.
   A) prospects   B) speculations   C) stakes   D) provisions

5. I suffered from mental _____ because of stress from my job.
   A) damage   B) release   C) relief   D) fatigue

6. The rest of the day was entirely at his _____ for reading or recreation.
   A) dismissal   B) survival   C) disposal   D) arrival

7. You will not be _____ about your food in time of great hunger.
   A) special   B) particular   C) peculiar   D) specific

8. Crime is increasing worldwide, and there is every reason to believe the _____ will continue into the next decade.
   A) emergency   B) trend   C) pace   D) schedule

9. You shouldn't have written in the _____ since the book belongs to the library.
   A) interval   B) border   C) margin   D) edge

10. The _____ of airplane engines announced a coming air raid.
    A) roar   B) exclamation   C) whistle   D) scream

11. This ticket _____ you to a free boat tour on the lake.
    A) entitles   B) appoints   C) grants   D) credits

12. This is the nurse who _____ to me when I was ill in hospital.
    A) accompanied   B) attended   C) entertained   D) shielded
13. I was about to _____ a match when I remembered Tom's warning.
    A) rub   B) hit   C) scrape   D) strike
14. The advertisement says this material doesn't _____ in the wash, but it has.
    A) contract   B) shrink   C) slim   D) dissolve
15. He was proud of being chosen to participate in the game and he _____ us that he would try as hard as possible.
    A) insured   B) guaranteed   C) assumed   D) assured
16. Not only the professionals but also the amateurs will _____ from the new training facilities.
    A) derive   B) acquire   C) benefit   D) reward
17. The work was almost complete when we received orders to _____ no further with it.
    A) progress   B) proceed   C) march   D) promote
18. I waited for him half an hour, but he never _____.
    A) turned in   B) turned down   C) turned off   D) turned up
19. A house with a dangerous gas _____ can be broken into immediately.
    A) leak   B) split   C) mess   D) crack
20. A dark suit is _____ to a light one for evening wear.
    A) favourable   B) suitable   C) preferable   D) proper
21. It was in the United States that I made the _____ of Professor Jones.
    A) association   C) recognition
    B) acquaintance   D) acknowledgement
22. Could you take a _____ sheet of paper and write your name at the top?
    A) bare   B) vacant   C) hollow   D) blank
23. A culture in which the citizens share similar religious beliefs and values is more likely to have laws that represent the wishes of its people than is a culture where citizens come from _____ backgrounds.
    A) extensive   B) influential   C) diverse   D) identical
24. Areas where students have particular difficulty have been treated _____ particular care.
    A) by   B) in   C) under   D) with
25. He gave a _____ to handle the affairs in a friendly manner.
    A) pledge   B) mission   C) plunge   D) motion
26. Don't let the child play with scissor _____ she cuts himself.
    A) in case   B) so that   C) now that   D) only if
27. _____ the danger from enemy action, people had to cope with a severe shortage of food, clothing, fuel, and almost everything.
    A) As far as   B) As long as   C) As well as   D) As soon as
28. Many people lost their jobs during the business _____.
    A) desperation   B) decrease   C) despair   D) depression
29. Whenever a big company _____ a small one, the product almost always gets worse.
    A) gets on with   B) cuts down   C) takes over   D) puts up with
30. Mr. Smith was the only witness who said that the fire was _____.
    A) mature   B) deliberate   C) meaningful   D) innocent

Unit 2

1. He asked us to _____ them in carrying through their plan.
   A）provide B）arouse C）assist D）persist
2. A good many proposals were raised by the delegates, _____ was to be expected.
   A）that B）what C）so D）as
3. He was such a _____ speaker that he held our attention every minute of the three-hour lecture.
   A）specific B）dynamic C）heroic D）diplomatic
4. Arriving home, the boy told his parents about all the _____ which occurred in his dormitory.
   A）occasions B）matters C）incidents D）issues
5. The opening between the rocks was very narrow, but the boys managed to _____ through.
   A）press B）squeeze C）stretch D）leap
6. They are trying to _____ the waste discharged by the factory for profit.
   A）expose B）exhaust C）exhibit D）exploit
7. The manager urged his staff not to _____ the splendid opportunity.
   A）drop B）miss C）escape D）slide
8. _____ I admire David as a poet, I do not like him as a man.
   A）Much as B）Only if C）If only D）As much
9. Because of a _____ engagement, Lora couldn't attend my birthday party last Saturday.
   A）pioneer B）premature C）prior D）past
10. The continuous rain _____ the harvesting of the wheat crop by two weeks.
    A）set back B）set off C）set out D）set aside
11. Not having a good command of English can be a serious _____ preventing you from achieving your goals.
    A）obstacle B）fault C）offense D）distress
12. It's very _____ of you not to talk aloud while the baby is asleep.
    A）concerned B）careful C）considerable D）considerate
13. Many a player who had been highly thought of has _____ from the tennis scene.
    A）disposed C）discouraged
    B）disappeared D）discarded
14. She's fainted. Throw some water on her face and she'll _____.
    A）come round B）come along C）come on D）come out
15. All their attempts to _____ the child from the burning building were in vain.
    A）regain B）recover C）rescue D）reserve
16. Computer technology will _____ a revolution in business administration.
    A）bring around C）bring out
    B）bring about D）bring up
17. The university has launched a research center to develop new ways of _____ bacteria which have become resistant to drug treatments.
    A）regulating B）halting C）interrupting D）combating

18. The _____ goal of the book is to help bridge the gap between research and teaching, particularly the gap between researchers and teachers.

    A) joint   B) intensive   C) overall   D) decisive

19. The rapid development of communications technology is transforming the _____ in which people communicate across time and space.

    A) route   B) transmission   C) vision   D) manner

20. When I go out in the evening I use the bike _____ the car if I can.

    A) rather than   C) in spite of

    B) regardless of   D) other than

21. There is no _____ evidence that people can control their dreams, at least in experimental situations in a lab.

    A) rigid   B) solid   C) smooth   D) harsh

22. Every culture has developed _____ for certain kinds of food and drink, and equally strong negative attitudes toward others.

    A) preferences   B) expectations   C) fantasies   D) fashions

23. It is reported that Uruguay understands and _____ China on human rights issues.

    A) grants   B) changes   C) abandons   D) backs

24. Only a few people have _____ to the full facts of the incident.

    A) access   B) resort   C) contact   D) path

25. His trousers _____ when he tried to jump over the fence.

    A) cracked   B) split   C) broke   D) burst

26. So far, _____ winds and currents have kept the thick patch of oil southeast of the Atlantic coast.

    A) governing   B) blowing   C) prevailing   D) ruling

27. The author was required to submit an _____ of about 200 words together with his research paper.

    A) edition   B) editorial   C) article   D) abstract

28. As the old empires were broken up and new states were formed, new official tongues began to _____ at an increasing rate.

    A) bring up   B) build up   C) spring up   D) strike up

29. Many patients insist on having watches with them in hospital, _____ they have no schedules to keep.

    A) even though   B) for   C) as if   D) since

30. Some plants are very _____ to light; they prefer the shade.

    A) sensible   B) flexible   C) objective   D) sensitive

Unit 3

1. I went along thinking of nothing _____, only looking at things around me.

    A) in particular   B) in harmony   C) in doubt   D) in brief

2. Critics believe that the control of television by mass advertising has _____ the quality of the programs.

    A) lessened   B) declined   C) affected   D) effected

3. I must _____ you on the excellent design of the new bridge.

    A）impose   B）dispose   C）contribute   D）congratulate

4. There is a fully _____ health center on the ground floor of the main office building.

    A）installed   B）equipped   C）provided   D）projected

5. For more than 20 years, we've been supporting educational programs that _____ from kindergartens to colleges.

    A）move   B）shift   C）range   D）spread

6. The _____ at the military academy is so rigid that students can hardly bear it.

    A）convention   B）confinement   C）principle   D）discipline

7. The test results are beyond _____; and they have been repeated in labs all over the world.

    A）negotiation   B）conflict   C）bargain   D）dispute

8. I was so _____ in today's history lesson. I didn't understand a thing.

    A）amazed   B）neglected   C）confused   D）amused

9. It _____ you to at least 50% off the regular price of either frames or lenses when you buy both.

    A）presents   B）entitles   C）credits   D）tips

10. Deserts and high mountains have always been a _____ to the movement of people from place to place.

    A）barrier   B）fence   C）prevention   D）jam

11. In order to make things convenient for the people, the department is planning to set up some _____ shops in the residential area.

    A）flowing   B）drifting   C）mobile   D）unstable

12. Mr. Smith says: "The media are very good at sensing a mood and then _____ it."

    A）overtaking   B）enlarging   C）widening   D）exaggerating

13. This is not an economical way to get more water; _____, it is very expensive.

    A）or else   C）in short

    B）on the contrary   D）on the other hand

14. It was the first time that such a _____ or else had to be taken at a British nuclear power station.

    A）presentation   B）precaution   C）preparation   D）prediction

15. _____ that he wasn't happy with the arrangements, I tried to book a different hotel.

    A）Perceiving   B）Penetrating   C）Puzzling   D）Preserving

16. The board of the company has decided to _____ its operations to include all aspects of the clothing business.

    A）multiply   B）lengthen   C）expand   D）stretch

17. His business was very successful, but it was at the _____ of his family life.

    A）consumption   B）credit   C）exhaustion   D）expense

18. First published in 1927, the charts remain an _____ source for researchers.

    A）identical   B）indispensable   C）intelligent   D）inevitable

19. Joe is not good at sports, but when it _____ mathematics, he is the best in the class.

    A）comes to   B）comes up to   C）comes on to   D）comes around to

20. Doctors warned against chewing tobacco as a _____ for smoking.

    A）relief   B）revival   C）substitute   D）succession

21. When carbon is added to iron in proper _____ the result is steel.

    A）rates   B）thicknesses   C）proportions   D）densities

22. You should try to _____ your ambition and be more realistic.

    A）reserve   B）restrain   C）retain   D）replace

23. Nancy is only a sort of _____ of her husband's opinion and has no ideas of her own.

    A）sample   B）reproduction   C）shadow   D）echo

24. Now that spring is here, you can _____ these fur coats till you need them again next winter.

    A）put over   B）put away   C）put off   D）put down

25. There is a _____ of impatience in the tone of his voice.

    A）hint   B）notion   C）dot   D）phrase

26. Please _____ dictionaries when you are not sure of word spelling or meaning.

    A）seek   B）inquire   C）search   D）consult

27. At yesterday's party, Elizabeth's boyfriend amused us by _____ Charlie Chaplin.

    A）copying   B）following   C）imitating   D）modeling

28. She keeps a supply of candles in the house in case of power _____.

    A）failure   B）lack   C）absence   D）drop

29. The group of technicians are engaged in a study which _____ all aspects of urban planning.

    A）inserts   B）grips   C）performs   D）embraces

30. The lecture which lasted about three hours was so _____ that the audience couldn't help yawning.

    A）tedious   B）bored   C）clumsy   D）tired

Unit 4

1. The machine looked like a large, _____, old-fashioned typewriter.

    A）forceful   B）clumsy   C）intense   D）tricky

2. Though she began her _____ by singing in a local pop group, she is now a famous Hollywood movie star.

    A）employment   B）career   C）occupation   D）profession

3. Within two weeks of arrival, all foreigners had to _____ with the local police.

    A）inquire   B）consult   C）register   D）resolve

4. Considering your salary, you should be able to _____ at least twenty dollars a week.

    A）put forward   B）put up   C）put out   D）put aside

5. As he has _____ our patience, we'll not wait for him any longer.

    A）torn   B）wasted   C）exhausted   D）consumed

6. These teachers try to be objective when they _____ the integrated ability of their students.

    A）justify   B）evaluate   C）indicate   D）reckon

7. Mrs. Morris' daughter is pretty and _____ and many girls envy her.

    A）slender   B）light   C）faint   D）minor

8. Tomorrow the mayor is to _____ a group of Canadian businessmen on a tour of the city.

    A）coordinate   B）cooperate   C）accompany   D）associate

9. I'm _____ enough to know it is going to be a very difficult situation to compete against three strong teams.

    A）realistic   B）conscious   C）aware   D）radical

10. Can you give me even the _____ clue as to where her son might be?

    A）simplest   B）slightest   C）least   D）utmost

11. Norman Davis will be remembered by many with _____ not only as a great scholar but also as a most delightful and faithful friend.

    A）kindness   B）friendliness   C）warmth   D）affection

12. Salaries for _____ positions seem to be higher than for permanent ones.

    A）legal   B）optional   C）voluntary   D）temporary

13. Most people agree that the present role of women has already affected U.S. society. _____, it has affected the traditional role of men.

    A）Above all   B）In all   C）At most   D）At last

14. Science and technology have _____ in important ways to the improvement of agricultural production.

    A）attached   B）assisted   C）contributed   D）witnessed

15. As an actor he could communicate a whole _____ of emotions.

    A）frame   B）range   C）number   D）scale

16. This is what you should bear in mind: Don't ____ a salary increase before you actually get it.

    A）hang on   B）draw on   C）wait on   D）count on

17. The ship's generator broke down, and the pumps had to be operated _____ instead of mechanically.

    A）artificially   B）automatically   C）manually   D）synthetically

18. The little girl was so frightened that she just wouldn't _____ her grip on my arm.

    A）loosen   B）remove   C）relieve   D）dismiss

19. He never arrives on time, and my _____ is that he feels the meetings are useless.

    A）preference   B）conference   C）inference   D）reference

20. Mrs. Smith was so _____ about everything that no servants could please her.

    A）specific   B）special   C）precise   D）particular

21. Last night he saw two dark _____ enter the building, and then there was the explosion.

    A）features   B）figures   C）sketches   D）images

22. It is obvious that this new rule is applicable to everyone without _____.

    A）exception   B）exclusion   C）modification   D）substitution

23. His temper and personality show that he can become a soldier of the top _____.

    A）circle   B）rank   C）category   D）grade

24. During the lecture, the speaker occasionally _____ his point by relating his own experiences.

    A）illustrated   B）hinted   C）cited   D）displayed

25. Only those who can _____ to lose their money should make high-risk investments.

    A）maintain   B）sustain   C）endure   D）afford

26. He found the _____ media attention intolerable and decided to go abroad.

    A）sufficient   B）constant   C）steady   D）plenty

27. There has been a collision _____ a number of cars on the main road to town.

    A）composing   B）consisting   C）involving   D）engaging

28. _____ elephants are different from wild elephants in many aspects, including their tempers.

    A）Cultivated   B）Regulated   C）Civil   D）Tame

29. Ten days ago the young man informed his boss of his intention to _____.

    A）resign   B）reject   C）retreat   D）replace

30. As one of the world's highest paid models, she had her face _____ for five million dollars.

    A）deposited   B）assured   C）measured   D）insured

Unit 5

1. A word processor is much better than a typewriter in that it enables you to enter and _____ your text more easily.

    A）register   B）edit   C）propose   D）discharge

2. We don't know why so many people in that region like to wear dresses of such _____ colors.

    A）low   B）humble   C）mild   D）dull

3. The news has just _____ that the president is going to visit China next month.

    A）come down   B）come up   C）come out   D）come about

4. The _____ that exists among nations could certainly be lessened if misunderstanding and mistrust were removed.

    A）tension   B）strain   C）stress   D）intensity

5. The other day, Mum and I went to St. James's Hospital, and they did lots and lots of tests on me, most of them were _____ and frightening.

    A）cheerful   B）horrible   C）hostile   D）friendly

6. In the Mediterranean seaweed is so abundant and so easily harvested that it is never of great _____.

    A）fare   B）payment   C）worth   D）expense

7. The writer was so _____ in her work that she didn't notice him enter the room.

    A）absorbed   B）abandoned   C）focused   D）centered

8. Actually, information technology can _____ the gap between the poor and the rich.

    A）link   B）break   C）ally   D）bridge

9. Some research workers completely _____ all those facts as though they never existed.

    A）ignore   B）leave   C）refuse   D）miss

10. Computer power now allows automatic searches of fingerprint files to match a print at a crime _____.

    A）stage   B）scene   C）location   D）occasion

11. The most basic reason why dialects should be preserved is that language helps to _____ a culture.

    A）retain   B）relate   C）remark   D）review

12. Companies are struggling to find the right _____ between supply and demand, but it is no easy task.

    A）equation   B）formula   C）balance   D）pattern

13. Mass advertising helped to ___ the emphasis from the production of goods to their consumption.
  A）vary   B）shift   C）lay   D）moderate

14. Because of his excellent administration, people lived in peace and _____ and all previously neglected matters were taken care of.
  A）conviction   B）contest   C）consent   D）content

15. I know you've got a smooth tongue, so don't talk me _____ buying it.
  A）away   B）down   C）out   D）into

16. Showing some sense of humor can be a(n) _____ way to deal with some stressful situations.
  A）effective   B）efficient   C）favorable   D）favorite

17. The situation described in the report _____ terrible, but it may not happen.
  A）inclines   B）maintains   C）sounds   D）remains

18. The company is trying every means to _____ the wholesale price of its products.
  A）pull down   B）put down   C）set down   D）bring down

19. The mayor _____ the police officer a medal of honor for his heroic deed in rescuing the earthquake victims.
  A）rewarded   B）awarded   C）credited   D）prized

20. The native Canadians lived in _____ with nature, for they respected nature as a provider of life.
  A）coordination   B）acquaintance   C）contact   D）harmony

21. Many people are asking whether traditional research universities in fact have any future _____.
  A）at all   B）so far   C）in all   D）on end

22. I was impressed _____ the efficiency of the work done in the company.
  A）in   B）about   C）with   D）for

23. Now in Britain, wines take up four times as much _____ in the storehouse as both beer and spirits.
  A）block   B）land   C）patch   D）space

24. His hand shook a little as he _____ the key in the lock.
  A）squeezed   B）inserted   C）stuffed   D）pierced

25. For professional athletes, _____ to the Olympics means that they have a chance to enter the history books.
  A）access   B）attachment   C）appeal   D）approach

26. In the long _____, the new information technologies may fundamentally alter our way of life.
  A）view   B）distance   C）jump   D）run

27. All the arrangements should be completed _____ your departure.
  A）prior to   B）superior to   C）contrary to   D）parallel to

28. We need to create education standards that prepare our next generation who will be _____ with an even more competitive market.
  A）tackled   B）encountered   C）dealt   D）confronted

29. By the late seventies, the amount of fixed assets required to produce one vehicle in Japan was _____ equivalent to that in the United States.
  A）rudely   B）roughly   C）readily   D）coarsely

30. Many people believe we are heading for environmental disaster _____ we radically change the way we live.
  A）but   B）although   C）unless   D）lest

Unit 6

1. Some people believe that since oil is scarce, the _____ of the motor industry is uncertain.

    A）terminal   B）benefit   C）fate   D）estimate

2. To speed up the _____ of letters, the Post Office introduced automatic sorting.

    A）treatment   B）delivery   C）transmission   D）departure

3. These overseas students show great _____ for learning a new language.

    A）enthusiasm   B）authority   C）convention   D）faith

4. The defense lawyer was questioning the old man who was one of the _____ of the murder committed last month.

    A）observers   B）witnesses   C）audiences   D）viewers

5. Politically these nations tend to be _____, with very high birth rates but poor education and very low levels of literacy.

    A）unstable   B）reluctant   C）rational   D）unsteady

6. The chairman was blamed for letting his secretary _____ too much work last week.

    A）take to   B）take out   C）take away   D）take on

7. "You try to get some sleep. I'll _____ the patient's breakfast," said the nurse.

    A）see to   B）stick to   C）get to   D）lead to

8. The London Marathon is a difficult race. _____, thousands of runners participate every year.

    A）Therefore   B）Furthermore   C）Accordingly   D）Nevertheless

9. The bank refused to _____ him any money, so he had to postpone buying a house.

    A）credit   B）borrow   C）loan   D）lease

10. The more a nation's companies _____ factories abroad, the smaller that country's recorded exports will be.

    A）lie   B）spot   C）stand   D）locate

11. Being ignorant of the law is not accepted as an _____ for breaking the law.

    A）excuse   B）intention   C）option   D）approval

12. Within two days, the army fired more than two hundred rockets and missiles at military _____ in the coastal city.

    A）goals   B）aims   C）targets   D）destinations

13. It is said in some parts of the world, goats, rather than cows, serve as a vital _____ of milk.

    A）storage   B）reserve   C）resource   D）source

14. "This light is too _____ for me to read by. Don't we have a brighter bulb somewhere?" said the elderly man.

    A）mild   B）dim   C）minute   D）slight

15. We have arranged to go to the cinema on Friday, but we can be _____ and go there another day.

    A）reliable   B）probable   C）feasible   D）flexible

16. We are quite sure that we can _____ our present difficulties and finish the task according to schedule.

    A）get across   B）get over   C）get away   D）get off

17. _____ recent developments we do not think your scheme is practical.

    A）In view of   B）In case of   C）In memory of   D）In favor of

18. Jessica was _____ from the warehouse to the accounting office, which was considered a promotion.

    A）delivered   B）exchanged   C）transferred   D）transformed

19. Mr. Smith asked his secretary to _____ a new paragraph in the annual report she was typing.

    A）inject   B）install   C）invade   D）insert

20. There's the living room still to be _____, so that's my next project.

    A）abandoned   B）decorated   C）dissolved   D）assessed

21. The old paper mill has been _____ to make way for a new shopping centre.

    A）cut down   B）kept down   C）torn down   D）held down

22. It may be necessary to stop _____ in the learning process and go back to the difficult points in the lessons.

    A）at a distance   B）at intervals   C）at ease   D）at length

23. You can hire a bicycle in many places. Usually you'll have to pay a _____.

    A）fare   B）fund   C）deposit   D）deal

24. My grandfather had always taken a _____ interest in my work, and I had an equal admiration for the stories of his time.

    A）splendid   B）weighty   C）vague   D）keen

25. _____ quantities of water are being used nowadays with the rapid development of industry and agriculture.

    A）Excessive   B）Extensive   C）Extreme   D）Exclusive

26. John cannot afford to go to university, _____ going abroad.

    A）nothing but   C）not to speak of

    B）anything but   D）nothing to speak of

27. Most laboratory and field studies of human behavior _____ taking a situational photograph at a given time and in a given place.

    A）involve   B）compose   C）enclose   D）attach

28. If you don't like to swim, you _____ as well stay at home.

    A）should   B）may   C）can   D）would

29. Dr. Smith was always _____ the poor and the sick, often providing them with free medical care.

    A）reminded of   C）tended by

    B）absorbed in   D）concerned about

30. Thomas Jefferson and John Adams died in July 1826, the fiftieth _____ of American Independence.

    A）ceremony   B）occasion   C）occurrence   D）anniversary

Part IV   Vocabulary Exercises for CET 6

Directions: For each sentence there are four choices marked A), B), C) and D). Choose the ONE answer that best completes the sentence.

Unit 1

1. He suggested that we put the scheme into effect, for it is quite _____.
   A) probable   B) sustainable   C) feasible   D) eligible

2. This book is about how these basic beliefs and values affect important _____ of American life.
   A) facets   B) formats   C) formulas   D) fashions

3. It is one thing to locate oil, but it is quite another to _____ and transport it to the industrial centers.
   A) permeate   B) extract   C) distinguish   D) concentrate

4. Students are expected to be quiet and _____ in an Asian classroom.
   A) obedient   B) overwhelming   C) skeptical   D) subsidiary

5. Our reporter has just called to say that rescue teams will _____ to bring out the trapped miners.
   A) effect   B) affect   C) conceive   D) endeavour

6. The Spanish team, who are not in superb form, will be doing their best next week to _____ themselves on the German team for last year's defeat.
   A) remedy   B) reproach   C) revive   D) revenge

7. Creating so much confusion, Mason realized he had better make _____ what he was trying to tell the audience.
   A) exclusive   B) explicit   C) objective   D) obscure

8. One of the examination questions _____ me completely and I couldn't answer it.
   A) baffled   B) mingled   C) provoked   D) diverted

9. The vision of that big black car hitting the sidewalk a few feet from us will never be _____ from my memory.
   A) ejected   B) escaped   C) erased   D) omitted

10. At present, it is not possible to confirm or to refute the suggestion that there is a causal relationship between the amount of fat we eat and the _____ of heart attacks.
    A) incidence   B) impetus   C) rupture   D) emergence

11. There are many who believe that the use of force _____ political ends can never be justified.
    A) in search of   B) in pursuit of   C) in view of   D) in light of

12. Sometimes the bank manager himself is asked to _____ checks if his clerks are not sure about them.
    A) credit   B) assure   C) certify   D) access

13. It is believed that the authorities are thinking of _____ new taxes to raise extra revenue.
    A) impairing   B) imposing   C) invading   D) integrating

14. When she heard the bad news, her eyes ____ with tears as she struggled to control her emotions.
    A) sparkled   B) twinkled   C) radiated   D) glittered

15. There are occasions when giving a gift _____ spoken communication, since the message it offers can cut through barriers of language and cultural diversity.
    A) overtakes   B) nourishes   C) surpasses   D) enforces

16. In order to keep the line moving, customers with lengthy _____ are required to do their banking inside.
    A）transit   B）transactions   C）turnover   D）tempos
17. President Wilson attempted to _____ between the powers to end the war, but neither side was prepared to give in.
    A）segregate   B）whirl   C）compromise   D）mediate
18. The police have installed cameras at dangerous road _____ to film those who drive through red traffic lights.
    A）trenches   B）utilities   C）pavements   D）junctions
19. It is reported that thirty people were killed in a _____ on the railway yesterday.
    A）collision   B）collaboration   C）corrosion   D）confrontation
20. Since a circle has no beginning or end, the wedding ring is accepted as a symbol of _____ love.
    A）successive   B）consecutive   C）eternal   D）insistent
21. Executives of the company enjoyed an _____ lifestyle of free gifts, fine wines and high salaries.
    A）exquisite   B）extravagant   C）exotic   D）eccentric
22. If you want to get into that tunnel, you first have to _____ away all the rocks.
    A）haul   B）repel   C）dispose   D）snatch
23. Some crops are relatively high yielders and could be planted in preference to others to _____ the food supply.
    A）enhance   B）curb   C）disrupt   D）heighten
24. Astronomers at the University of California discovered one of the most distant _____.
    A）paradoxes   B）paradises   C）galaxies   D）shuttles
25. Many great scientists _____ their success to hard work.
    A）portray   B）ascribe   C）impart   D）acknowledge
26. The sign set up by the road _____ drivers to a sharp turn.
    A）alerts   B）refreshes   C）pleads   D）diverts
27. The doctors don't _____ that the patient will live much longer.
    A）monitor   B）manifest   C）articulate   D）anticipate
28. Call your doctor for advice if the _____ persist for more than a few days.
    A）responses   B）signals   C）symptoms   D）reflections
29. We find it impossible to _____ with the latest safety regulations.
    A）accord   B）unify   C）obey   D）comply
30. Professor Smith and Professor Brown will _____ in presenting the series of lectures on American literature.
    A）alter   B）alternate   C）substitute   D）exchange

Unit 2

1. It is generally known that New York is a city for _____ and a center for odd bits of information.
    A）veterans   B）victims   C）pedestrians   D）eccentrics

2. High grades are supposed to _____ academic ability, but John's actual performance did not confirm this.

    A）certify   B）clarify   C）classify   D）notify

3. In spite of the _____, it seemed that many of the invited guests would still show up.

    A）deviation   B）distinction   C）controversy   D）comparison

4. The relatives of those killed in the crash got together to seek_____.

    A）premium   B）compensation   C）repayment   D）refund

5. At first everything went well with the project but recently we have had a number of _____ with the machinery.

    A）disturbances   B）setbacks   C）outputs   D）distortions

6. He tried to hide his _____ patch by sweeping his hair over to one side.

    A）barren   B）bare   C）bald   D）bleak

7. The old couple now still _____ for their beloved son, 30 years after his death.

    A）cherish   B）groan   C）immerse   D）mourn

8. Coffee is the _____ of this district and brings local farmers a lot of money.

    A）majority   B）staple   C）spice   D）elite

9. Before we move, we should _____ some of the old furniture, so that we can have more room in the new house.

    A）discard   B）dissipate   C）cancel   D）conceal

10. You cannot imagine how _____ I feel with my duties sometimes.

    A）overflowed   C）overwhelmed

    B）overthrown   D）overturned

11. Anyone not paying the registration fee by the end of this month will be _____ to have withdrawn from the program.

    A）contemplated   B）deemed   C）acknowledged   D）anticipated

12. Although he was on a diet, the delicious food _____ him enormously.

    A）distracted   B）stimulated   C）inspired   D）tempted

13. The police are trying to _____ what really happened.

    A）ascertain   B）assert   C）avert   D）ascribe

14. He said that ending the agreement would _____ the future of small or family-run shops, lead to fewer books being published and increase prices of all but a few bestsellers.

    A）venture   B）expose   C）jeopardize   D）legalize

15. As we know, computers are used to store and _____ information efficiently.

    A）reclaim   B）reconcile   C）reassure   D）retrieve

16. His illness first _____ itself as severe stomach pains and headaches.

    A）expressed   B）manifested   C）reflected   D）displayed

17. The _____ they felt for each other was obvious to everyone who saw them.

    A）affection   B）adherence   C）sensibility   D）sensitivity

18. When construction can begin depends on how soon the _____ of the route is completed.

    A）conviction   B）identity   C）orientation   D）survey

19. The government _____ a heavy tax on tobacco, which aroused opposition from the tobacco industry.

    A）pronounced   B）imposed   C）complied   D）prescribed

20. Years after the accident he was still _____ by images of death and destruction.
     A）twisted   B）dipped   C）haunted   D）submerged

21. The boxer _____ and almost fell when his opponent hit him.
     A）staggered   B）shattered   C）scattered   D）stamped

22. In mountainous regions, much of the snow that falls is _____ into ice.
     A）dispersed   B）embodied   C）compiled   D）compacted

23. These continual _____ in temperature make it impossible to decide what to wear.
     A）transitions   B）transformations C）exchanges   D）fluctuations

24. The post-World War II baby _____ resulted in a 43 percent increase in the number of teenagers in the 1920s and 1970s.
     A）boost   B）boom   C）production   D）prosperity

25. Elizabeth did not enter the museum at once, but _____ in the courtyard.
     A）resided   B）dwelled   C）lingered   D）delayed

26. Henry went through the documents again carefully for fear of _____ any important data.
     A）relaying   B）overlooking   C）deleting   D）revealing

27. The bank is offering a _____ to anyone who can give information about the robbery.
     A）reward   B）bonus   C）prize   D）compliment

28. It is a(n) _____ that the French eat so much rich food and yet have a relatively low rate of heart disease.
     A）analogy   B）paradox   C）correlation   D）illusion

29. For many years the Japanese have _____ the car market.
     A）presided   B）occupied   C）operated   D）dominated

30. The subject of safety must be placed at the top of the _____.
     A）agenda   B）bulletin   C）routine   D）timetable

Unit 3

1. My grandfather, a retired worker, often _____ the past with a feeling of longing and respect.
     A）considers   B）contemplates   C）contrives   D）contacts

2. Medical students are advised that the wearing of a white coat _____ the acceptance of a professional code of conduct expected of the medical profession.
     A）supplements   B）simulates   C）signifies   D）swears

3. The doctors _____ the newly approved drug into the patient when he was critically ill.
     A）injected   B）ejected   C）projected   D）subjected

4. Apart from philosophical and legal reasons for respecting patients' wishes, there are several practical reasons why doctors should _____ to involve patients in their own medical care decisions.
     A）enforce   B）endow   C）endeavor   D）enhance

5. This is a long _____ — roughly 13 miles down a beautiful valley to the little church below.
     A）terrain   B）descent   C）degeneration   D）tumble

6. She was deeply _____ by the amount of criticism her play received.
     A）deported   B）deprived   C）involved   D）frustrated

7. Some scientists are dubious of the claim that organisms _____ with age as an inevitable outcome of living.

   A）depress   B）default   C）deteriorate   D）degrade

8. Many manufacturers were accused of concentrating too heavily on cost reduction, often at the _____ of the quality of their products.

   A）expense   B）exposure   C）expansion   D）expectation

9. One witness _____ that he'd seen the suspect run out of the bank after it had been robbed.

   A）convicted   B）conformed   C）retorted   D）testified

10. Nothing Helen says is ever _____. She always thinks carefully before she speaks.

   A）simultaneous   B）homogenous   C）spontaneous   D）rigorous

11. She gave _____ directions about the way the rug should be cleaned.

   A）explicit   B）brisk   C）transient   D）opaque

12. It took a lot of imagination to come up with such a(n) _____ plan.

   A）inherent   B）ingenious   C）vigorous   D）exotic

13. A _____ official is one who is irresponsible in his work.

   A）timid   B）tedious   C）suspicious   D）slack

14. Most mathematicians trust their _____ in solving problems and readily admit they would not be able to function without it.

   A）conception   B）perception   C）intuition   D）cognition

15. He had an almost irresistible _____ to talk to the crowd when he entered Hyde Park.

   A）impulse   B）instinct   C）stimulation   D）surge

16. Encouraged by their culture to voice their opinions freely, the Canadians are not afraid to go against the group _____, and will argue their viewpoints enthusiastically, though rarely aggressively.

   A）consent   B）conscience   C）consensus   D）consciousness

17. He still _____ the memory of his carefree childhood spent in that small wooden house of his grandparents .

   A）nourishes   B）cherishes   C）fancies   D）scans

18. She expressed her strong determination that nothing could _____ her to give up her career as a teacher.

   A）induce   B）deduce   C）reduce   D）attract

19. The microscope and telescope, with their capacity to enlarge, isolate and probe, demonstrate how details can be _____ and separated from the whole.

   A）radiated   B）extended   C）prolonged   D）magnified

20. Lighting can be used not only to create an atmosphere, but also to _____ features of the house, such as ornaments or pictures.

   A）highlight   B）underline   C）activate   D）upgrade

21. By turning this knob to the right you can _____ the sound from the radio.

   A）intensify   B）amplify   C）enlarge   D）reinforce

22. One of the attractive features of the course was the way the practical work had been _____ with the theoretical aspects of the subject.

   A）embedded   B）embraced   C）integrated   D）synthesized

23. They couldn't see a _____ of hope that they would be saved by a passing ship.
    A）grain   B）span   C）slice   D）gleam
24. The traditional markets retain their _____ for the many Chinese who still prefer fresh food like live fish, ducks, chickens over packaged or frozen goods.
    A）appeal   B）pledge   C）image   D）survival
25. _____ efforts are needed in order to finish important but unpleasant tasks.
    A）Consecutive   B）Condensed   C）Perpetual   D）Persistent
26. A number of students _____ in flats, and others live in the nearby holiday resorts, where there is a reasonable supply of competitively low priced accommodation.
    A）revive   B）inhabit   C）gather   D）reside
27. He bought his house on the _____ plan, paying a certain amount of money each month.
    A）division   B）premium   C）installment   D）fluctuation
28. He could not _____ ignorance as his excuse; he should have known what was happening in his department.
    A）petition   B）plead   C）resort to   D）reproach
29. Many ecologists believe that lots of major species in the world are on the _____ of extinction.
    A）margin   B）border   C）verge   D）fringe
30. Any salesperson who sells more than the weekly _____ will receive a bonus.
    A）ratio   B）quota   C）allocation   D）portion

Unit 4

1. Susan has _____ the elbows of her son's jacket with leather patches to make it more durable.
    A）reinforced   B）sustained   C）steadied   D）confirmed
2. Although we tried to concentrate on the lecture, we were _____ by the noise from the next room.
    A）distracted   B）displaced   C）dispersed   D）discarded
3. The reason why so many children like to eat this new brand of biscuit is that it is particularly sweet and _____.
    A）fragile   B）feeble   C）brisk   D）crisp
4. Don't trust the speaker any more, since the remarks he made in his lectures are never _____ with the facts.
    A）symmetrical   B）comparative   C）compatible   D）harmonious
5. They had to eat a(n) _____ meal, or they would be too late for the concert.
    A）temporary   B）hasty   C）immediate   D）urgent
6. Having a(n) _____ attitude towards people with different ideas is an indication that one has been well educated.
    A）analytical   B）bearable   C）elastic   D）tolerant
7. No form of government in the world is _____; and each system reflects the history and present needs of the region or the nation.
    A）dominant   B）influential   C）integral   D）drastic

8. In spite of the _____ economic forecast, manufacturing output has risen slightly.

    A）faint   B）dizzy   C）gloomy   D）opaque

9. Too often Dr. Johnson's lectures ____ how to protect the doctor rather than how to cure the patient.

    A）look to   B）dwell on   C）permeate into   D）shrug off

10. Located in Washington D.C., the Library of Congress contains an impressive _____ of books on every conceivable subject.

    A）flock   B）configuration   C）pile   D）array

11. Some felt that they were hurrying into an epoch of unprecedented enlightenment, in which better education and beneficial technology would _____ wealth and leisure for all.

    A）maintain   B）ensure   C）certify   D）console

12. Fiber optic cables can carry hundreds of telephone conversations _____.

    A）homogeneously B）spontaneously   C）simultaneously D）ingeniously

13. Excellent films are those which _____ national and cultural barriers.

    A）transcend   B）traverse   C）abolish   D）suppress

14. The law of supply and demand will eventually take care of a shortage or _____ of dentists.

    A）surge   B）surplus   C）flush   D）fluctuation

15. One third of the Chinese in the United States live in California, ____ in the San Francisco area.

    A）remarkably   B）severely   C）drastically   D）predominantly

16. After the terrible accident, I discovered that my ear was becoming less _____.

    A）sensible   B）sensitive   C）sentimental   D）sensational

17. Now the cheers and applause _____ in a single sustained roar.

    A）mingled   B）tangled   C）baffled   D）huddled

18. Among all the public holidays, National Day seems to be the most joyful to the people of the country; and on that day the whole country is _____ in a festival atmosphere.

    A）trapped   B）sunk   C）soaked   D）immersed

19. The wooden cases must be secured by overall metal strapping so that they can be strong enough to stand rough handling during _____.

    A）transit   B）motion   C）shift   D）traffic

20. Nowadays many rural people flock to the city to look for jobs on the assumption that the streets there are _____ with gold.

    A）overwhelmed   C）paved

    B）stocked   D）overlapped

21. It is a well-known fact that the cat family _____ lions and tigers.

    A）enriches   B）accommodates   C）adopts   D）embraces

22. My boss has failed me so many times that I no longer place any _____ on what he promises.

    A）assurance   B）probability   C）reliance   D）conformity

23. The English language contains a _____ of words which are comparatively seldom used in ordinary conversation.

    A）latitude   B）multitude   C）magnitude   D）longitude

24. It was such a(n) _____ when Pat and Mike met each other in Tokyo. Each thought that the other was still in Hong Kong.
    A）occurrence   B）coincidence   C）fancy   D）destiny
25. Parents have to learn how to follow a body's behavior and adapt the tone of their _____ to the baby's capabilities.
    A）perceptions   B）consultations   C）interactions   D）interruptions
26. Governments today play an increasingly larger role in the _____ of welfare, economics, and education.
    A）scopes   B）ranges   C）ranks   D）domains
27. If businessmen are taxed too much, they will no longer be _____ to work hard, with the result that tax revenues might actually shrink.
    A）cultivated   B）licensed   C）motivated   D）innovated
28. Jack is not very decisive, and he always finds himself in a _____ as if he doesn't know what he really wants to do.
    A）fantasy   B）dilemma   C）contradiction   D）conflict
29. He is a promising young man who is now studying at our graduate school. As his supervisor, I would like to _____ him to your notice.
    A）commend   B）decree   C）presume   D）articulate
30. It was a wonderful occasion which we will _____ for many years to come.
    A）conceive   B）clutch   C）contrive   D）cherish

Unit 5

1. It seems somewhat _____ to expect anyone to drive 3 hours just for a 20-minute meeting.
   A）eccentric   B）impossible   C）absurd   D）unique
2. This area of the park has been specially _____ for children, but accompanying adults are also welcome.
   A）inaugurated   B）designated   C）entitled   D）delegated
3. The girl's face _____ with embarrassment during the interview when she couldn't answer the tough question.
   A）beamed   B）dazzled   C）radiated   D）flushed
4. Slavery was _____ in Canada in 1833, and Canadian authorities encouraged the slaves, who escaped from America, to settle on its vast virgin land.
   A）diluted   B）dissipated   C）abolished   D）resigned
5. Unfortunately, the new edition of this dictionary is _____ in all major bookshops.
   A）out of reach   C）out of business
   B）out of stock   D）out of season
6. The hands on my alarm clock are _____, so I can see what time it is in the dark.
   A）exotic   B）gorgeous   C）luminous   D）spectacular
7. Psychologists have done extensive studies on how well patients _____ with doctors' orders.
   A）comply   B）correspond   C）interfere   D）interact

48

8. In today's class, the students were asked to _____ their mistakes on the exam paper and put in their possible corrections.

    A) cancel   B) omit   C) extinguish   D) erase

9. The Government's policies will come under close _____ in the weeks before the election.

    A) appreciation   B) specification   C) scrutiny   D) apprehension

10. Police and villagers unanimously _____ the forest fire to thunder and lightning.

    A) ascribed   B) approached   C) confirmed   D) confined

11. In some remote places there are still very poor people who can't afford to live in _____ conditions.

    A) gracious   B) decent   C) honorable   D) positive

12. Since our knowledge is _____, none of us can exclude the possibility of being wrong.

    A) controlled   B) restrained   C) finite   D) delicate

13. You shouldn't _____ your father's instructions. Anyway he is an experienced teacher.

    A) deduce   B) deliberate   C) defy   D) denounce

14. The company management attempted to _____ information that was not favorable to them, but it was all in vain.

    A) suppress   B) supplement   C) concentrate   D) plug

15. It is my hope that everyone in this class should _____ their errors before it is too late.

    A) refute   B) exclude   C) expel   D) rectify

16. The boy's foolish question _____ his mother who was busy with housework and had no interest in talking.

    A) intrigued   B) fascinated   C) irritated   D) stimulated

17. Millions of people around the world have some type of physical, mental, or emotional _____ that severely limits their abilities to manage their daily activities.

    A) scandal   B) misfortune   C) deficit   D) handicap

18. It is believed that the feeding patterns parents _____ on their children can determine their adolescent and adult eating habits.

    A) compel   B) impose   C) evoke   D) necessitate

19. If the value-added tax were done away with, it would act as a _____ to consumption.

    A) progression   B) prime   C) stability   D) stimulus

20. The bride and groom promised to _____ each other through sickness and health.

    A) nourish   B) nominate   C) foster   D) cherish

21. They're going to build a big office block on that _____ piece of land.

    A) void   B) vacant   C) blank   D) shallow

22. Without any hesitation, she took off her shoes, ___ up her skirt and splashed across the stream.

    A) tucked   B) revolved   C) twisted   D) curled

23. Very few people could understand his lecture because the subject was very _____.

    A) faint   B) obscure   C) gloomy   D) indefinite

24. Professor Smith explained the movement of light _____ that of water.

    A) by analogy with   B) by virtue of   C) in line with   D) in terms of

25. Tom is bankrupt now. He is desperate because all his efforts _____ failure.
    A）tumbled to   C）inflicted on
    B）hinged upon   D）culminated in

26. While fashion is thought of usually _____ clothing, it is important to realize that it covers a much wider domain.
    A）in relation to   B）in proportion to   C）by means of   D）on behalf of

27. The meaning of the sentence is _____; and you can interpret it in several ways.
    A）skeptical   B）intelligible   C）ambiguous   D）exclusive

28. Cancer is a group of diseases in which there is uncontrolled and disordered growth of _____ cells.
    A）irrelevant   B）inferior   C）controversial   D）abnormal

29. At that time, the economy was still undergoing a _____, and job offers were hard to get.
    A）concession   B）supervision   C）recession   D）deviation

30. I could hear nothing but the roar of the airplane engines which _____ all other sounds.
    A）overturned   B）drowned   C）deafened   D）smoothed

Unit 6

1. Because of the _____ of its ideas, the book was in wide circulation both at home and abroad.
    A）originality   B）subjectivity   C）generality   D）ambiguity

2. With its own parliament and currency and a common _____ for peace, the European Union declared itself — in 11 official languages — open for business.
    A）inspiration   B）assimilation   C）intuition   D）aspiration

3. America has now adopted more _____ European style inspection systems, and the incidence of food poisoning is falling.
    A）discrete   B）solemn   C）rigorous   D）autonomous

4. Mainstream pro-market economists all agree that competition is an _____ spur to efficiency and innovation.
    A）extravagant   B）exquisite   C）intermittent   D）indispensable

5. In the late 19th century, Jules Verne, the master of science fiction, foresaw many of the technological wonders that are _____ today.
    A）transient   B）commonplace   C）implicit   D）elementary

6. I was so _____ when I used the automatic checkout lane in the supermarket for the first time.
    A）immersed   B）assaulted   C）thrilled   D）dedicated

7. His arm was _____ from the shark's mouth and reattached, but the boy, who nearly died, remained in a delicate condition.
    A）retrieved   B）retained   C）repelled   D）restored

8. Bill Gates and Walt Disney are two people America has _____ to be the Greatest American.
    A）appointed   B）appeased   C）nicknamed   D）nominated

9. The _____ majority of citizens tend to believe that the death penalty will help decrease the crime rate.

    A) overflowing   B) overwhelming   C) prevalent   D) premium

10. We will also see a _____ increase in the number of televisions per household, as small TV displays are added to clocks, coffee makers and smoke detectors.

    A) startling   B) surpassing   C) suppressing   D) stacking

11. The advance of globalization is challenging some of our most _____ values and ideas, including our idea of what constitutes "home".

    A) enriched   B) enlightened   C) cherished   D) chartered

12. Researchers have discovered that _____ with animals in an active way may lower a person's blood pressure.

    A) interacting   B) integrating   C) migrating   D) merging

13. The Beatles, the most famous British band of the 1960s, traveled worldwide for many years, _____ cultural barriers.

    A) transporting   B) transplanting   C) transferring   D) transcending

14. In his last years, Henry suffered from a disease that slowly _____ him of much of his sight.

    A) relieved   B) jeopardized   C) deprived   D) eliminated

15. Weight lifting, or any other sport that builds up your muscles, can make bones become denser and less _____ to injury.

    A) attached   B) prone   C) immune   D) reconciled

16. He has _____ to museums hundreds of his paintings as well as his entire personal collection of modern art.

    A) ascribed   B) attributed   C) designated   D) donated

17. Erik's website contains _____ photographs and hundreds of articles and short videos from his trip around the globe.

    A) prosperous   B) gorgeous   C) spacious   D) simultaneous

18. Optimism is a _____ shown to be associated with good physical health, less depression and longer life.

    A) trail   B) trait   C) trace   D) track

19. The institution has a highly effective program which helps first-year students make a successful _____ into college life.

    A) transformation   B) transmission   C) transition   D) transaction

20. Philosophers believe that desire, hatred and envy are "negative emotions" which _____ the mind and lead it into a pursuit of power and possessions.

    A) distort   B) reinforce   C) exert   D) scramble

21. The term "glass ceiling" was first used by the Wall Street Journal to describe the apparent barriers that prevent women from reaching the top of the corporate _____.

    A) seniority   B) superiority   C) height   D) hierarchy

22. Various efforts have been made over the centuries to predict earthquakes, including observing lights in the sky and _____ animal behavior.

    A) abnormal   B) exotic   C) absurd   D) erroneous

23. Around 80 percent of the _____ characteristics of most white Britons have been passed down from a few thousand Ice Age hunters.
    A）intelligible   B）random   C）spontaneous   D）genetic
24. Picasso gained popularity in the mid-20th century, which was _____ of a new attitude towards modern art.
    A）informative   B）indicative   C）exclusive   D）expressive
25. The country was an island that enjoyed civilized living for a thousand years or more with little _____ from the outside world.
    A）disturbance   B）discrimination   C）irritation   D）irregularity
26. Fashion designers are rarely concerned with vital things like warmth, comfort and _____.
    A）stability   B）capabilit   C）durability   D）availability
27. Back in the days when people traveled by horse and carriage, Karl Benz _____ the world with his extraordinary three-wheeled motor vehicle.
    A）inhibited   B）extinguished   C）quenched   D）stunned
28. If we continue to ignore the issue of global warming, we will almost certainly suffer the _____ effects of climatic changes worldwide.
    A）dubious   B）drastic   C）trivial   D）toxic
29. According to the theory of evolution, all living species are the modified _____ of earlier species.
    A）descendants   B）dependants   C）defendants   D）developments
30. The panda is an endangered species, which means that it is very likely to become _____ without adequate protection.
    A）intact   B）insane   C）extinct   D）exempt

提高篇
Skill & Practice

一、英语听力考试中的预判

在听力考试正式开始前应该对试题的选项进行预览，并根据选项所给的线索，判断出即将进行的听力内容是关于哪一方面的对话或题材。预判有利于加深考试印象。从而在随后的听力考试中对听力对话和朗读的内容更清楚地把握。更为重要的是，这样的预判有利于考生抓住考点，从而保证答题的准确率。**预览答案应该放在完成试卷一，听力考试正式开始之前**。听力考试正式开始前共有六七分钟的时间，可以用来预览长对话或文章听力的选项，做出预判。

二、考生应掌握的技能

理论化的技巧要通过亲身实践才能转化为现实的能力。本书高屋建瓴，首先通过听力考试时间分布的实际情况，帮助考生有效利用考试空隙时间，进行有效的预判。其次，本书在讲解各种题型的答题技巧之后，附有大量的实践练习，旨在通过实践让考生将答题技巧在做题过程中消化掌握，真正提高考生的应试能力。总结起来考生应掌握以下基本技能。

（一）语言基础与文化背景知识

扎实的语言基础是指熟练掌握语音、语法、基本词汇以及常用句型，包括口语中的一些习惯表达方法等，更为重要的是同学们在平时学习的过程中，要养成朗诵单词的良好习惯，注意发音准确,这对听力提高非常重要。

不熟悉文化背景知识，往往会造成理解的障碍。在听力训练中，要逐步熟悉有关的文化背景知识，这样有利于对听力细节的把握。文化背景知识不仅对听力理解很重要，也是提高基础语言能力的有效途径，还是一名英语学习者综合文化素质的表现。

背景知识虽然重要，但在考试过程中终究不能代替对语言的基础能力的掌握。如果没有听懂语言点，单凭背景知识进行猜测，同样不可能找到正确的答案。语言理解虽然与背景知识密切相关，但提高听力理解能力的基本条件依然是掌握好语言本身。

（二）基本的听力技能

具备一定的听力技能是提高听力理解能力的有效途径。听力技能主要指捕捉重要信息、进行正确推理、通过综合归纳推断对话或短文中心意思等。捕捉重要信息是听力理解的首要任务，遗漏了重要信息就不可能听清和理解讲话的基本意思。有时重要信息出现在段首或段尾，听者往往受故事情节的干扰而忽略了关键性的段首或段尾句。

在对话中，说话人常常出于某种考虑而不直接表示肯定或否定，而是间接回答。这时，听话者必须从间接回答中领悟说话人的确切含义。正确理解各种委婉的表达方法也是考生必须掌握的一项重要听力技能。

另外，考生还必须学会归纳和总结，善于抓住中心思想。

（三）良好的听音习惯

在听音过程中必须全神贯注，积极思考，**边听边记录要点**。考生还要注意训练和加强短时记忆能力。短时记忆对短文的听力理解尤为重要。因为能否记住刚听完的内容，是理解全文内容和选择正确答案的前提。我们把听音后记忆的信息分为两种：**正信息**（information positive）**与负信息**（information negative）。正信息是有助于答题的相关信息，负信息是对答题形成干扰的冗余信息。听音时做记录是为了重点记忆与答题相关联的正信息。记忆中存储的信息并非越多越好，记忆的内容力求相关与准确。储存的正信息越多，理解的条件就越充分，答对题的把握也就越大。

总之，具备预判能力是提高听力理解能力的重要保证，在听的过程中对可能出现的信息要有所判断。如果新出现的信息与预期信息截然相反，就要善于迅速调整，不断修正自己做出的判断。这是重要的听力技能，在平时训练时要予以充分重视。

三、听力考题的分布

大学英语四级听力考试时间为35分钟。包括三篇新闻（7道题），两篇长对话（8道题），三篇听力文章（10道题）。

四、考试流程及听力预判的准备

如前所述，预判是四、六级听力考试答题的关键。如果能事先进行有效预判，那么考生就可以做到在听题时心中有数，运筹帷幄，取得事半功倍的理想效果了。那么如何才能正确预判呢？这得首先从四级考试的时间分布着手。四级考试新题型考试时间为两小时十分钟。上午9：00～11：20考四级。试卷分**答题卡1，答题卡2**和试题册。9：00发放试卷，9：10考试正式开始，9：55收**答题卡1**（包括作文和快速阅读部分，即作文答题时间30分钟，快速阅读答题时间15分钟）。10：00听力考试正式开始。显然，9：55～10：00五分钟的收卷时间加上约两分多钟的试音和朗读指令的时间，同学们应充分加以利用。完成答题卡1的考生可以利用这个时间预览长对话和短文听力的答案项。因为每一篇长对话或短文听力的3～4个答案项它们在逻辑上应该是彼此关联的，所以聪明的考生可以从答案项的预览中，整理出一个逻辑线索，然后做出一定程度的预判。预判包括**内容的预判和答案的预判**。内容的预判即根据答案性的预览判断出听力对话或文章是有关哪一方面的内容；答案的预判包括某一道题将可能涉及什么问题，答案有可能是选项中的哪一项。只要考生能根据自己的逻辑做出预判，不论答案是否和考生听完听力录音后做出的判断一致，预览预判对考生的帮助都是非常明显的。有的考生尚未听录音，通过预览就能预判出相当一部分正确答案。其实，预判的目的并不是在听力录音前就判断出答案，而是通过预览预判使得考生对即将读出的内容有所了解，加深印象。即使在预判中做出与后来正确答案完全不同的（这种可能性是很大的）答案，也不要紧。毕竟通过预判，考生增加了对听力内容的印象，这有利于在听后做出正确的选择。

> **注意**：准备听力考试的考生务必在听前合理安排预览，可能的话做出一定程度的预判，要记住听力考试中这样一句至理名言："尽可能地预判，即便是错误预判也远胜于无预判。"

短对话与长对话

听力考试最先测试短对话，但短对话的选项可以在朗读 Section A（听力的对话部分）的指令时开始预览，也就是说短对话虽然是听力考试的第一部分，短对话选项的预览却是安排在最后的。因为短对话有八道题，每题之间有 13 ～ 14 秒的停顿，而它们之间又不存在逻辑联系。因此，短对话的选项完全可以在听力考试的短对话正式开始后，一个一个浏览，浏览后听题，听完后立刻做出选择，再利用 13 ～ 14 秒的空隙浏览下一题的答案。**注意答题节奏**，一个对话结束后应该迅速做出判断，不要影响下一道题的回答。

词汇热身

（一）易混淆的多义词

1. **bank** 表示（1）银行。（2）河岸。

2. **tip** 表示（1）建议。例，some useful tips 表示一些有益的建议；（2）小费、给……小费。例，I tipped the man several dollars. 我给了他几美元小费。（3）尖、顶端。例，finger tip：指尖。常用习语：on the tip of one's tongue 表示话就在嘴边却说不出来。

3. **awful** 表示丑陋的、非常差的；但是，awfully 表示很、非常。例，awfully nervous：相当紧张。awfully good：相当好。

4. **be worn out** 表示（1）筋疲力尽。例，I was completely worn out at the end of the day. 那天要结束时，我疲惫不堪。（2）褴褛的、破旧不堪的。例，After many years my shirt was worn out. 许多年后我的衬衫已经穿破了。

5. **check** 表示（1）检查、核实。check-in 表示登机检查。（2）支票。

6. **count** 表示（1）数、计算。（2）count on 表示依赖，等于 rely on. 例，You can count on me to deal with the emergent case. 你可以指望我处理紧急情况。

7. **ring** 表示（1）鸣、敲响、按铃。例，ring the bell：鸣钟，按门铃。（2）打电话。例，Please give me a ring tonight. 今晚请给我打电话。（3）环状物。（4）戒指。例，give her an engagement ring：给她订婚戒指。（5）团伙。例，a criminal ring：犯罪团伙。

8. **drop** 表示（1）滴。例，drops of water：水滴。（2）下降。例，a drop in the price of gold：金价下跌。（3）拜访。常用词组：drop in、drop in on，表示顺道拜访。（4）放弃。例，I'll have to drop the case. 我不得不放弃这件事了。

9. **film** 表示（1）电影。（2）胶卷。

10. **kid** 表示（1）孩子。（2）开玩笑。例，Are you kidding？你不是在开玩笑吧？表示不太相信。

（二）场景必备词

1. **Hotel**。single room：单人房 / double room：双人房 / reservation：预订 / front desk：前台 / a honey-moon suite：蜜月套房 / book：预订

2. **Restaurant**。menu：菜单 / order：订单 / salad：沙拉 / soft drink：软饮料 / dessert：饭后甜点 / ice cream：冰激淋 / soup：汤 / go Dutch：AA 制、各付各账 / beef steak：牛排 / mutton：羊肉 / make a reservation：预订、预约

3. **Library**。borrow：借 / due：到期 / over-due：逾期 / fine：罚款 / renew：续借 / catalogue：目录 / volume：卷，册 English version：英文版本

4. **Post Office**。mail：信件 / parcel：包裹 / airmail：航空邮件 / registered letter：挂号信 /

postage：邮费

5．**Store**。discount：折扣 / bargain：讨价还价 / medium-sized：中等尺寸的、中号的 / old-fashioned：过时的 / counter：柜台 / catalog：商品目录

6．**Bank**。open an account：开户 / deposit：存款 / signature：签名

7．**Hospital**。flu：流行性感冒 / fever：发烧 / cough：咳嗽 / pills：药丸 / tablet：药片 / take medicine：吃药 / stomachache：胃疼 / temperature：体温 / prescribed drug：处方药 / symptom：症状 / indigestion：消化不良 / operation：手术 / vaccine injection：疫苗注射 / immune system：免疫系统 / appointment：预约

8．**School**。Bachelor's degree：学士学位 / Master's degree：硕士学位 / Doctor's degree：博士学位 / dormitory：宿舍 / semester：学期 / term paper：学期报告 / tuition fee：学费 / registration：注册、登记 / required course：必修课 / optional course：选修课 / failing：不及格 / quit school：辍学 / credits：学分 / course：课程 / signature：签名 /cafeteria：自助食堂 / canteen：食堂

9．**Airport**。flight：航班 / take off：起飞 / land：使着陆 /boarding：登机 / fasten your seatbelt：系好安全带 /check-in：登机前检查 / departure time：起飞时间 / airlines：航空公司

10．**Street**。driving license：驾照 / run a red light：闯红灯 / speeding：超速 / fine：罚款 / lane line：分道线 / bicycle lane：自行车车道 / vehicle：机动车

短对话题型归类、技巧与实践

一、常考题型

（一）数字与计算题

"数字与计算"是早年大学英语四级统考中听力测试最常考的项目之一。常见的计算题包括时间、价格、年龄、距离、速度等。出题形式可分为计算型、辨认型和替换型。以加减计算题为主。

相关词汇与表达：ahead of schedule/ delay/ postpone/ double/ a quarter/ deadline

例一

A）At 10:30.　　B）At 10:25.　　C）At 10:40.　　D）At 10:45.

原文

M: So when are the other guys going to get here? The train is leaving in 10 minutes. We can't wait here forever.

W: It's 10:30 already? They are supposed to be here by now. I told everybody to meet here by 10:15.

Q: When is the train leaving?

解：有关数字和时间题的回答（从答案项可判断）一定要尽可能地速记下对话中提到的每一个数字和时间，如本题考生在听的过程中应记录下三个时间：10 minutes（迟到10分钟）、10:30（现在时间）和10:15（应该到达的时间）。同时对每个时间对应什么要有大概的印象。如同样是该题，如果问题问的是 How long have the other guys already been late?

A）10 minutes　　B）15 minutes　　C）20 minutes　　D）25 minutes

如果在听的过程中未能对各个时间做出相应的反应，显然很难做出正确的回答。另外，

要注意英语中的十几和几十的发音，除了长短音不同，更重要的区分在于它们的重音不同，前者重音在后，后者重音在前。

提示：ten fifty 也可以表达为ten to eleven同样指10:50（差10分11点）的意思，请同学们记住这种表达方法。

（二）职业、身份和相互关系题

考查考生的社会基本常识、逻辑判断，涉及大量固定场所的专用词，请参考 3. 地点与场所题。

（三）地点与场所题

最常见的提问方式是：

Where does the conversation most probably take place?

Where are the two speakers now?

例一（1996.1）

A）At home. 　　　　　　　　C）At the health center.

B）At the riverside. 　　　　　D）At his office.

原文

M: Hello, this is John Hopkins at the Riverside Health Center. I'd like to speak to Mr. Jones.

W: I'm sorry, Mr. Hopkins, my husband isn't at home. But I can give you his office phone number. He won't be back until 6 o'clock.

Q: Where does Mrs. Jones think her husband is now?

例二（2004.1）

A）At a booking office. 　　　　C）On a busy street.

B）In a Hong Kong hotel. 　　　D）At an airport.

原文

W: Can I help you, Sir?

M: Yes. Can you show me the way to gate 9 for flight 901 to Hong Kong? I'm quite confused here.

Q: Where does the conversation most probably take place?

（四）态度与反应题

涉及的主要是对话中男女双方对某人某事的看法。主要测试考生的分析判断能力，考生务必注意转折类信息词。

例一（2005.6）

A）The man hates to lend his tools to other people.

B）The man hasn't finished working on the bookshelf.

C）The tools have already been returned to the woman.

D）The tools the man borrowed from the woman are missing.

原文

W: Simon, oh, well, could you return the tools I lent you for building the bookshelf last month?

M: Oh, I hate to tell you this, but I can't seem to find them.

Q: What do we learn from the conversation?

解：先开口讲话的女士说了一大通繁杂的信息，其中像 bookshelf 等词汇考生并不熟悉，听到这里考生不免沮丧。但是前面的很多信息跟答题并没有关系，考生只要记住女士是要男士归还工具（return the tools），然后男士说了 I hate to tell you this, but I can't seem to find them（但是我好像找不到了）。后面的内容才是回答问题的关键，这是英语四级听力考试一个非常明显的特征，请同学们务必牢记。这里还考查了学生逻辑上的一个简单的判断，即工具找不到了，那么就是不见了：missing。

例二（2002.6）

A）He wishes to have more courses like it.   C）He wishes the teacher would talk more.

B）He finds it hard to follow the teacher.   D）He doesn't like the teacher's accent.

原文

W: You took an optional course this semester, didn't you? How is it going?

M: Terrible! It seems like the more the professor talks, the less I understand.

Q: How does the man feel about the course?

解：考查 the more ... the less 句型。

（五）推理判断题

推理判断是英语四级听力测试中最常见的题型之一，难度较大。因为说话人表达思想的方法比较含蓄，不能为答案选择提供直接的信息，这就要求考生利用语音语调和逻辑推理的思维过程来判断对话的内在含义，领会说话人的真实意图。听力理解不但要听懂具体的话语，而且要听懂隐含的意义，能判断讲话人的意图等。

这类题型在近几年的考试中题量大，而且有增加的趋势。

例一（2002.6）

A）Go on with the game.   C）Review his lessons.

B）Draw pictures on the computer.   D）Have a good rest.

原文

W: Mark is playing computer game.

M: Should he do that when the final exam is drawing near?

Q: What does the man think Mark should do?

解："**Should he do that** when the final exam is drawing near?" 言下之意指 "**He shouldn't do that** when the final exam is drawing near?"。

例二（2004.1）

The man is usually the last to hand in his test paper.

The man has made a mess of his midterm exam.

The man has bad study habits.

The man is a diligent student.

原文

M: I'm exhausted. I stayed up the whole night studying for my midterm math exam.

W: But why do you always wait until the last minute?

Q: What does the woman imply?

解："但是你为什么总是要等到最后一分钟呢？"言下之意指不应该拖到考试前才复习。

例三（2004.6）

A）She has learned a lot from the novel.

B）She also found the plot difficult to follow.

C）She usually has difficulty remembering name.

D）She can recall the names of most characters in the novel.

原文

M: I had a hard time getting through this novel.

W: I share your feeling, who can remember the names of 35 different characters?

Q: What does the woman imply?

解："我和你感觉相同，谁能记得住 35 个不同人物的名字呢？"，言下之意指记不住那么多名字。

例四（2005.1）

A）Tony should continue taking the course.

B）She approves of Tony's decision.

C）Tony can choose another science course.

D）She can't meet Tony so early in the morning.

原文

M: I'm going to drop my Information Science class. It meets too early in the morning.

W: Is that really a good reason to drop the class, Tony?

Q: What does the woman mean?

解："那真是退出学习班的好理由吗？"，言下之意指不是好理由，不应该退出学习班。

例五（2005.1）

A）Move the washing machine to the basement.

B）Turn the basement into a workshop.

C）Repair the washing machine.

D）Finish his assignment.

原文

M: Allen is in the basement trying to repair the washing machine.

W: Shouldn't he be working on his term paper?

Q: What does the woman think Allen should do?

解："他不应该在做论文吗？"，言下之意指"他应该在做论文"。

例六（2005.6）

A）Save time by using a computer.　　C）Borrow Martha's computer.

B）Buy her own computer.　　D）Stay home and complete her paper.

原文

W: I am going to Martha's house. I have a paper to complete. And I need to use her computer.

M: Why don't you buy one yourself?　Think how much time you could save.

Q: What does the man suggest the woman do?

解："你自己为什么不买一台呢？"言下之意指女士应该自己买一台。

> 提示：从以上的解析中，同学们应该注意到推论题或建议题的说话者的态度或建议往往是以反义疑问句的形式出现的。答题时一定要注意听说话者的语气，同时要熟悉反义疑问句的句式，否则在考试的时候就可能来不及反应，破坏答题的节奏。

二、谨防陷阱、精彩博弈

出题者针对听力考试的 Section A 答案项往往都会设计对话陷阱，特别是在短对话中，出题者抓住没有听懂对话的同学的心理，利用对话的结束语中的一部分设计干扰项。因为，没有听懂对话的考生，通常能听懂对话中的只言片语，此时，考生往往有抓救命稻草的心理，看到选项中有自己听到的单词，就"欣然"做出选择，结果恰恰跌入了出题者精心设计的陷阱。所以考生在没有听懂对话的意思只靠听到的部分词作为选择依据时，一定要慎重了，此时与其以词（听到的只言片语）为据，不如体会语气。

虽然用结束语设计选项作为干扰的听力题在近几年有所减少，但是这依然是短对话的一个重要的方面，请同学们在平时做题时注意积累，熟悉这些题型，培养自己的"直觉"，真正做到熟能生巧。

例一（2004.1）

A）The woman is watching an exciting film with the man.

B）The woman can't take a photo of the man.

C）The woman is running toward the lake.

D）The woman is filming the lake.

原文

M: Look! The view is fantastic. Could you take a picture of me with the lake in the background?

W: I'm afraid I just ran out of film.

Q: What do we learn from the conversation?

解：选项 A、D 完全是利用女士的结束语中的 film 进行干扰，因为 film 一词，许多同学更熟悉它作为"电影"之意，而不是很熟悉它作为胶卷的意思。

例二（2006.1）

A）The 2:00 train will arrive earlier.

B）The 2:30 train has a dining car.

C）The woman prefers to take the 2:30 train.

D）They are going to have some fast food on the train.

原文

M: There is a non-stop train for Washington and it leaves at 2:30.

W: It's faster than the 2 o'clock train. Besides, we can have something to eat before getting on the train.

Q: What do we learn from the conversation?

解：女士的结束语为"have something to eat before getting on the train"，D 项就是利用结束语设计的干扰选项，都提到了吃点东西，对话中是指上车前吃，而 D 项则表示在车上吃。有不少考生没理解对话，只听懂了只言片语（have something to eat），于是误选了 D。

例三（2006.1）

A）Alice didn't seem to be nervous during her speech.

B）Alice needs more training in making public speeches.

C）The man can hardly understand Alice's presentation.

D）The man didn't think highly of Alice's presentation.

原文

W: Did you attend Alice's presentation last night? It was the first time for her to give a speech to a large audience.

M: How she could be so calm in front of so many people is really beyond me!

Q: What do we learn from the conversation?

解：男士的结束语，"is really beyond me" 是指不知道、弄不清楚。C 项明显是利用这个结束语设计的干扰选项，但是男士说的是 "他真不知道 Alice 可以在那么多人面前如此沉着"，而不是 C 项 "不理解 Alice 的陈述"。

例四（2006.1）

A）Help the company recruit graduate students.

B）Visit the electronics company next week.

C）Get a part-time job on campus before graduation.

D）Apply for a job in the electronics company.

原文

M: You know the electronics company is coming to our campus to recruit graduate students next week.

W: Really? What day? I'd like to talk to them and hand in my resume.

Q: What does the woman want to do?

解：男士的结束语用了 "the company is coming to recruit graduate students next week"，A 项就是利用该结束语（recruit graduate students）设计的干扰选项。不过由于很多考生当时并不知道 recruit（招聘、招募）一词的意思，没有听懂，反而因祸得福没有错选 A 项。

> 提示：近年来，利用结束语的只言片语所设计的干扰项已经比前些年的考试更为复杂化了。以前用结束语的只言片语设计干扰项往往用一两个单词进行简单干扰（如例一），现在有一种新的趋势，即不是用原字进行干扰，而是用对话的部分意思，断章取义地进行干扰。

Practice makes perfect!

Exercise 1

1. A）The man enjoys traveling by car.

   B）The man lives far from the subway.

   C）The man is good at driving.

   D）The man used to own a car.

2. A）Tony should continue taking the course.

   B）She approves of Tony's decision.

C）Tony can choose another science course.

D）She can't meet Tony so early in the morning.

3．A）She has to study for the exam.

B）She is particularly interested in plays.

C）She's eager to watch the new play.

D）She can lend her notes to the man.

4．A）They will be replaced by on-line education sooner or later.

B）They will attract fewer kids as on-line education expands.

C）They will continue to exist along with on-line education.

D）They will limit their teaching to certain subjects only.

5．A）Most students would like to work for a newspaper.

B）Most students find a job by reading advertisements.

C）Most students find it hard to get a job after they graduate.

D）Most students don't want jobs advertised in the newspapers.

6．A）Move the washing machine to the basement.

B）Turn the basement into a workshop.

C）Repair the washing machine.

D）Finish his assignment.

7．A）Some students at the back cannot hear the professor.

B）The professor has changed his reading assignment.

C）Some of the students are not on the professor's list.

D）The professor has brought extra copies of his assignment.

8．A）She doesn't want to talk about the contest.

B）She's modest about her success in the contest.

C）She's spent two years studying English in Canada.

D）She's very proud of her success in the speech contest.

9．A）Talking about sports.   C）Reading newspapers.

   B）Writing up local news.   D）Putting up advertisements.

10．A）They shouldn't change their plan.   C）The tennis game won't last long.

    B）They'd better change their mind.   D）Weather forecasts are not reliable.

Exercise 2

1．A）The man hates to lend his tools to other people.

B）The man hasn't finished working on the bookshelf.

C）The tools have already been returned to the woman.

D）The tools the man borrowed from the woman are missing.

2．A）Give the ring to a policeman.

B）Wait for the owner of the ring in the rest room.

C）Hand in the ring to the security office.

D）Take the ring to the administration building.

3．A）Save time by using a computer.   C）Borrow Martha's computer.

    B）Buy her own computer.   D）Stay home and complete her paper.

4. A) The man doesn't have money for his daughter's graduate studies.

   B) The man doesn't think his daughter will get a business degree.

   C) The man insists that his daughter should pursue her studies in science.

   D) The man advises his daughter to think carefully before making her decision.

5. A) The cinema is some distance away from where they are.

   B) He would like to read the film review in the newspaper.

   C) They should wait to see the movie at a later time.

   D) He'll find his way to the cinema.

6. A) He's been to Seattle many times.　　　C) He has a high position in his company.

   B) He has chaired a lot of conferences.　　D) He lived in Seattle for many years.

7. A) Teacher and student.　　　　　　　　C) Manager and office worker.

   B) Doctor and patient.　　　　　　　　　D) Travel agent and customer.

8. A) She knows the guy who will give the lecture.

   B) She thinks the lecture might be informative.

   C) She wants to add something to her lecture.

   D) She'll finished her report this weekend.

9. A) An art museum.　　　　　　　　　　C) A college campus.

   B) A beautiful park.　　　　　　　　　　D) An architectural exhibition.

10. A) The houses for sale are of poor quality.

    B) The houses are too expensive for the couple to buy.

    C) The housing developers provide free trips for potential buyers.

    D) The man is unwilling to take a look at the houses for sale.

Exercise 3

1. A) See a doctor.　　　　　　　　　　　C) Get treatment in a better hospital.

   B) Stay in bed for a few days.　　　　　D) Make a phone call to the doctor.

2. A) The 2:00 train will arrive earlier.

   B) The 2:30 train has a dining car.

   C) The woman prefers to take the 2:30 train.

   D) They are gong to have some fast food on the train.

3. A) She has been longing to attend Harvard University.

   B) She'll consider the man's suggestion carefully.

   C) She has finished her project with Dr. Garcia's help.

   D) She'll consult Dr. Garcia about entering graduate school.

4. A) Alice didn't seem to be nervous during her speech.

   B) Alice needs more training in making public speeches.

   C) The man can hardly understand Alice's presentation.

   D) The man didn't think highly of Alice's presentation.

5. A) It's worse than 30 years ago.

   B) It remains almost the same as before.

   C) There are more extremes in the weather.

   D) There has been a significant rise in temperature.

6. A）At a publishing house.   C）In a reading room.
    B）At a bookstore.   D）In Prof. Jordan's office.

7. A）The man can stay in her brother's apartment.
    B）Her brother can help the man find a cheaper hotel.
    C）Her brother can find an apartment for the man.
    D）The man should have booked a less expensive hotel.

8. A）Priority should be given to listening.
    B）It's most helpful to read English newspapers every day.
    C）It's more effective to combine listening with reading.
    D）Reading should come before listening.

9. A）It can help solve complex problems.   C）It is a new weapon against terrorists.
    B）It will most likely prove ineffective.   D）It will help detect all kinds of liars.

10. A）Help the company recruit graduate students.
    B）Visit the electronics company next week.
    C）Get apart-time job on campus before graduation.
    D）Apply for a job in the electronics company.

Exercise 4

1. A）The girls got on well with each other.
    B）It's understandable that girls don't get along.
    C）She was angry with the other young stars.
    D）The girls lacked the courage to fight.

2. A）The woman does her own housework.   C）The woman's house is in a mess.
    B）The woman needs a housekeeper.   D）The woman works as a housekeeper.

3. A）The Edwards are quite well-off.
    B）The Edwards should cut down on their living expenses.
    C）It'll be unwise for the Edwards to buy another house.
    D）It's too expensive for the Edwards to live in their present house.

4. A）The woman didn't expect it to be so warm at noon.
    B）The woman is sensitive to weather changes.
    C）The weather forecast was unreliable.
    D）The weather turned cold all of a sudden.

5. A）At a clinic.   C）At a restaurant.
    B）In a supermarket.   D）In an ice cream shop.

6. A）The woman did not feel any danger growing up in the Bronx.
    B）The man thinks it was quite safe living in the Bronx district.
    C）The woman started working at an early age to support her family.
    D）The man doesn't think it safe to send an 8-year-old girl to buy things.

7. A）The man has never seen the woman before.
    B）The two speakers work for the same company.
    C）The two speakers work on the same floor.
    D）The woman is interested in market research.

8. A）The woman can't tolerate any noise.

   B）The man is looking for an apartment.

   C）The man has missed his appointment.

   D）The woman is going to take a train trip.

答案与原文

Exercise 1

答案

（1-5）DAACB　　（6-10）DCBCA

原文

1. **W:** You've sold your car. You don't need one?

   M: Not really. I've never liked driving anyway. Now we've moved to a place near the subway entrance. We can get about quite conveniently.

   Q: What do we learn from the conversation?

2. **M:** I'm going to drop my Information Science class. It meets too early in the morning.

   W: Is that really a good reason to drop the class, Tony?

   Q: What does the woman mean?

3. **M:** If you aren't doing anything particular, shall we see the new play at the Grand Theater tonight?

   W: Sounds great. But I've got to go over my notes for tomorrow's midterm.

   Q: What does the woman imply?

4. **M:** What do you think of the prospects for online education? Is it going to replace the traditional school?

   W: I doubt it. Schools are here to stay, because there are much more than just book learning. Even though more and more kids are going online, I believe fewer of them will quit school altogether.

   Q: What does the woman think of the conventional schools?

5. **M:** How do most students find a job after they graduate?

   W: They usually look for a job by searching the want ads in the newspapers.

   Q: What does the woman mean?

6. **M:** Allen is in the basement trying to repair the washing machine.

   W: Shouldn't he be working on his term paper?

   Q: What does the woman think Allen should do?

7. **W:** Professor Newman, a few of us at the back didn't get a copy of your reading assignment.

   M: Well, there're only 38 names on my class list. And I didn't bring any spare copies.

   Q: What do we learn from the conversation?

8. **M:** Congratulations, Li Ming. You are the talk of the town, and the proud of our class now.

   W: If you are referring to my winning the English speech contest, I don't think it's such a big deal. You know I've spent two summer vacations learning English in Canada.

   Q: What do we learn about Li Ming from the conversation?

9. **M:** Would you pass me the sports section, please?

W: Sure, if you give me the classified ads and local news section.

Q: What are the speakers doing?

10. W: If the weather is this hot tomorrow, we may as well give up the idea of playing tennis in the afternoon.

M: Oh, I don't think it'll last long. The weather forecast says it will cloud over by midafternoon.

Q: What does the man mean?

Exercise 2

答案

（1-5）DCBDA　　（6-10）ACBCD

原文

1. W: Simon, oh, well, could you return the tools I lent you for building the bookshelf last month?

M: Oh, well, I hate to tell you this, but I can't seem to find them.

Q: What do we learn from the conversation?

2. W: I found an expensive diamond ring in the restroom this morning.

M: If I were you, I'd turn it in to the security office. It is behind the administration building.

Q: What does the man suggest the woman do?

3. W: I'm going to Martha's house. I have a paper to complete. And I need to use her computer.

M: Why don't you buy one yourself? Think how much time you could save.

Q: What does the man suggest the woman do?

4. W: Daddy, I've decided to give up science and go to business school.

M: Well, it's your choice as long as pay your own way, but I should warn you that not everyone with a business degree will make a successful manager.

Q: What do we learn from the conversation?

5. W: I've just read in the newspaper that Lord of the Rings is this year's greatest hit. Why don't we go and see it at the Grand Cinema?

M: Don't you think that cinema is a little out of the way?

Q: What does the man mean?

6. W: Bob said that Seattle is a great place for conferences.

M: He's certainly in the position to make that comment. He has been there so often.

Q: What does the man say about Bob?

7. W: Mr. Watson, I wonder whether it's possible for me to take a vacation early next month?

M: Did you fill out a request form?

Q: What is the probable relationship between the two speakers?

8. M: Do you want to go to the lecture this weekend? I hear that the guy who is going to deliver the lecture spent a year living in the rainforest.

W: Great, I am doing a report on the rain forest. Maybe I can get some new information to add to it.

Q: What does the woman mean?

9. **W:** Wow, I do like this campus. All the big trees, the green lawns, and the old buildings with tall columns. It's really beautiful.

M: It sure is. The architecture of these buildings is in the Greek style. It was popular in the 18th century here.

Q: What are the speakers talking about?

10. **M:** This article is nothing but advertising for housing developers. I don't think the houses for sale are half that good.

W: Come on, David. Why so negative? We are thinking of buying a home, aren't we? Just a trip to look at the place won't cost us much.

Q: What can be inferred form the conversation?

Exercise 3

答案

（1-5）ACDAC　（6-10）BACBD

原文

1. **W:** Carol told us on the phone not to worry about her. Her left leg doesn't hurt as much as it did yesterday.

M: She'd better have it examined by a doctor anyway. And I will call her about it this evening.

Q: What does the man think Carol should do?

2. **M:** There is a non-stop train for Washington and it leaves at 2:30.

W: It's faster than the 2 o'clock train. Besides, we can have something to eat before getting on the train.

Q: What do we learn from the conversation?

3. **M:** Hi, Melissa, how's your project going? Have you thought about going to graduate school? Perhaps you can get into Harvard.

W: Everything is coming along really well. I have been thinking about graduate school. But I'll talk to my tutor Dr. Garcia first and see what she thinks.

Q: What do you learn about the woman from the conversation?

4. **W:** Did you attend Alice's presentation last night? It was the first time for her to give a speech to a large audience.

M: How she could be so calm in front of so many people is really beyond me!

Q: What do we learn from the conversation?

5. **W:** You've been doing weather reports for neatly 30 years. Has the weather got any worse in all these years?

M: Well, not necessarily worse. But we've seen more swings.

Q: What does the man say about the weather?

6. **M:** Excuse me, I am looking for the textbook by Professor Jordon for the marketing

course.

W: I am afraid it's out of stock. You'll have to order it. And it will take the publisher 3 weeks to send it to us.

Q: Where did this conversation most probably take place?

7. M: I am going to New York next week, but the hotel I booked is really expensive.

W: Why book a hotel? My brother has 2 spare rooms in his apartment.

Q: What does the woman mean?

8. W: In my opinion, watching the news on TV is a good way to learn English. What do you think?

M: It would be better if you could check the same information in English newspapers afterwards.

Q: What does the man say about learning English?

9. M: I hear a newly-invented drug can make people tell the truth and it may prove useful in questioning terrorists. Isn't it incredible?

W: Simple solutions to complex problems rarely succeed. As far as I know, no such drugs are ever known to work.

Q: What does the woman think of the new drug?

10. M: You know the electronics company is coming to our campus to recruit graduate students next week.

W: Really? What day? I'd like to talk to them and hand in my resume.

Q: What does the woman want to do?

Exercise 4

答案

（1-8）AACDCABB

原文

1. M: What would be like working with those young stars?

W: It was a great group, I always got mad when people said that we didn't get along, just because we were girls, there was never a fight. We had a great time.

Q: What does the woman mean?

2. M: Are you telling me you don't have a housekeeper?

W: No, we don't. If you make a mess, you clean it up yourself.

Q: What do we learn from this conversation?

3. W: I hear that the Edwards are thinking of buying another house.

M: Should they be doing that with all the other expenses they have to pay? Anyhow, they are over 70 now, their present house is not too bad.

Q: What does the man imply?

4. M: You look like you are freezing to death. Why don't you put this on?

W: Thank you. It was so warm at noon. I didn't expect the weather to change so quickly.

Q: What do we learn from the conversation?

5. M: I'll have the steak, French Fries, and let's see, chocolate ice-cream for dissert.

W: Oh, Oh, you know these things will ruin your health, too much fat and sugar. How about ordering some vegetables and fruit instead?

Q: Where does the conversation most probably take place?

6. M: What was it like growing up in New York's Bronx District? Was it safe?

W: To me, it was. It was all I knew. My mom would send me to the shop and I'd go and buy things when I was about 8 years old.

Q: What do we learn from the conversation?

7. M: Nice weather, isn't it? Oh, I've seen you around the office, but I don't think we've met. I am Henry Smith. I work in the Market Research Section.

W: Nice to meet you, Henry. I am Helen Grant. I am in the Advertising Section on the ninth floor.

Q: What can we infer from the conversation?

8. M: Mam, I hear you have an apartment for rent, can I take a look at it?

W: Sure, you're welcome any time by appointment, but I have to tell you the building is close to a railway with the noise. You might as well save the trip.

Q: What do we learn from the conversation?

长对话技巧与实践

长对话的准备，除了同样要熟悉掌握对话中一些场景的必备词汇，作为一个整体，对长对话的理解和答题还需要注意以下几点。

（1）利用指令和试音时间做好预览、预判。

（2）试题基本遵循顺序对应原则，即长对话中三个或四个问题的答题依据是前对前，后对后，相互对应的。

（3）题量分布均匀，长对话一般包括不止一个话题，要注意往往话题一转就意味着可能要考另外一道题。

（4）注意对话中的提问，出题者往往喜欢在此设计考点。

例一

Questions 19 to 22 are based on the conversation you have just heard.

19. A）The benefits of strong business competition.
    B）A proposal to *lower the cost of production.*
    C）*Complaints about the expense* of modernization.
    D）Suggestions concerning new business strategies.

20. A）It *cost much more than its worth.*
    B）It should be brought up-to-date（与 modernize 同义）.
    C）It calls for immediate repairs.
    D）It can still be used for a long time.

21. A）The personnel manager should be fired for inefficiency.
    B）A few engineers should be employed to modernize the factory.
    C）The entire staff should be retrained.
    D）Better-educated employees should be promoted.

22. A）Their competitors have long been advertising on TV.
    B）TV commercials *are less expensive.*

C）Advertising in newspapers alone is not sufficient.

D）TV commercials attract more investments.

预判：从 19 题选项 A）、B）、D）看，对话似乎是关于公司运营的建议或主张的，且 19 题极有可能问的是本篇对话是关于什么的。从 20 题选项来看，对话者在谈论一种东西，这种东西似乎不那么令人满意了，因此，对它的处理意见有 A）"花费高于其本身价值"B）"应该及时更新了"C）"需要立即修理了"D）"还能用上一段时间"。

总体上似乎有两条线，第一条线（粗体斜字）是关于降低成本的一条线：从 19 题 B）降低生产成本的建议到 20 题 A）和 22 题 B）似乎都和节约成本有关；第二条线（下划线）是关于企业需要及时更新设备或人员，使企业实现现代化。而不论是节约成本还是使企业现代化或者是其他建议，都是从属于采取一种新的营销策略，所以，19 题 D）"有关新的经营策略的建议"可能是正确的。而 21 题 A）"人事经理效率低下应该被解雇"，似乎不像是一种合理化建议，更像是在"打小报告"所以可以大胆预判 A）不正确。

> **提示**：对话的主题和线索主要依靠选项中的重复词、同义词和同类别词等关键词确定。例如，本对话中的 modernize（重复词）、19 题的 proposal 与 suggestions（同义词）和 22 题的 advertising 与 commercials（同类别词）。考生也无须担心预判是否与对话（或文章）的事实相符，前面已经说过即便是"错误预判，也要强于没有预判"。例如 21 题，假如文章真的是说人事经理的效率不高，应该被解雇，可以肯定的是，你之前的预判给你留下的印象足以轻而易举地帮你选出正确的答案。

请听录音答题

答案

19. D   20. B   21. B   22. C

原文

W: Hello, Gary. How're you?

M: Fine! And you?

W: Can't complain. (19) Did you have time to look at my proposal（建议）?

M: No, not really. Can we go over it now?

W: Sure. (19) I've been trying to come up with some new production and advertising strategies. First of all, if we want to stay competitive, we need to modernize our factory. (20) New equipment should've been installed long ago.

（第一个话题：女士关于生产和广告新策略的建议，请男士参考，继而提出第二个话题：早就应该安装新设备以实现企业的现代化）

M: How much will that cost?

W: We have several options ranging from one hundred thousand dollars all the way up to half a million.

M: OK. We'll have to discuss these costs with finance.

（第三个话题：有关安装新设备的成本，没有具体谈，一带而过，该处没有设题）

W: We should also consider human resources. I've been talking to personnel as well as our staff at the factory.

M: And what's the picture?

W: (21) We'll probably have to hire a couple of engineers to help us modernize the factory.

（第四个话题：需要新的人员来帮助实现企业的现代化）

M: What about advertising?

W: Marketing has some interesting ideas for television commercials.

M: TV? Isn't that a bit too expensive for us? (22) What's wrong with advertising in the papers, as usual?

W: Quite frankly, (22) it's just not enough anymore. We need to be more aggressive in order to keep ahead of our competitors.

（第五个话题：关于广告营销策略）

M: Will we be able to afford all this?

W: I'll look into it, but I think higher costs will be justified. These investments will result in higher profits for our company.

M: We'll have to look at the figures more closely. Have finance draw up a budget for these investments.

W: All right. I'll see to it.

（第六个话题：关于广告营销的成本，该处没有设题）

Questions 19 to 20 are based on the conversation you have just heard.

Question 19: What are the two speakers talking about?

Question 20: What does the woman say about the equipment of their factory?

Question 21: What does the woman suggest about human resources?

Question 22: Why does the woman suggest advertising on TV?

> 提示：对于19题，一些心急的同学会仓促地选择C)，modernization的确是对话的一个主题，但是对话并没有涉及modernization的成本，更谈不上对进行现代化所要花费的成本的抱怨。对话涉及modernization和promotion (advertising)，都是建议公司采取一种新的营销策略。另外，答案依据都已经在原文中标出，同学们请注意，题目的设计基本是遵循对话的前后顺序的原则进行的，所以在后面的练习中，一定要训练边听边扫描答案项的"一心二用"的答题技能，才能真正让长对话和短文听力的答题变得轻松起来。

下面请花 50 秒的时间浏览分析例二的选项，然后答题。

例二

Questions 23 to 25 are based on the conversation you have just heard.

23. A）Searching for reference material.   C）Writing a course book.

    B）Watching a film of the 1930s.   D）Looking for a job in a movie studio.

24. A）It's too broad to cope with.   C）It's controversial.

    B）It's a bit outdated.   D）It's of little practical value.

25. A）At the end of the online catalogue.

    B）At the Reference Desk.

    C）In the New York Times.

    D）In the Reader's Guide to Periodical Literature.

请听录音答题

解：分析选项，可以做出这样的预判（在此强调，不要在意预判的是否与对话内容一致），23 题问的可能是某人要做什么的；24 题问的是某一样东西的缺陷；25 题问的是应该在哪里做一件事或得到一样东西。

答案

23．A   24．A   25.D

原文

W: Sir, you've been using the online catalogue for quite a while. Is there anything I can do to help you?

M: Well, (23) I've got to write a paper about Hollywood in the 1930s and 1940s, and I'm really struggling. There are hundreds of books, and I just don't know where to begin.

W: (24) Your topic sounds pretty big. Why don't you narrow it down to something like...uh... the history of the studios during that time?

M: You know, I was thinking about doing that, but more that 30 books came up when I typed in "movie studios."

W: You could cut that down even further by listing the specific years you want. Try adding "1930s" or "1940s" or maybe "Golden Age."

M: "Golden Age" is a good idea. Let me type that in ... Hey, look, just 6 books this time. That's a lot better.

W: Oh... another thing you might consider... have you tried looking for any magazine or newspaper articles?

M: No, I've only been searching for books.

W: Well, (25) you can look up magazine articles in the Reader's Guide to Periodical Literature.And we do have the Los Angeles. Times available over there. You might go through their indexes to see if there's anything you want.

M: Okay, I think I'll get started with these books and then I'll go over the magazines.

W: If you need any help, I'll be over at the Reference Desk.

M: Great, thanks a lot.

Questions 23 to 25 are based on the conversation you have just heard.

Question 23: What is the man doing?

Question 24: What does the librarian think of the topic the man is working on ?

Question 25: Where can the man find the relevant magazine articles?

特别提示：对于25题的回答，如果考生能够一边浏览答案项，一边听放音，可以很容易地选对答案，否则，很难做出选择。由于选项中往往不止一项被涉及（不再机械的考听单词的能力，而是考学生对听力材料的理解），就要求考生在听放音时，浏览答案，把听到的选项定位，找到它对应的内容，答题时就可以一目了然了。本题的B）At the Reference Desk.和D) In the Reader's Guide to Periodical Literature.在对话中都提到了，考生通过一边听放音，一边浏览答案，并进行线索速记。知道at the reference desk对应的是男士，而in the Reader's Guide to Periodical Literature对应的是查询期刊文章，记下适量的线索（magazine articles）就可以比较容易地选出正确的答案了。

注意：有的考生认为没有这么多时间去预判，其实不然。在听力考试正式开始前（9：55～10：00）收答题卡一，做好答题卡一的考生不应浪费这段时间，而应充分对其加以利用，预览长对话和短文听力的选项。10：00听力考试正式开始，这时还有试音部分（从2007年6月恢复包括Example在内试音），持续大约三分钟的时间。这些时间完全可以继续用来预览长对话和短文听力的选项，做出一定程度的预判。如果不能在答案上有所预判，至少在逻辑上要能判断出对话或文章是关于哪一方面的。更需考生注意的是，在放Section A的时候，就可以回来浏览短对话第一题的选项了。Section A的指令持续大约52秒，足够同学们浏览一两个选项了，然后平静一下心情，等待听力考试的正式开始。听力每一问题问完大约留有13～14秒的时间让同学们答题，同学们应迅速做出判断和选择，再预览下一题。不要下一道题马上就要开始了，还在犹豫上一题应该选什么，从而影响下一题的回答。在听力考试中把握答题的节奏非常重要，需要考生在平时训练中多加练习。另外，在听Section B的指令时（大约持续30秒），应该再看一下自己的预判，有准备地去听题、做题，效果无疑会更佳。

Practice makes perfect!

Part I   Warm-up Exercises

Unit 1

Conversation One

1. A）Go to Germany to live with his friend.
   B）Return to Germany for further studies.
   C）Set up a company in Shanghai.
   D）Find a job in a large multinational company in Shanghai.
2. A）Because his girlfriend works there.
   B）Because he can earn a good salary and get a good experience.
   C）Because he can contribute more to his native land.
   D）Because he cannot find a job abroad.
3. A）They take away the most educated people from developing countries.
   B）They often send their employees to work abroad.
   C）They always give immigrants high-wage jobs.
   D）They are in favor of cross-cultural communication.

Conversation Two

1. A）Gail   B）Mark   C）Susan   D）His parents
2. A）Mark and Gail's marriage plan.   C）Culture differences in a mixed marriage.
   B）Race views in Gail's parents.   D）Waiting won't hurt a marriage.
3. A）Gail's happiness.   C）Mark's being of a different race.
   B）Mark's citizenship status.   D）How their children will be treated.

4. A）They will wait for a while.

   B）They will get married as planned.

   C）They will be realistic and resolve all doubts before they get married.

   D）No answer is provided.

Unit 2

Conversation One

1. A）They have some fun and games in their lives.

   B）They save money for a trip to the Middle East.

   C）They begin to plan a trip around the world.

   D）They work hard to improve their living standards.

2. A）Different countries have different policies regarding travel and immigration.

   B）Travel and immigration will cost them a lot of money.

   C）The policies regarding travel and immigration in some countries aren't realistic.

   D）All the countries just have the same policies regarding travel and immigration.

3. A）People there are hostile to foreigners.

   B）The traffic conditions in that region are very backward.

   C）There is a lot of conflict in the region.

   D）Foreigners usually find it hard to get along with the local people there.

Conversation Two

1. A）They are very modern.   C）They are very relaxing.

   B）They are very beautiful.   D）They are very expensive.

2. A）No, he doesn't.   C）No, because he hasn't got one.

   B）Yes, he sometimes does.   D）Yes, he always does.

3. A）She plays tennis.   C）She plays golf and table tennis.

   B）She plays mah-jong.   D）She plays table-tennis.

4. A）By E-mail.   B）By phone.   C）By post.   D）By fax.

Unit 3

Conversation One

1. A）Obedient.   B）Complaining.   C）Efficient.   D）Capable.

2. A）Robots can do everything for human being.

   B）Robots can make the impossible possible.

   C）Robots can ultimately replace human brains.

   D）Robots can do many things we may not imagine possible.

3. A）robots are the most creative and powerful creatures on earth.

   B）machines can do the kind of work that is physically unbearable to humans.

   C）Feng Yi is fairly emotional when talking about robot.

   D）they both believe that robot will free humans from boring work.

Conversation Two

1. A) Dense fog.   C) Plentiful winter sunshine.
   B) A story about a blind woman.   D) Clean air and water.
2. A) Since the Thames River was full of fish.
   B) When the average winter sunshine doubled.
   C) Before the government took steps to solve the problem.
   D) After the Clean Air Act was enforced.
3. A) The old factories.
   B) The newly-built factories.
   C) The old factories as well as some newly-built ones.
   D) Neither the old factories nor the newly-built ones.
4. A) Factories are built far away from residential areas.
   B) The industrial zone has been set up in the suburban areas.
   C) The air and water in the city is considerably polluted.
   D) The suburban areas are full of polluted air.

Unit 4

Conversation One

1. A) To the supermarket.   B) To his home.   C) To school.   D) To the woman's house.
2. A) To earn money for holidays.   C) To earn money for school.
   B) To earn money for his family.   D) To earn money for his sister's education.
3. A) To clean the yard for her neighbors.   C) To cut grass for her neighbors.
   B) To do some shopping for her neighbors.   D) To plant trees for her neighbors.

Conversation Two

1. A) Because she is tired of staying home all day.
   B) Because there is a good film in the neighborhood theatre.
   C) Because she enjoys going to the movies.
   D) Because she is tired of watching TV.
2. A) She prefers to spend money on something else.
   B) It would cost them more to see a movie in downtown than in the neighborhood.
   C) People cannot help buying things if they go downtown.
   D) It would take a long drive to get there.
3. A) Because the movie theatre is too far away.
   B) Because the film is too old.
   C) Because she doesn't want to see it a second time.
   D) Because it's a popular film so the tickets would be quite expensive.
4. A) People are tired of watching TV nowadays.
   B) Baseball games attract more people than films do.
   C) There aren't any films worth seeing in local theatres.
   D) The woman is rather hard to please.

Part II Test Yourself

Conversation One

Questions 19 to 21 are based on the conversation you have just heard.

19. A）To make a business report to the woman.
    B）To be interviewed for a job in the woman's company.
    C）To resign from his position in the woman's company.
    D）To exchange stock market information with the woman.

20. A）He is head of a small trading company.
    B）He works in an international insurance company.
    C）He leads a team of brokers in a big company.
    D）He is a public relations officer in a small company.

21. A）The woman thinks Mr. Saunders is asking for more than they can offer.
    B）Mr. Saunders will share one third of the woman's responsibilities.
    C）Mr. Saunders believes that he deserves more paid vacations.
    D）The woman seems to be satisfied with Mr. Saunders' past experience.

Conversation Two

Questions 22 to 25 are based on the conversation you have just heard.

22. A）She's worried about the seminar.
    B）The man keeps interrupting her.
    C）She finds it too hard.
    D）She lacks interest in it.

23. A）The lecturers are boring.
    B）The course is poorly designed.
    C）She prefers Philosophy to English.
    D）She enjoys literature more.

24. A）Karen's friend.
    B）Karen's parents.
    C）Karen's lecturers.
    D）Karen herself.

25. A）Changing her major.
    B）Spending less of her parents' money.
    C）Getting transferred to the English Department.
    D）Leaving the university.

答案与原文

Unit 1

📋 **答案**

（1）DBA   （2）CACD

📄 **原文**

Conversation One

W: What do you plan to do after you finish your university work?

M: (1) I've got a friend in Germany who says that he can get me a job with a large multinational company here in Shanghai.

W: (1) <u>So you'll work here?</u>

M: (2) <u>Well, I can earn a very good salary and get good experience.</u>

W: Would you leave for a foreign country if they ask you to go?

M: It depends what they want and how long they want me to stay away from home.

W: Did you know that (3) <u>some people say that both foreign companies and foreign countries take the most talented people away from their homes in developing countries on purpose?</u>

M: Why would they do that?

W: Highly educated people often make large contributions to both a country's economy and society.

M: So it would be to the advantage of a country to allow skilled immigrants in?

W: Yes, of course it would.

Q 1： What does the man plan to do after finishing his university work?

Q 2： Why does the man want to work in Shanghai?

Q 3： What did the woman say about foreign companies and foreign countries?

Conversation Two

M: (2) <u>What do you think of Mark and Gail's marriage plans,</u> (1) <u>Susan</u>?

W: I don't know. It seems the situation is quite difficult.

M: What do you mean?

W: Well, to begin with, Gail's parents have many reservations about their marriage.

M: How do you know?

W: For instance, (3) <u>Gail's father is concerned about both Mark's citizenship status and how their children will be treated.</u>

M: These are both real concerns because people do get married just to acquire citizenship and children from mixed marriages do often receive bad treatment from other children.

W: Yes, and yet Gail thinks that racial and culture differences can often be a gift in a relationship, even though people often feel full of doubt about a mixed marriage.

M: So who's right?

W: Maybe there is no right answer. The situation is really difficult.

M: I see.

Q 1： Who is the man talking with?

Q 2： What are they talking about?

Q 3： Gail's parents seem concerned about all of the following except _____.

Q 4： What will Mark and Gail probably do?

Unit 2

📋 **答案**

（1）CAC　　　　（2）CAAA

📑 **原文**

Conversation One

M: Honey, after all these stressful years, (1) <u>I suggest we go on a trip around the world next year.</u>

W: That sounds fun.

M: Yes, but I think it's also going to take us a lot of work.

W: Why is that?

M: You know, (2) each country has its own policies regarding travel and immigration.

W: Wouldn't it be easier if every country had the same policy?

M: Of course. It would, but that just wouldn't be realistic.

W: No, you're probably right.

M: For instance, in the Middle East, it is often very difficult to go from one country to another.

W: Why is that?

M: (3) There's a lot of conflict in the region so countries are reluctant to allow people to move from place to place easily.

Q 1： What does the man suggest to the woman?

Q 2： Why does the man say that a trip around the world take them a lot of work?

Q 3： Why is it often difficult to move from country to country in the Middle East?

Conversation Two

W: How does time affect you?

M: I actually spend time deciding how I will conduct my day.

W: That sounds like a good way to budget some leisure time for you.

M: Yes, (1) I like the relaxed feeling of the surroundings at the golf course.

W: Do you take your cell phone with you?

M: No, (2) I like to avoid such devices when I am at the golf course because if the phone rings, I will want to answer it.

W: (3) I spend my leisure time playing tennis.

M: That's a superb way to stay in shape and also have a good time.

W: I'm not a very good player; I just want to play for a brief time and make friends by playing tennis.

M: I have met some interesting people at the golf course too and (4) I can contact them by E-mail when I don't have leisure time.

W: I always like to meet people face-to-face because I am able to explore my questions more thoroughly than I can by E-mail or electronic communication.

M: Yes, I think face-to-face interaction is very important and should be used when possible.

W: Well, I couldn't agree with you more. Also, playing tennis also allows me to get away from my work environment.

M: Yes, I also enjoy getting away.

Q 1： What does the man think about the surroundings at the golf course?

Q 2： Does the man take his cell phone with him to the golf course?

Q 3： What does the woman do in her leisure time?

Q 4： How does the man contact his golf friends when he has no leisure time?

Unit 3

📋 **答案**

（1）BDA （2）ADCC

原文

Conversation One

F(Feng Yi)： Suppose I let you make a wish, Simon, what would you wish?

S(Simon): If so, I'd wish I had a robot.

F： Why a robot, of all things?

S: (1) A robot is clever, capable, efficient, and obedient. It'll work with precision. And it'll work round the clock without complaint.

F： Yes, it'll relieve us of hard and tedious work. But what would you do if you had a robot to work for you?

S: (2) Work wonders, such as farming, manufacturing, construction, transportation, telecommuni-cation, medical treatment, things you may not even imagine possible.

F： But aren't you creating a world of machines, a world of cold, emotionless, mechanical creatures?

S: I don't think so. Robots can provide us with all kinds of entertainment imaginable, including both artistic and popular forms of entertainment. (3) And no human culture can match its variety and creativity.

F： (3) It depends on what you mean by variety and creativity. I consider humans the most varied, sophisticated, creative and powerful creatures on earth. Any mechanical culture is simply lifeless, and it's harmful to the human world.

S: Don't get so emotional. We can live in peace with our robots. You know robots would willingly do the kind of work that is physically unbearable to humans.

F: Hmm, you may be right.

Q 1： Which of the following is inappropriate to describe "robot" according to Simon?

Q 2： What does Simon mean by saying "working wonders"?

Q 3： All of the following statements are true except_____.

Conversation Two

(Zhao Lei, an engineer in British Oxygen Company, is talking about pollution control with his British colleague, David.)

Z (Zhao Lei): So you are from London, David. Some time ago I read an interesting story about London fog.

D (David): Oh, yeah, I think I know the one you mean. It's about a blind woman leading a man with good eyesight to his home in a dense fog.

Z: That's right. Since then, (1) I've always thought of London as a city full of fog. It must be terrible living there.

D: That's already history. London is no longer like that. (2) The yellow-black winter fog has disappeared since the Clean Air Act was enforced in 1956. Since then the average winter sunshine has doubled.And the Thames is swarming with fish.

Z: Really? I wish we could do away with air pollution and dust here. It's been tormenting us for years.

D: It's not that bad, is it? I've found the city fairly clean.

Z: Ah, but this is a suburban area.(4) Go to the industrial zone and you'll be bothered by the air and water pollution.

D: The factories must have been set up a long time ago. (3) <u>Old factories are usually not equipped with pollution control devices.</u> That was the same in my country. It took us many years to make our industrial cities clean and healthy.

Z: (3) <u>But the trouble we have is that even some of the newer factories didn't include pollution control measures when they were built.</u> Besides, quite a number of factories were built in the middle of residential areas.

D: Oh, that's too bad. New factories should have been built out of town.

Z: Fortunately, our government has already realized the importance of environmental protection. We can expect a cleaner and healthier city in the future.

Q 1： What was London famous for in the past?

Q 2： When did London do away with its air pollution?

Q 3： According to the two speakers what kind of factories has contributed to the environmental pollution in the cities in China?

Q 4： Which statement is true to the city Zhao Lei lives in?

Unit 4

答案

（1）BCD　　　　　（2）DBCD

原文

Conversation One

M: Hello, how are you?

W: I'm fine, where are you going?

M: (1) <u>Oh, I'm on my way home from work.</u>

W: I didn't know you have a job.

M: Ya, I work part-time at the supermarket.

W: What do you do there?

M: I work in the produce section, trimming and wrapping fresh fruit and vegetables. I also stock shelves. Sometimes when it really gets busy, I work at the check-out counter. Have you got a job?

W: Ya, I do yard work for people. You know, cutting grass, raking leaves, falling weeds, things like that.

M: I'd like doing that. It must be nice to work outdoors.

W: Sometimes it is, except when it rains, snows or gets too hot or too cold.

M: I guess every job has its drawbacks. There are times when I get pretty tired of carrying things around at my job.But a job is a job.(2) <u>Got to earn money for school.</u>

W: Me, too, tuition sure is high, isn't it? Well, (3) <u>I'd better get going, I have to plant some trees for my neighbors this afternoon.</u>

Q 1： Where is the man going when the woman meets him?

Q 2： Why does the man have to work?

Q 3： Why does the woman have to go?

Conversation Two

W: (1) <u>I'm tired of watching television. Let's go to cinema tonight.</u>

M: All right. Do you want to go downtown? Or is there a good movie in the neighborhood?

W: I'd rather not spend a lot of money. (2) <u>What does the paper say about neighborhood theaters?</u>

M: Here's the list on page 18, Column 6. Here it is. Where's the Denton? There's a perfect movie there.

W: That's too far away. And it's hard to find a place to park there.

M: Well, the Grand Theater has Gone with the Wind.

W: (3) <u>I saw that years ago. I don't want to see it again. Moreover, it's too long. We wouldn't get home until midnight.</u>

M: The Center has a horror film. You wouldn't want to see that.

W: No, indeed.I wouldn't be able to sleep tonight.

M: That's about all there is. Unless we change our decision and go downtown.

W: No, we just can't pay for it. There must be something we haven't seen.

M: Here, look for yourself. I can't find anything else.

W: Look at this!

M: What?

W: In the television timetable, there is a baseball game tonight.

M: I wasn't looking for a TV program. I was looking at the movie ads.

W: I know, but I just happened to notice it. New York is playing in Boston. I suppose we'd better stay home. We can go to cinema Friday.

M: That must be good. I wouldn't mind watching that.

Q 1： Why does the woman want to go to the movie?

Q 2： What does "I'd rather not spend a lot of money" imply?

Q 3： Why does the woman say she doesn't want to see the movie "Gone with the wind"?

Q 4： What may you infer from the conversation?

Part Ⅱ Test Yourself

答案

（19-21）BCD   （22-25）DCBD

原文

Conversation One

W: Please have a seat, Mr. Thunders. I received your resume last week, and was very impressed.

M: Thank you!

W: We are a small financial company trading mostly stocks and bonds. May I ask why you are interested in working for us?

M: Your company has an impressive reputation and (19) <u>I've always wanted to work for a smaller company.</u>

W: That's good to hear. Would you mind telling me a little bit about your present job?

M: (20) <u>I'm currently working in a large international company in charge of a team of 8 brokers</u>（经纪人）. We buy and sell stocks for major clients worldwide.

W: Why do you think you are the right candidate for this position?

M: As a head broker, I have a lot of experience in the stock market. I deal with the clients on the daily bases, and I enjoy working with people.

W: (21) <u>Well, you might just be the person we've been looking for.</u> Do you have any questions?

M: Uh-hum, if I were hired, how many accounts would I be handling?

W: You will be working with two other head brokers, in another words, you will be handling about a third of our clients.

M: And who would I report to?

W: Directly to me.

M: I see. What kind of benefits package do you offer?

W: Two weeks of paid vacation（带薪假期）in your first year employment. You are also been entitled to medical and dental insurance, but (21) <u>this is something you should discuss with our Personnel Department（人事部）.</u> Do you have any other questions?

M: No, not at the moment.

W: Well, I have to discuss your application with my colleagues and we'll get back to you early next week.

M: OK, thanks, it's been nice meeting you!

W: Nice meeting you too! And thanks for coming in today.

Conversation Two

M: Hey, Karen, you are not really reading it, are you?

W: Pardon?

M: The book! You haven't turned the page in the last ten minutes.

W: No, Jim, I suppose I haven't. I need to get through although, (22) <u>but I keep drifting away.</u>

M: So it doesn't really hold your interest?

W: (22) <u>No, not really. I wouldn't bother with it, to be honest,</u> but I have to read it for a seminar. I'm at the university.

M: It's a labor of labor then rather than a labor of love.

W: I should say, I don't like Dickens at all really, the author, indeed, I am starting to like the whole course less and less.

M: It's not just the book, it's the course as well?

W: Yeah, in a way, although the course itself isn't really that bad, a lot of it is pretty good, in fact, and the lecturers are fine. It's me, I suppose. You see, (23) <u>I wanted to do philosophy rather than English,</u> but my parents took me out of it.

M: So the course is OK as such. It's just that hadn't been left to you. You would have chosen a different one.

W: Oh, they had my best interest at heart, of course, my parents. They always do, don't they? (24)<u>They believe that my job prospects（工作前景）would be pretty limited with the degree of Philosophy,</u> plus they give me really a generous allowance（可观的津贴）, but I am beginning to feel that I'm wasting my time and their money. They would be so disappointed, though, (25)<u>if I told them I was quitting.</u>

Q 22：Why can't Karen concentrate on the book?

Q 23：Why is Karen starting to like the course less and less?

Q 24：Who thinks Philosophy graduates have limited job opportunities?

Q 25：What is Karen thinking of doing?

短文听力应试策略

相对第一部分（Section A）的对话来说，短文难度较大。这是因为短文篇幅较长，信息量大，题材广泛，包括英、美等英语国家的文化、社会习俗、地理、教育、科普、人物传记和一般性知识等。

短文听力应试技巧

如前所述，考生通过利用 9:55 ～ 10:00 的试卷 1 交卷时间以及朗读指令等空余时间已经浏览了短文听力的选项，并做出了一定程度的预判。等到 Section A Conversation 全部完成，**就再利用朗读 Section B 的指令（大约持续 30 秒）的时间，立刻回顾一下之前所做的预判，进一步加深印象**，然后做题。这样有助于加深对重要信息的记忆，有助于提高解题的正确率。在听的过程中一旦发现内容和自己预期的不一样，要善于及时调整。紧张的考试中记忆的持续是非常短暂的，这就要求考生利用边听边浏览的答题方法，**在题目选项旁边及时标注**，等问题问完后根据自己的标注更准确地回答问题。所以考生务必养成一边听一边在选项旁做标注的良好习惯，标注可以用符号、字母甚至汉字，只要能帮助你回忆所听的内容即可。

如果短文是一篇故事，那么听的时候应抓住地点、时间、人物、因果等要素，抓住了这些也就抓住了故事的框架。在抓住框架的前提下记下一些细节。如果能做到这一步，那么对于故事之后的提问就能应答自如。有时从选项中看不出要听的短文是故事还是其他类型的，但听完开头几句便能知分晓。

例一

请预览选项

Questions 26 to 29 are based on the passage you have just heard.

26. A）Rent a grave.
    B）Burn the body.
    C）Bury the dead near a church.
    D）Buy a piece of land for a grave.

27. **A）To solve the problem of lack of land.**
    B）To see whether they have decayed.
    C）To follow the Greek religious practice.
    D）To move them to a multi-storey graveyard.

28. A）They should be buried lying down.
    B）They should be buried standing up.
    C）They should be buried after being washed.
    D）They should be buried when partially decayed.

29. **A）Burning dead bodies to ashes.**
    B）Storing dead bodies in a remote place.
    C）Placing dead bodies in a bone room.
    D）Digging up dead bodies after three years.

预判：分析选项，从短文选项的关键词 grave 和 bury、storing、placing（后三者在文中表示相同意思，都表示尸体的安葬）很快可以推断本文是关于人死后应该如何安葬的。而从 27 题 A）我们可以做出这样一个假定，随着人口的迅速扩张，似乎连墓地也"尸满为患"，土地愈发紧缺，人们不得不想出新办法来解决这一问题。粗体字选项可以作为一条逻辑链条，27 题 A）、28 题 B）和 29 题 A）与 B）似乎都是与我们的假定——墓地紧张有关。另外，28 题 D）"它们应该在部分开始腐烂后再安葬"与 29 题 D）"在埋葬三年后再把尸体挖上来"似乎过于荒谬，我们在预览的时候可以把它们假定为错误选项而预先予以排除。当然，我们在正式听音之前的预判并非总是正确的。假定之后在听音过程中发现，我们预览时的判断与文章并不一致，甚至预判中认为是荒谬的东西正是文章所表述的东西，这也没有关系。由于预览时留下的印象，我们同样可以很快排除错选的答案，然后确定正确答案，这就是我们说的**"即便是错误的预判也胜于无预判"**。

请听录音答题

原文

　　In Greece, only rich people will rest in peace for ever when they die. Most of the population, however, will be undisturbed for only three years, then they will be dug up, washed, compressed into a small tin box, and placed in a bone room. If the body has only partially decayed (部分腐烂), it is reburied in a smaller cheaper grave, but not for long, the body will be dug up again some time later when it has fully decayed. (26) <u>Buying a piece of land for a grave is the only way to avoid this process.</u> The cost of the grave is so great that most people choose to rent a grave for three years and even after being dug up, lasting peace is still not guaranteed. If no one pays for renting space in the bone room, the skeleton is removed and stored in a building in a poor part of the town. (27) <u>Lack of space in Athens is the main reason why the dead are dug up after three years.</u> The city is so overcrowded that sometimes dead bodies are kept in hospitals for over a week until a grave is found. Athens city council wants to introduce cremation (火葬) that (29) <u>is burning the dead bodies as a means of dealing with the problem.</u> But the Greek Church resists this practice; they believe the only place where people burn is a hell, so burning dead bodies is against the Greek concept of life after death. (28) <u>To save space, the church suggested burying the bodies standing up instead of lying down.</u> Some people proposed building multi-storey underground grave yards.

Questions 26 to 29 are based on the passage you have just heard.
Question 26: What must Greeks do to keep the dead resting in ever-lasting peace?
Question 27: Why are most dead bodies in Athens dug up after three years?
Question 28: What suggestions does the church give about the burying of the dead bodies?
Question 29: What practice does the Greek church object to?

解析：26～29 题的答案依据已分别用下划线在原文中标出，看来雅典人也主张入土为安，只不过由于土地资源稀缺（Lack of space in Athens is the main reason why the dead are dug up after three years），活着的人支付不起昂贵的墓穴费，很多逝去的人的尸体又被重新挖掘起来。政府主张火葬，而教会却反对，认为人只有在地狱中才被火焚烧，所以教会提出新的主张：尸体以直立的状态被埋葬（第 28 题答案）。本篇短文 27 题的预判：由于墓地紧张而产生的一系列问题，而 28 题 D）"它们应该在部分开始腐烂后再安葬"与 29 题 D）"在埋葬三年后再把尸体挖上来"在预判中被排除。其实根据文章的叙述确有其事，只不过它们都不是正确答案，因为即便是希腊人也不希望出现 28 题与 29 题 D）所描述的情况，之所以有这样情况存在，完全是由于土地资源稀缺所致，所以最终还是会到达我们预判所确定的那条主线上：土地稀缺。

　　答案：D　A　B　A

重要提示：（1）答案在文中的定位发生了对顺序原则的偏离，主要是28题与29题在文中的定位没有按照顺序下来。但是答案在文中的定位总体上依然遵循顺序的原则，这对考生边听短文边浏览选项是非常有利的。（2）不少听力教材所总结出一些所谓"技巧"：原文朗读到的就一定是正确的答案。本篇短文的许多选项（包括不正确的选项）的内容在文中都以原话形式被提及，但是并没有成为正确的答案，这也是近几年听力考试的新的发展趋势。新的听力考试注重考察考生对听力材料的理解，而不是机械地考察考生的听力，选项中的内容在文章中被提及，并不一定表示它是正确答案，对此务必请考生注意。

例二

请预览选项

Questions 30 to 32 are based on the passage you have just heard.

30. A）Many foreign tourists visit the United States every year.
    B）Americans enjoy eating out with their friends.
    C）The United States is a country of immigrants.
    D）Americans prefer foreign foods to their own food.

31. A）They can make friends with people from other countries.
    B）They can get to know people of other cultures and their lifestyles.
    C）They can practice speaking foreign languages there.
    D）They can meet with businessmen from all over the world.

32. A）The couple cook the dishes and the children help them.
    B）The husband does the cooking and the wife serves as the waitress.
    C）The mother does the cooking while the father and children wait on the guests.
    D）A hired cook prepares the dishes and the family members serve the guests.

预判：分析选项，可以判断本文可能是有关外国人（或移民）在美国生活的情况。31题的选项涉及外国人到美国（或者美国人去外国）的目的或者好处。32题更明确，问题大概是问有客人来访时，是丈夫、妻子或者夫妻一起做饭招待客人还是雇一个厨师做饭招待客人。带着这些问题去听，显然更容易选出正确的答案。

请听录音答题

原文

If you visit a big city anywhere in the world, you will probably find a restaurant would serve the food of your own native country. Most large cities in the United States offer international sample of foods. Many people enjoy eating the food of other nations. This is probably one reason why there are so many different kinds of restaurants in the United States. (30) A second reason is that many Americans come from other parts of the world. They enjoy tasting the foods of their native lands. In the city of Detroit, for example, there are many people from western Europe, Greece, Latin America, and the Far East. There are many restaurants in Detroit which serve the foods of these areas. There are many other international restaurants too. Americans enjoy the foods in these restaurants (31) as well as the opportunity to better understand the people and their way of life. One of the most common international restaurants to be found in the United States is the Italian restaurant. The restaurant may be a small business run by a single family. (32) <u>The mother of the family cooks all of the dishes, and the father and children serve the people who come to eat there.</u> Or it may be a large restaurant owned by several different people who worked together in the business. Many Italian dishes that Americans enjoy are made with meats, tomatoes and cheese. They are very delicious and tasty.

Questions 30 to 32 are based on the passage you have just heard.

Questions 30: Why are there so many international restaurants in the United States?

Questions 31: Why do Americans like to go to international restaurants apart from enjoying the foods there?

Questions 32: How is a typical Italian family restaurant run in the United States?

解析：本篇预判的内容出现了部分偏差，如 31 题并不是问美国人到外国去的目的而是问美国人到外国餐厅就餐的原因。其实大同小异，这样的偏差并不会影响正确答案的选择。

答案：C B C

例三

请预览选项

Questions 33 to 35 are based on the passage you have just heard.

33．A）He took them to watch a basketball game.
   B）He trained them to play European football.
   C）He let them compete in getting balls out of a basket.
   D）He taught them to play an exciting new game.

34．A）The players found the basket too high to reach.
   B）The players had trouble getting the ball out of the basket.
   C）The players had difficulty understanding the complex rules.
   D）The players soon found the game boring.

35．A）By removing the bottom of the basket.　　C）By simplifying the complex rules.
   B）By lowering the position of the basket.　　D）By altering the size of the basket.

预判：本题的预判并不难，33 题问的是一个人带领一群人干什么（A）"观看篮球赛"、B）"踢足球"、C）"把球从篮子中拿出"、D）"教他们一种新的令人兴奋的游戏"）。32 题大概问的是参加游戏的人遇到了什么困难或不便。35 题是逻辑的自然延伸，即如何解决困难或不便的。我们可以假设 34 题正确答案是 A）或 B），那么 35 题的答案很自然地就应该是 B）（对应 34 题 A 选项）或 A）（对应 34 题 B 选项）。更可能的预判是 34 题 B）、35 题 A），因为这很像在叙述早期的篮球运动及其发展。

请听录音答题

原文

One winter day in 1891, a class of training school in Massachusetts, U. S. A, went into the gym for their daily exercises. Since the football season had ended, most of young men felt they were in for a boring time. But their teacher, James Nasmyth had other ideas. (33) <u>He had been working for a long time on the new game that would have the excitement of American football.</u> Nasmyth showed the men a basket he had hung at each end of the gym, and explained that they were going to use a round European football. At first everybody tried to throw the ball into the basket no matter where he was standing. "Pass! Pass!" Nasmyth kept shouting, blowing his whistle to stop the excited players. Slowly, they began to understand what was wanted of them. (34) <u>The problem with the new game, which was soon called "basketball", was getting the ball out of the basket.</u> They used ordinary food baskets with bottoms, and the ball, of course, stayed inside. At first, someone had to climb up every time a basket was scored. (35) <u>It was several years before someone came up with the idea of removing the bottom of the basket and letting the ball fall through.</u> There have been many changes in the rules since then, and basketball has become one of the world's most popular sports.

Questions 33 to 35 are based on the passage you have just heard.

Questions 33: What did Nasmyth do to entertain his students one winter day?

Questions 34: According to the speaker, what was the problem with the new game?

Questions 35: How was the problem with the new game solved?

解析：怎么样，都预判对了吧？是不是听力的预判真的很神奇！

答案：D B A

例四

请预览选项

Questions 14 to 17 are based on the passage you have just heard.

14. A）A basket.　　　B）A cup　　　C）An egg.　　　D）An oven.
15. A）To let in the sunshine.　　　C）To keep the nest cool.
 B）To serve as its door.　　　D）For the bird to lay eggs.
16. A）Branches.　　　B）Grasses.　　　C）Mud.　　　D）Straw.
17. A）Some are built underground.　　　C）Most are sewed with grasses.
 B）Some can be eaten.　　　D）Most are dried by the sun.

预判：本篇答案项很短，没有太多答题的线索。不过文章似乎与鸟的筑巢有关，其中 14 题似乎在问鸟巢的形状，16 题似乎问的是用什么筑巢，17 题似乎问的是所建巢穴的情况（是建在地下？可以吃？用草缝起来？大部分被太阳烘干？）。对于这些选项很短的题的回答，最重要的是边听录音边浏览选项，并做标注，做与选项相对应的"对点记忆"。

请听录音答题

原文

Did you know that there is a kind of bird that can sew? This bird, called the tailor bird, uses its mouth as a needle. (14) <u>It sews leaves together in the shape of a cup.</u> Then it adds a layer of straw to the inside of the cup and lays its eggs there.

Each bird species builds its own special kind of nest. The most common materials used for nests are grasses, branches and feathers. A bird must weave these materials into a nest. Just imagine building a house without cement or nails to hold it together!

Another bird is called the weaver bird. The weaver bird builds a nest that looks like a basket. The nest's shape is like a pear with a hole in the middle. (15) <u>The hole is the door of the nest.</u> a third bird is called the oven bird. (16) <u>The oven bird makes the nest that is very solid. The nest is made of mud.</u> The oven bird forms the mud into the shape of an oven, and then lets it dry in the sun. The sun bakes the mud, making it very hard.

Not all birds make their homes in branches. Some birds build their nests on the ground, while others bury their eggs under the ground. And some birds do not build nests at all. (17) <u>So, when you look for nests and eggs in the branches of trees and bushes, remember, that some nests may be right under your feet.</u>

Questions 14: What does the nest built by a tailor bird look like?

Questions 15: Why is there a hole in the weaver bird's nest?

Questions 16: What is the oven bird's nest made of?

Questions 17: What might surprise us about birds' nests according to the speaker?

解析：本文 14 和 16 题的对点记忆

14. A）A basket. (weaver bird).　　　　　　C）An egg.

　　B）A cup (tailor bird).　　　　　　　　D）An oven (oven bird).

16. A）Branches (most common materials used for nests).

　　B）Grasses (most common materials used for nests).

　　C）Mud (oven bird).

　　D）Straw.

在进行对点记忆后，问题的回答会变得简单很多。

答案：B　B　C　A

特别提示：考生在实践中，会发现这样一种状况：对于文字较长的选项可以在预览中整理出一定的逻辑线索来，但是对于只有一两个单词的选项似乎很难整理出一条逻辑线索并做出预判。情况的确如此，由于选项过短，考生很难通过预览做出预判。这就涉及四、六级听力考试有关长对话和短文听力的另一个重要技巧——一心二用，边听边看（选）。这种技巧较难，考生在准备考试过程中只有通过做真题和模拟题的实践练习，才能掌握。特别需要边浏览选项边答题，除了长对话与短文听力中选项本身较短的题目外，不论是对话题，还是短文听力，凡是涉及数字、时间、地点、人物的听力题选项一般都很短。对于这些选项，许多考生并不是听不出来，只是很难判断应该去抓住哪些信息。对此，考生应该做的就是根据选项"对点记忆"。即，一边听朗读，一边在选项旁做出相应的标注，进行"对点记忆"，再根据朗读后的提问做出相应的选择。据统计，对于大部分580分以上的考生而言，四、六级考试中的短文听力题的答题，70%以上是在文章阅读完毕已经做出选择，而并不是在听完每道题才做出选择的。对于这些优秀的考生而言，在文章朗读过程中，利用"边听边看"的答题方法已经基本完成试题的回答了，而随后的问题提问时的答题时间，只是对已选答案的核对和补充而已。

这样做到"一心二用"，其实需要考生注意力更为集中，它的要求很高。考生必须能够做到一边听录音，一边扫描选项，这样在听录音的时候便能做出比较有依据、有把握的选择了。

注意：每一篇长对话或短文听力题目的设计，总的来说是按照听力录音朗读的顺序安排的。因此，考生在扫描完一道题的答案，感觉这一道题在文章的对应部分已经朗读完毕，就应该开始浏览下一题的答案，然后每道题依次进行下去，直到完成所有Section A的长对话和Section B问题的回答。这是在做短文听力时考生应该把握的回答问题的正确的节奏。

Practice makes perfect!

Exercise 1

Passage One

Questions 11 to 13 are based on the passage you have just heard.

11. A）The art of saying thank you.
    B）The secret of staying pretty.
    C）The importance of good manners.
    D）The difference between elegance and good manners.
12. A）They were nicer and gentler.
    B）They paid more attention to their appearance.
    C）They were willing to spend more money on clothes.
    D）They were more aware of changes in fashion.
13. A）By decorating our homes.
    B）By being kind and generous.
    C）By wearing fashionable clothes.
    D）By putting on a little make-up.

Passage Two

Questions 14 to 16 are based on the passage you have just heard.

14. A）Children don't get enough education in safety.
    B）Children are keen on dangerous games.
    C）The playgrounds are in poor condition.
    D）The playgrounds are overcrowded.
15. A）They should help maintain the equipment.
    B）They should keep a watchful eye on their children.
    C）They should stop their children from climbing ladders.
    D）They should teach their children how to use the equipment.
16. A）They tend to stay within shouting or running distance of their parents.
    B）They should be aware of the potential risks on the playground.
    C）They may panic in front of high playground equipment.
    D）They can be creative when they feel secure.

Passage There

Questions 17 to 20 are based on the passage you have just heard.

17. A）It takes skill.
    B）It pays well.
    C）It's a full-time job.
    D）It's admired worldwide.
18. A）A mother with a baby in her arms.
    B）A woman whose bag is hanging in front.
    C）A lone female with a handbag at her right side.
    D）An old lady carrying a handbag on the left.
19. A）The back pocket of his tight trousers.
    B）The top pocket of his jacket.
    C）A side pocket of his jacket.
    D）A side pocket of his trousers.

20. A）Theater lobbies with uniformed security guards.
    B）Clothing stores where people are relaxed and off guard.
    C）Airports where people carry a lot of luggage.
    D）Hotels and restaurants in southeast London.

Exercise 2

Passage One

Questions 11 to 13 are based on the passsage you have just heard.

11. A）Synthetic fuel.   C）Alcohol.
    B）Solar energy.   D）Electricity.
12. A）Air traffic conditions.   C）Road conditions.
    B）Traffic jams on highways.   D）New traffic rules.
13. A）Go through a health check.   C）Arrive early for boarding.
    B）Carry little luggage.   D）Undergo security checks.

Passage Two

Questions 14 to 17 are based on the passsage you have just heard.

14. A）In a fast-food restaurant.   C）At a county fair.
    B）At a shopping center.   D）In a bakery.
15. A）Avoid eating any food.
    B）Prepare the right type of pie to eat.
    C）Wash his hands thoroughly.
    D）Practice eating a pie quickly.
16. A）On the table.   C）Under his bottom.
    B）Behind his back.   D）On his lap.
17. A）Looking sideways to see how fast your neighbor eats.
    B）Eating from the outside toward the middle.
    C）Swallowing the pie with water.
    D）Holding the pie in the right position.

Passage Three

Questions 18 to 20 are based on the passsage you have just heard.

18. A）Beauty.   B）Loyalty.   C）Luck.   D）Durability.
19. A）He wanted to follow the tradition of his country.
    B）He believed that it symbolized an everlasting marriage.
    C）It was thought a blood vessel in that finger led directly to the heart.
    D）It was supposed that the diamond on that finger would bring good luck.
20. A）The two people can learn about each other's likes and dislikes.
    B）The two people can have time to decide if they are a good match.
    C）The two people can have time to shop for their new home.
    D）The two people can earn enough money for their wedding.

Exercise 3

Passage One

Questions 11 to 13 are based on the passage you have just heard.

11. A) It has been proven to be the best pain-killer.
    B) It is a possible cure for heart disease.
    C) It can help lower high body temperature effectively.
    D) It reduces the chance of death for heart surgery patients.

12. A) It keeps blood vessels from being blocked.
    B) It speeds up their recovery after surgery.
    C) It increases the blood flow to the heart.
    D) It adjusts their blood pressure.

13. A) It is harmful to heart surgery patients with stomach bleeding.
    B) It should not be taken by heart surgery patients before the operation.
    C) It will have considerable side effects if taken in large doses.
    D) It should not be given to patients immediately after the operation.

Passage Two

Questions 14 to 16 are based on the passage you have just heard.

14. A) They strongly believe in family rules.
    B) They are very likely to succeed in life.
    C) They tend to take responsibility for themselves
    D) They are in the habit of obeying their parents.

15. A) They grow up to be funny and charming.
    B) They often have a poor sense of direction.
    C) They get less attention from their parents.
    D) They tend to be smart and strong-willed.

16. A) They usually don't follow family rules.
    B) They don't like to take chances in their lives.
    C) They are less likely to be successful in life.
    D) They tend to believe in their parent's ideas.

Passage Three

Questions 17 to 20 are based on the passage you have just heard.

17. A) They wanted to follow his example.
    B) They fully supported his undertaking.
    C) They were puzzled by his decision.
    D) They were afraid he wasn't fully prepared.

18. A) It is more exciting than space travel.
    B) It is much cheaper than space travel.
    C) It is much safer than space travel.
    D) It is less time-consuming than space travel.

19. A）They both attract scientists' attention.

    B）They can both be quite challenging.

    C）They are both thought-provoking.

    D）They may both lead to surprising findings.

20. A）To show how simple the mechanical aids for diving can be.

    B）To provide an excuse for his changeable character.

    C）To explore the philosophical issues of space travel.

    D）To explain why he took up underwater exploration.

Exercise 4

Passage One

Questions 11 to 13 are based on the passage you have just heard.

11. A）It has done more harm than good in the southern USA.

    B）It was brought to the northern USA by Asian farmers.

    C）It was introduced into the USA to kill harmful weeds.

    D）It can be used by farmers to protect large buildings.

12. A）They will become to hard to plough.

    B）They will soon be overgrown with Kudzu.

    C）People will have to rely on Kudzu for a living.

    D）People will find it hard to protect the soil.

13. A）The soil there is not so suitable for the plant.

    B）The factories there have found a good use for it.

    C）The farmers there have brought it under control.

    D）The climate there is unfavorable to its growth.

Passage Two

Questions 14 to 16 are based on the passage you have just heard.

14. A）The universe as a whole.   C）An association of teachers and scholars.

    B）A society of legal professionals.   D）A business corporation.

15. A）Provincial colleges were taken over by larger universities.

    B）Its largest expansion took place during that period.

    C）Small universities combined to form bigger ones.

    D）Its role in society went through a dramatic change.

16. A）Private donations.   C）Government funding.

    B）Fees paid by students.   D）Grants from corporations.

Passage Three

Questions 17 to 20 are based on the passage you have just heard.

17. A）He was interested in the study of wild animals.

    B）He started the organization of Heifer International.

    C）He was wounded in the Spanish civil war.

    D）He sold many cows to many countries in the world.

18. A）To make plans for the development of poor countries.
    B）To teach people how to use new skills to raise animals.
    C）To help starving families to become self-supporting.
    D）To distribute food to the poor around the world.
19. A）They should submit a report of their needs and goals.
    B）They should provide food for the local communities.
    C）They should offer all baby animals to their poor neighbors.
    D）They should help offer animals the way they have been helped.
20. A）It has helped relieve hunger in some developing countries.
    B）It has improved animal breeding skills all over the world.
    C）It has bridged the gap between the rich and the poor in America.
    D）It has promoted international exchanged of farming technology.

答案与原文

Exercise 1

答案

（11-15）CABCB   （16-20）DACAB

原文

Passage One

(11) Do you remember a time when people were a little nicer and gentler with each other? I certainly do. And I feel that much of the world has somehow gotten away from that. Too often I see people rushing into elevators without giving those inside a chance to get off first, or never saying "Thank you" when others hold the door open for them. We get lazy, and in our laziness, we think that something like a simple "Thank you" doesn't really matter. But it can matter very much. The fact is that no matter how nicely we dress or how beautifully we decorate our homes, we can't be truly elegant without good manners, because elegance (优雅) and good manners always go hand in hand. In fact, I think of good manners as a sort of hidden beauty secret. (12) Haven't you noticed that the kindest, most generous people seem to keep getting prettier? It's funny how that happens. But it does. Take the long lost art of saying "Thank you". Like wearing a little makeup (化妆) or making sure your hair is neat, getting into the habit of saying "Thank you" can make you feel better about yourself. (13) Good manners add to your image, while an angry face makes the best-dressed person look ugly.

Questions 11 to 13 are based on the passage you have just heard.
Question 11: What is the passage mainly about?
Question 12: What does the speaker say about people of the past?
Question 13: According to the speaker, how can we best improve our image?

Passage Two

"Go to the playground and have fun!" Parents will often say to their kids. But they should remember playground can be dangerous. Each year, about 200,000 children end up in hospital emergency rooms with playground injuries. Many injuries involve falls from too high equipment onto too hard surfaces. Nearly 70% of the injuries happen on public playgrounds. (14) Recent studies show they may be badly designed, their protective surfaces are inadequate, and their equipment is poorly maintained. Parents should make sure that the equipment on the playground is safe and that children are playing safely.

Last year, the national program for playground safety gave the nation's playgrounds a grade of C for safety, after visiting more than 3,000 playgrounds nationwide. (15) Parents should watch closely. They should always be within shouting and running distance of their children. Young children don't understand cause and effect, so they may run in front of moving swings. They are also better at climbing up than getting down, so they may panic at the top of a ladder.

It's important for children to know you're watching them. (16) Once they feel that sense of security (安全感), that's when they can be creative.

Questions 14 to 16 are based on the passage you have just heard.

Question 14: What is the cause of playground injuries?

Question 15: What should parents do to prevent playground injuries?

Question 16: What does the speaker say about young children?

Passage Three

For 25 years, I was a full-time thief, specializing in picking pockets. Where I come from in southeast London, that's an honorable profession. (17) Anyone can break in a house and steal things, but picking somebody's pocket takes skill. My sister and I were among the most successful pickpocket teams in London. We worked in hotel and theater lobbies, airports, shopping centers and restaurants.

Now we don't steal any more. But this crime is worldwide. Here's how to protect yourself: Professional pickpockets do not see victims, only handbags, jewels and money. Mothers with babies, the elderly, the disabled are all fair game. (18) My preferred target was the lone female, handbag at her side, the right side to be exact. So if I'm next to her, I can reach it cautiously with my right hand across my body. Only about one woman in a thousand carries her bag on the left, and I tended to steer clear of (远离) them. Women, whose bags are hanging in front of them are tricky for the pickpocket, as there isn't a blind side. If you want to make it even harder, use a bag with handles rather than a strap. (19) For men, one of the best places to keep a wallet is in the back pocket of tight trousers. You'll feel any attempts to move it. Another good place is in the buttoned-up inside pocket of a jacket; there is just no way in. Even better, keep wallets attached to a cord or chain that is fastened to a belt.

(20) A pickpocket needs targets who are relaxed and off guard. The perfect setting is a clothing store. When customers wander among the racks, they are completely absorbed in the items they hold up. The presence of a uniformed security guard is even better. A false sense of security makes a pickpocket's job much simpler.

Questions 17 to 20 are based on the passage you have just heard.

Question 17: Why does the speaker say that picking somebody's pocket is an honorable profession in southeast London?

Question 18: According to the speaker, who is most likely to become a victim of pickpockets?

Question 19: In the speaker's opinion, what's the best place for a man to keep his wallet?

Question 20: What is the perfect setting for picking pockets according to the speaker?

Exercise 2

📋 **答案**

（11-15）DABCA　　　　　（16-20）BBACB

📻 **原文**

Passage One

In the next few decades, people are going to travel very differently from the way they do today. (11) Everyone is going to drive electrically-powered cars, so in a few years, people won't worry about running out of gas. Some of the large automobile companies are really moving ahead with this new technology. F&C Motors, a major auto company, for example, is holding a press conference next week. After the press conference, the company will present its new electronically operated models. Transportation in the future won't be limited to the ground. Many people predict that traffic will quickly move to the sky. In the coming years, instead of radio reports about road conditions and highway traffic, (12) news reports will talk about traffic jams in the sky. But the sky isn't the limit. In the future, you will probably even be able to take a trip to the moon. Instead of listening to regular airplane announcements, you will hear someone say: The spacecraft to the moon leaves in 10 minutes. Please check your equipment. (13) And remember no more than 10 ounces of carry-on baggage are allowed.

Questions 11 to 13 are based on the passage you have just heard.
Question 11: What will be used to power cars in the next few decades?
Question 12: What will future news reports focus on when talking about transportation?
Question 13: What will passengers be asked to do when they travel to the moon?

Passage Two

(14) County fairs are a tradition in New England towns. They offer great entertainment. One popular event is the pie-eating contest. If you want to take part in the contest, it is a good idea to remember these guidelines: (15) First, make sure your stomach is nearly empty of food. Eating a whole pie can be hard if you have just finished a meal. Next, it is helpful to like the pie you are going to eat. The cream types are a good choice. They slide down the throat more easily. Placing your hands in the right position adds to the chances of winning. There is a temptation to reach out and help the eating process. This will result in becoming disqualified. Don't just sit on your hands, (16) if your hands are tied behind your back, you will not be tempted to make use of them.

Now you are ready to show your talent at eating pies. The object of course, is to get to the bottom of the pie plate before the other people. (17) It is usually better to start at the outside and work toward the middle. This method gives you a goal to focus on. Try not to notice what the other people near you are doing. Let the cheers from the crowd spur you on. But do not look up. All you should think about is eating that pie.

Questions 14 to 17 are based on the passage you have just heard.
Question 14: Where is a pie-eating contest usually held?
Question 15: What should a person do before entering into the pie-eating contest?

Question 16: Where is a person advised to put his hands during the contest?

Question 17: What suggestion is offered for eating up the pie quickly?

Passage Three

The period of engagement is the time between the marriage proposal and the wedding ceremony. Two people agree to marry when they decide to spend their lives together. The man usually gives the woman a diamond engagement ring. That tradition is said to have started when an Austrian man gave a diamond ring to the woman he wanted to marry. (18) The diamond represented beauty. He placed it on the third finger of her left hand. He chose that finger (19) because it was thought that the blood vessel in that finger went directly to the heart. Today we know that this is not true, yet the tradition continues.

Americans generally are engaged for a period of about one year, if they are planning a wedding ceremony and a party. During this time, friends of the bride may hold a party at which women friends and family members give the bride gifts that she will need as a wife. These could include cooking equipment or new clothing. Friends of the man who is getting married may have a bachelor party for him. This usually takes place the night before the wedding. Only men are invited to the bachelor party.

During the marriage ceremony, the bride and her would-be husband usually exchange gold rings that represent the idea that their union will continue forever. The wife often wears both the wedding ring and the engagement ring on the same finger. The husband wears his ring on the third finger on his left hand. Many people say the purpose of the engagement period is to permit enough time to plan the wedding. (20) But the main purpose is to let enough time pass so the two people are sure that they want to marry each other. Either person may decide to break the engagement, if this happens, the woman usually returns the ring to the man. They also return any wedding gifts they have received.

Questions 18 to 20 are based on the passage you have just heard.

Question 18: What was the diamond ring said to represent?

Question 19: Why did the Austrian man place the diamond ring on the third finger of the left hand of his would-be wife?

Question 20: What is the chief advantage of having the engagement period?

Exercise 3

答案

（11-15）DAABC   （16-20）ACBBD

原文

Passage One

(11) A new study reports the common drug aspirin greatly reduces life threatening problems after an operation to replace blocked blood vessels to the heart. More than 800,000 people around the world have this heart surgery each year. (11) The doctors who carried out the study say giving aspirin to patients soon after the operation could save thousands of lives. People usually take aspirin to control pain and reduce high body temperature. Doctors also advise some people to take aspirin to help prevent heart attacks. About 10 to 15 percent of these heart operations end in death

or damage to the heart or other organs. The new study shows that even a small amount of aspirin reduced such threats. The doctors said the chance of death for patients who took aspirin would fall by 67%. They claimed this was true if the aspirin was given within 48 hours of the operation. (12) The doctors believe aspirin helps heart surgery patients because it can prevent blood from thickening and blood vessels from being blocked (阻止血液浓度变稠，进而防止血管堵塞). However, (13) the doctors warned that people who have stomach bleeding (胃出血) or other bad reactions from aspirin should not take it after heart surgery.

Questions 11 to 13 are based on the passage you have just heard.

Question 11: What is the finding of the new study of aspirin?

Question 12: In what way can aspirin help heart surgery patients according to the doctors?

Question 13: What warning did the doctors give about the use of aspirin?

Passage Two

Were you the first or the last child in you family? Or were you a middle or only child? Some people think it matters how you were born in your family. But there are different ideas about what birth order means. (14) Some people say that oldest children are smart and strong-willed. They are very likely to be successful. The reason for this is simple. Parents have a lot of time for their first child. They give him or her a lot of attention. So this child is very likely to do well. (14) An only child will succeed for the same reason. What happens to the other children in the family? (15) Middle children don't get so much attention, so they don't feel that important. If a family has many children, the middle one sometimes gets lost in the crowd. The youngest child, though, often gets special treatment. He or she is the baby. Often this child grows up to be funny and charming. Do you believe these ideas about birth order too? A recent study saw things quite differently. The study found that the first children believed in family rules. They didn't take many chances in their lives. They usually followed orders. (16) Rules didn't mean as much to later children in the family. They went out and followed their own ideas. They took chances and they often did better in life.

Questions 14 to 16 are based on the passage you have just heard.

Question 14: According to common belief, in what way are the first child and the only child alike?

Question 15: What do people usually say about middle children?

Question 16: What do we learn about later children in a family from a recent study of birth order?

Passage Three

(17) When my interest shifted from space to the sea, I never expected it would cause such confusion among my friends, yet I can understand their feelings. (20) As I have been writing and talking about space flight for the best part of 20 years, a sudden switch of interest to the depth of the sea does seem peculiar. To explain, I'd like to show my reasons behind this unusual change of mind. The first excuse I give is an economic one. (18) Underwater exploration is so much cheaper than space flight. The first round-trip ticket to the moon is going to cost at least 10 billion dollars if you include research and development. By the end of this century, the cost will be down to a few million. On the other hand, the diving suit and a set of basic tools needed for skin-diving can be bought for 20 dollars. My second argument is more philosophical. The ocean, surprisingly enough, has many things in common with space. (19) In their different ways, both sea and space are equally hostile. If we wish to survive in either for any length of time, we need to have mechanical aids. The diving suit helped the design of the space suit. The feelings and the emotions of a man beneath

the sea will be much like those of a man beyond the atmosphere.

Questions 17 to 20 are based on the passage you have just heard.

Question 17: How did the speaker's friends respond to his change of interest?

Question 18: What is one of the reasons for the speaker to switch his interest to underwater exploration?

Question 19: In what way does the speaker think diving is similar to space travel?

Question 20: What is the speaker's purpose in giving this talk?

Exercise 4

答案

（11-15）ABDCB　　　　（16-20）CBCDA

原文

Passage One

Unless you have visited the southern United States, you probably have never heard of Kudzu. Kudzu, as any farmer in the south will sadly tell you, is a super-powered weed. It is a strong climbing plant. Once it gets started, Kudzu is almost impossible to stop. It climbs to the tops of the tallest trees. It can cover large buildings. Whole barns and farm houses have been known to disappear from view. (11) Wherever it grows, its thick twisting stems（扭曲的干、茎）are extremely hard to remove.

Kudzu was once thought to be a helpful plant. Originally found in Asia, it was brought to America to help protect the land from being swallowed by the sea. It was planted where its tough roots which grow up to five feet long could help hold back the soil. (11) But the plant soon spread to places where it wasn't wanted. Farmers now have to fight to keep it from killing other plants.

(12) In a way, Kudzu is a sign of labor shortage in the south. Where there is no one to work in the fields, Kudzu soon takes over. The northern United States faces no threat from Kudzu. (13) Harsh winters kill it off. The plant loves the warmth of the south, but the south surely doesn't love it. If someone could invent some use for Kudzu and remove it from southern farmland, his or her fortune would be assured.

Questions 11 to 13 are based on the passage you have just heard.

Question 11: What do we learn about "Kudzu" from the passage?

Question 12: What will happen if the fields are neglected in the southern United States?

Question 13: Why isn't Kudzu a threat to the northern United States?

Passage Two

The word "university" comes from the Latin word "universitas", meaning "the whole". Later, in Latin legal language, "universitas" meant a society or corporation. (14) In the Middle Ages, the word meant "an association of teachers and scholars".

The origins of universities can be traced back to the 12th to14th centuries. In the early 12th century, long before universities were organized in the modern sense, students gathered together for higher studies at certain centers of learning. The earliest centers in the Europe were at Bolonia in Italy, founded in 1088. Other early centers were set up in France, the Czech Republic, Austria and Germany from 1150 to 1386. The first universities in Britain were Oxford and Cambridge. They were established in 1185 and 1209 respectively. The famous London University was founded in 1836. This was followed by the foundation of several universities such as Manchester and Birmingham, which developed from provincial colleges.

(15) It was in the 1960's that the largest expansion of higher education took place in Britain. This expansion took 3 basic forms: Existing universities were enlarged, new universities were developed from existing colleges and completely new universities were set up.

In Britain, finance for universities comes from three source: (16) The first, and the largest source, is grants (拨款) from the government, the second source is fees paid by students and the third one is private donations. All the British universities except one receive some government funding. The exception is Buckingham, which is Britain's only independent university.

Questions 14 to 16 are based on the passage you have just heard.

Question 14: What did the word "Universitas" mean in the Middle Ages?

Question 15: Why was the 1960's so significant for British Higher Education?

Question 16: What is the main financial source for British universities?

Passage Three

One of the biggest problems in developing countries is hunger. An organization called Heifer International is working to improve the situation. The organization sends farm animals to families and communities around the world.

(17) An American farmer, Dan West, developed the idea for Heifer International in the 1930's. Mr. West was working in Spain where he discovered a need for cows. Many families were starving because of the civil war in that county. So Mr. West asked his friends in the United States to send some cows. The first Heifer animals were sent in 1944. (20) Since that time, more than 4,000,000 people in 115 countries have had better lives because of Heifer animals.

To receive a Heifer animal, families must first explain their needs and goals. (18) They must also make a plan which will allow them to become self-supporting. Local experts usually provide training. The organization says that animals must have food, water, shelter, health care and the ability to reproduce. Without them, the animals will not remain healthy and productive. Heifer International also believes that families must pass on some of their success to others in need. This belief guarantees that each person who takes part in the program also becomes a giver. (19) Every family that receives a Heifer animal must agree to give that animal's first female baby to other people in need. Families must also agree to pass on the skills and training they receive from Heifer International. This concept helps communities become self-supporting.

Questions 17 to 20 are based on the passage you have just heard.

Question 17: What does the speaker tell us about Mr. West?

Question 18: What is the ultimate goal of Heifer International?

Question19: What are families required to do after they receive support from Heifer International?

Question 20: What is the major achievement of Heifer International?

复合式听写应试技巧

　　"复合式听写"是一种综合能力测试，它对学生的听力、书写能力以及单词（包括读音和拼写）、语法的熟练程度要求相当高，平时需打好基础，牢固掌握并做到活用语言知识，培养和锻炼语言能力，以不断增强语言的熟练程度和语感。在英语学习中，特别是背诵单词时要培养边听边看边记忆的好习惯。针对听写词组（通常不超过三个单词），记录时可以练习速记，使用缩写、简写，甚至一些符号，只要考生本人能看懂就行。复合式听写有以下应对策略。

　　（1）熟练掌握并不断扩充词汇量。单词的记忆必须做到准确，这样才能迅速而正确地拼写出来，本书的**"Listen & Learn"** 部分是重点针对复合式听写而精心设计的词汇强化训练。

　　（2）在做"复合式听写"测试题前，考生应充分利用朗读"复合式听写"的 Directions 的时间，尽快浏览短文，以期对全文的中心思想有所了解，做到心中有数。

　　（3）在听第一遍朗读期间，考生应该努力打好基础，将需要听写的单词听明白，然后尽可能拼写正确。

　　（4）考生切记，不要纠结于个别单词。因为停留在一个单词上会打乱整个听写的节奏，从而影响其他单词或词组的听写。

　　（5）第二遍听写时，把原来没有写好的单词拼写完整，核对要点内容，力求完整准确。第三遍听写时要检查自己所拼写的单词与朗读的发音是否一致。

　　（6）三遍全部听完后，对所填的词句进行检查，看填入的单词或词组与上下文意思是否协调。特别要注意单词的单、复数形式，大小写，时态和语态等常规语法知识，尽可能地避免语法及拼写错误。

例

请用 50 秒（Section C 指令朗读持续的时间）浏览文章。

请听录音

Directions: In this section, you will hear a passage three times. When the passage is read for the first time, you should listen carefully for its general idea. When the passage is read for the second time, you are required to fill in the blanks with the exact words you have just heard. Finally, when the passage is read for the third time, you should check what you have written.

Russia is the largest economic power that is not a member of the World Trade Organization. But that may change. Last Friday, the European Union said it would support Russia's (1) _____ to become a W.T.O. member.

Representatives of the European Union met with Russian (2) _____ in Moscow. They signed a trade agreement that took six years to (3) _____.

Russia called the trade agreement (4) _____. It agreed to slowly increase fuel prices within the country. It also agreed to permit (5) _____ in its communications industry and to remove some barriers to trade.

In (6) _____ for European support to join the W.T.O., Russian President Putin said that Russia would speed up the (7) _____ to approve the Kyoto Protocol, an international (8) _____ agreement to reduce the production of harmful industrial gases. These "greenhouse gas" trap heat in the atmosphere and (9) _____ changing the world's climate.

Russia had signed the Kyoto Protocol, but has not yet approved it. The agreement takes effect when it has been approved by nations that produce at least 55 percent of the world's greenhouse gases. But currently, nations producing only 44 percent have (10) _____. The United States, the world's biggest producer, withdrew from the Kyoto Protocol after President Bush took office in 2001. So, Russia's approval is required to put the Kyoto Protocol into effect.

To join the W.T.O., a country must reach trade agreements with major trading countries that are also W.T.O. members. Russia must still reach agreements with China, Japan, South Korea and the United States.

(1) effort	(2) officials	(3) negotiate	(4) balanced
(5) competition	(6) exchange	(7) process	(8) environmental
(9) are blamed for	(10) approved		

Practice Makes Perfect!

Exercise 1

What do young Americans think about the presidential candidates and social issues? A new public opinion study shows that the (1) _____ of young people support Democrats over Republicans. The young people also have (2) _____ positions on several social issues.

The results of the study were (3) _____ earlier this week by the New York Times newspaper. The study was (4) _____ on telephone calls to six hundred fifty-nine young people earlier this month. They were between the ages of 17 and 29.

Fifty-four percent of the young Americans questioned said they plan to (5) _____ a Democratic Party candidate for president in 2008. The study also found that many more young Americans are paying attention to the 2008 presidential (6) _____ than the last one in 2004. They share with the general public a (7) _____ opinion of President Bush. Only twenty-eight percent of this group approve of the job he is doing as president.

Almost half of young Americans questioned feel their generation will (8) _____ than their parents' generation. But more than seventy-five percent of them believe the votes of their generation would make a difference in the next presidential election.

The study found that young adults share the same opinions as the general population on some issues. But they have different opinions on several issues. For example, young Americans are more likely than the general public to support a government-controlled (9) _____ for all Americans. The young people are also more likely to support a liberal policy on immigration.

Forty-four percent of the young Americans said they believe couples of the same sex should be permitted to (10) _____. Only twenty-eight percent of the general population approve of the legalization of same-sex marriage.

Exercise 2

(1) _____ experts had a lot to discuss this week. President Bush (2) _____ to keep a (3) _____ top administration official out of prison. And last week the Supreme Court ended its

first full term with two Bush (4) _____.

Most experts agree that the appointments have created a more conservative high court. Just how much may (5) _____ to be seen. But some already think the changes may be remembered as the president's biggest success for the conservative movement.

In the most recent term, the four most conservative justices (6) _____ twice as many cases as they lost. One-third of all cases were decided by votes of five-to-four.

The (7) _____ vote was often Justice Anthony Kennedy. He was in the (8) _____ in every five-four decision. Over the years he has voted with conservatives as well as liberals on the court.

In this term, Justice Kennedy sided with the liberals in their most important case. The court ruled that the government has the power to (9) _____ the release of greenhouse gases. But he took the side of the conservatives in their most important decisions.

These included upholding a federal ban on a late-term abortion method. Another decision limited free speech rights of public students. And last week the court limited the ability of school systems to consider race in efforts to balance student populations.

On the last day of the term, the Supreme Court agreed to hear appeals by detainees at Guantanamo Bay, Cuba. The court had (10) _____ an earlier request in April. The detainees seek the right to appeal their detainment in federal court. The administration says they are enemy combatants (战士) and should not be given such rights. The Supreme Court will hear the arguments after its next term begins in October.

Exercise 3

For Americans, time is money. They say, "You only get so much time in this life; you'd better use it wisely." The future will not be better than the past or present as Americans are (1) _____ to see things, unless people use their time for constructive activities. Thus Americans (2) _____ a "well-organized" person, one who has a written list of things to do and a (3) _____ for doing them. The ideal person is (4) _____ and is (5) _____ of other people's time. They do not waste people's time with conversation or other activity that has no (6) _____ beneficial outcome.

The American attitude toward time is not (7) _____ shared by others, especially non-Europeans. They are more likely to regard time as something that is simply there around them, not something they can use. One of the more difficult things many students must (8) _____ in the states is the (9) _____ that time must be saved whenever possible and used wisely every day.

In the (10) _____, the fast food industry can be seen as a clear example of American culture product. McDonald's, KFC, and other fast food establishments are successful in a country where many people spend the least amount of time preparing and eating meals. As McDonald's restaurants spread around the world, they have been viewed as symbols of American society and culture, bringing not just hamburgers but an emphasis on speed, efficiency, and shiny cleanliness.

答案

Exercise 1

(1) majority   (2) liberal   (3) published   (4) based

(5) vote for   (6) race   (7) negative   (8) be worse off

(9) health care system   (10) legally marry

Exercise 2

(1) Legal   (2) intervened   (3) former   (4) appointees

(5) remain   (6) won   (7) deciding   (8) majority

(9) restrict   (10) denied

Exercise 3

(1) trained   (2) admire   (3) schedule   (4) punctual

(5) considerate   (6) visible   (7) necessarily   (8) adjust to

(9) notion   (10) context

Test Yourself

Unit 1

Section A

Directions: In this section, you will hear 8 short conversations and 2 long conversations. At the end of each conversation, one or more questions will be asked about what was said. Both the conversation and the questions will be spoken only once. After each question there will be a pause. During the pause, you must read the four choices marked A), B), C) and D), and decide which is the best answer. Then mark the corresponding letter on Answer Sheet 2 with a single line through the centre.

11. A）She doesn't think the shirt comes in a bigger size.
    B）She thinks this shirt will fit the man.
    C）A checked shirt won't look good on the man.
    D）The bigger sizes are more expensive.

12. A）She expects the man to have it.
    B）She's angry with the man for forgetting it.
    C）She doesn't know where it is.
    D）She'd like the man to return it by tonight.

13. A）She didn't buy the ticket.
    B）The ticket was expensive.
    C）She doesn't know how much the ticket cost.
    D）There are still a few tickets left.

14. A）Eat a bigger breakfast.
    B）Make time for lunch in her schedule.
    C）Take only morning classes next semester.
    D）Change her schedule after she eats lunch.

15. A）He's quitting the band for academic reasons.
    B）He didn't enjoy being a member of the band.
    C）He's getting academic credit for being in the band.
    D）He's taking time off from his studies to join the band.

16. A）His suit is too old to wear.   C）He doesn't want to wear a suit.
    B）He doesn't want to buy new clothes.   D）He'll go shopping with the woman.

17. A）Calculate the bill again.　　C）Invite the man to dinner.

    B）Refuse to pay the bill.　　D）Lend the man some money.

18. A）Sara rarely makes mistakes.　　C）Sara's boss is hard to work with.

    B）Sara usually says what she thinks.　　D）The secretary wasn't hard worker.

Questions 19 to 22 are based on the conversation you have just heard.

19. A）How different kinds of pepper are produced.

    B）Why white pepper is superior to dishes.

    C）How the pepper plant is grown.

    D）How various peppers are used in cooking.

20. A）He read about it in a cookbook.　　C）He heard about it from a friend.

    B）He grows his own herbs and spices.　　D）He studied it in cooking school.

21. A）It's preserved in liquid.　　C）It's dried.

    B）The skin is removed.　　D）It's freeze-dried.

22. A）Because it's more pure than other types of pepper.

    B）Because it's flavor is special.

    C）Because it keeps its original color.

    D）Because it's rare.

Questions 23 to 25 are based on the conversation you have just heard.

23. A）A story in prose.

    B）A poem that rhymes.

    C）A translation of a short literary work.

    D）A journal about the process of writing.

24. A）The class has been assigned to read it in English.

    B）He was able to read it in French.

    C）He isn't sure it's available in English.

    D）He thinks it's an example of what the professor wants.

25. A）It's pronounced differently in French.

    B）To write without using it is difficult both in English and in French.

    C）Every word in the French author's professor book contained it.

    D）It's commonly used in English to make poetry rhyme.

Section B

Directions: In this section, you will hear 3 short passages. At the end of each passage, you will hear some questions. Both the passage and the questions will be spoken only once. After you hear a question, you must choose the best answer from the four choices marked A）, B）, C）, and D）. Then mark the corresponding letter on the Answer Sheet with a single line through the center.

Passage One

Questions 26 to 28 are based on the passage you have just heard.

26. A）American industrialists.　　C）International leaders.

    B）French economists.　　D）Civil War veterans.

27. A）The rights of private business owners should be protected.

    B）The government shouldn't interfere in private business.

C）Politicians should support industrial growth.

D）Competition among companies should be restricted.

28. A）they did not have many restrictions from the government.

B）they had won strong support from the government.

C）they did not faced much competition from the overseas business.

D）they were very smart and experienced.

Passage Two

Questions 29 to 32 are based on the passage you have just heard.

29. A）The rate at which the universe is expanding.

B）Early models of the universe.

C）Newton's three laws of motion.

D）How gravity affects the stars and the universe.

30. A）That it can't be measured.

B）That it doesn't change.

C）That it's getting smaller.

D）That it's rapidly increasing.

31. A）Why stars move so quickly.

B）Why few stars have planets.

C）Why stars aren't moving toward one another.

D）Why stars haven't moved farther apart.

32. A）It has, to a large extent, resolved the earlier contradictions.

B）It has hardly resolved any contradictions.

C）It has resolved some contradictions but created more.

D）It has resolved all the earlier contradictions and proved to be successful.

Passage Three

Questions 33 to 35 are based on the passage you have just heard.

33. A）Men lie more often than women.

B）Women lie more often than man.

C）Men and women lie in different ways.

D）People who tell lies are unpopular.

34. A）They found themselves lying to appear more competent.

B）They found themselves lying to appear more likable.

C）They found themselves lying much more than they had thought.

D）They found themselves surprised at the way they lied to each other.

35. A）Children tend to lie more often than adults.

B）Children are confused as to whether they should always tell the truth.

C）Children will model their behavior on their parents.

D）Children won't pretend to like a birthday gift they don't really like.

Section C

Directions: In this section, you will hear a passage three times. When the passage is read for the first time, you should listen carefully for its general idea. When the passage is read for the second time, you are required to fill in the blanks numbered from 36 to 43 with the exact words you have heard. For blanks numbered from 44 to 46 you are required to fill in the missing information. For these blanks, you can either use the exact words you have just heard or write down the main points in your own words. Finally, when the passage is read for the third time, you should check what you have written.

A new report (36) _____ that eight million children each year are born with serious disorders caused at least partly by their genes. That is about six percent of all births worldwide. Researchers found that about ninety-five percent of births with serious defects happen in the developing world.

The study (37) _____ high birth-defect rates in developing countries to poor health care and (38) _____. The researchers also note higher than (39) _____ rates of marriage among blood relatives, and of older women having babies.

The most common (40) _____ defects include heart disorders, and (41) _____ formed backbones and brains.

Hundreds of thousands of other children are born with serious defects that are caused during pregnancy. Pregnant women risk harm to their babies from alcohol and tobacco. There is also a risk if they get (42) _____ with diseases like rubella or syphilis, or do not get enough nutrients like iodine and folic acid.

Researchers collected information on almost two hundred countries. They found that every year more than three million children under the age of five die from birth defects. Those who survive may have (43) _____ problems for life. The report suggests a number of ways to deal with the international problem. One step is to make sure women have a healthy diet during their (44) _____ years. Another is to test men and women to (45) _____ those at higher risk of having children with genetic disorders.

答案与原文

Unit 1

📋 答案

Section A

(11-15) BDBBA　　　(16-20) BABAD　　　(21-25) CBADB

Section B

(26-30) BBADB　　　(31-35) CACCB

Section C

(36) estimates　　(37) links　　(38) nutrition
(39) average　　(40) genetic　　(41) incorrectly
(42) infected　　(43) mental or physical　　(44) reproductive
(45) identify

📖 原文

Section A

Question 11

M: Do you have this style shirt in my size?

W: I'll check. But...to tell you the truth, I think this one is right for you.

Q: What does the woman mean?

Question 12

M: Oh, I'm sorry, I just realized that I forgot to bring the tape recorder you lent me. I left it back in my dorm.

W: That's all right. I won't need it until tonight as long as I've got it by then.

Q: What does the woman imply?

Question 13

M: So how much was your plane ticket?

W: More than I could really afford. I had to dip into my saving.

Q: What does the woman imply?

Question 14

W: Days are going to be busy for me next semester, three classes in the morning and then two more in the afternoon. I won't even have time for lunch.

M: You really should try to fit it in. You know, those afternoon classes would be tough to sit through if your stomach's rumbling.

Q: What does the man suggest the woman do?

Question 15

W: You are dropping out of the Marching Band? But I thought you loved traveling and playing before big crowds.

M: I do. But...with all that time away from my studies my grades are really starting to slip.

Q: What does the man mean?

Question 16

W: I'm thinking of getting a new pantsuit to wear to James' wedding.

M: I just hope that my old suit still fits. You know how I feel about shopping.

Q: What does the man imply?

Question 17

M: What's my share of the bill? 18.50? That can't be right! I only had a salad for dinner.

W: Don't get so excited. Let me check them out.

Q: What will the woman probably do next?

Question 18

M: I'm surprised that Sarah told her boss he was wrong to have fired his secretary.

W: I know. But that Sarah...if she has an opinion, everyone's got to know it.

Q: What does the woman mean?

Now you will hear two long conversations.

Conversation One

M: We are almost finished. Could you hand me the white pepper?

W: Why white pepper and not black? Aren't they the same thing?

M: Well, they are from the same plant, but white pepper is milder. I usually prefer it; it has a more mild flavor.

W: How? Aren't they from the same plant?

M: Well. It depends on how ripe it is when it's fixed. You surely have a lot of questions.

W: That's because you have all the answers. (20) Did you learn about this stuff in cooking school?

M: Yeah, we study all kinds of herbs and spices.

W: So go on. It's interesting. How do we get black pepper done?

M: Ehh. Well, the pepper corn is actually a fruit. It grows on ripe. It's not really black or white. It turns from green to yellow to red as it ripens. (21) For black pepper, you pick it when it's still a little immature, and then dry.

W: Dry in darkness?

M: Well, the skin turns dark as it dries.

W: Does that means white pepper is pepper without the skin.

M: Exactly. It is put to dry in the sun after the skin is wrapped up. It's also mature a little longer than black pepper.

W: So they do all that just to get a milder pepper corn (胡椒籽)?

M: Right.

W: This green pepper corns are interesting. I never see them before.

M: (22) Green pepper has a very distinctive flavor. Some people really like it.

W: So it must be picked really young.

M: Right. It's not sun dry. It's either put in a liquid or a freeze dry to keep the color.

W: Well, you are quite the pepper expert, aren't you?

M: Oh, a good chef gets to know about spices.

W: I'll be judge of that. Let me taste. Hmm, that's good.

Questions 19 to 22 are based on the conversation you have just heard.

Q 19: What are the speakers mainly discussing?

Q 20: How did the man learn about pepper?

Q 21: What happens to black pepper after it's picked?

Q 22: Why do some people like the green pepper?

Conversation Two

M: I didn't see you in creative writing class today. What happened?

W: Oh, just a dentist appointment. That's all. Say, did we get a new assignment for next week?

M: Yeah. A really interesting one, actually. (23) We're supposed to write a short story that has some sort of limitation or, constraints imposed on it.

W: What do you mean? Like rhyming in a Poem?

M: Well, that'll be ideal. (23) But what we write has to be prose, as prose poetry. Just to make rhyme in a poem is too easy, I guess. I think Prof. Johnson really wants to challenge us, to put our creativity to the test.

W: Well, did she give any hints about what's on her mind?

M: No really, (24) but I may have an idea the kind of thing what she's looking for. I just finished a really strange book by some French guy. He wrote a whole book without even using a single letter "e".

W: (25) A whole book without a single "e"? How's possible? But, wait a minute. I didn't know you can read French.

M: I can't. I read the English translation. (25) But get this. There's not one "e" in that either.

W: (25) No way. Think of the words you couldn't use.

M: (25) I know, but that translator manages it. I got the book at home if you want to check out for yourself. What's really amazing to me is that leaving "e" in English gonna involve a complete different group of words and ends in French.

W: Sometime you have to show me that book. But right now I'd better get going the writing for next week. I already have a couple of ideas thanks to you. And I think I just might be able to work on it to something interesting.

Questions 23 to 25 are based on the conversation you have just heard.

Q 23: What is the students' assignment to write?

Q 24: Why did the man mention a book by a French author?

Q 25: What the point does the man make about the letter?

Section B

Passage One

(26) In the 18th century French economists protested the excessive regulation of business by the government. Their motto was "lasser faire". Laisser faire means let the people do as they choose. In the economic sense, this meant that while the government should be responsible for things like maintaining peace and protecting property rights, (27) it should not interfere with private business. It shouldn't create regulations that might hinder (阻碍) business growth. In other words, governments should take a hand-off approach to business. For a while in the United States, laisser faire was a popular doctrine. But things quickly changed. After the Civil War, politicians rarely opposed the government's generous support of business owners. They were only too glad to support government land grants and loans to railroad owners for example. Their regulations kept tariffs high and that helped protect American industrialists against foreign competition. (28) Ironically in the late 19th century, a lot of people believed that the laisser faire policy was responsible for the country's industrial growth. It was generally assumed that because business owners did not have a lot of external restrictions placed on them by the government, they could pursue their own interests, and this was what made them so successful. But in fact, many of these individuals would not have been able to meet their objectives if not for government support.

Questions 26 to 28 are based on the passage you have just heard.

Q 26: Who first used the motto laisser faire?

Q 27: What is the principal idea of the laisser faire policy?

Q 28: According to the passage most Americans in the late 19th century believed that the business individuals were successful because _____.

Passage Two

Today most astronomers accept the notion that groups of stars that make up the universe are all moving father and farther away from each other. But until very recently this idea of an expanding universe was not a theory most European scholars believed in since ancient times and (30) up to about 17th century most of these scholars thought the size of the universe have remained unchanged since the moment of its creation or perhaps for ever, with all the stars remaining more or less in place in relation to each other. But that was challenged in the late 17th century by Isaac Newton's idea of gravity as a force of attraction, which contradicted to the idea of a universe that is static, unchanging. (31) If gravity causes all the stars out there in space to attract each other as Newton said, then they could not remain motionless. Sooner or later all the stars will fall in each other. (31) Scientists then propose a new model, taking Newton's theory into account, they didn't want to abandon the idea of motionless stars. But for this model to work the stars won't fall in each other; they had to modify Newton's law of gravity. So they theorize that for the distance as large as those between stars, the gravitation force repels rather than attracts. As we might guess, there are still other contradictions. But the problems in the past centuries are prettily resolved by currently accepted theory, (32) which says the universe is continuously expanding. You'll be reading all about that as your homework tonight.

Questions 29 to 32 are based on the passage you have just heard.

Q 29: What is the passage mainly about?

Q 30: What did most European scholars believe before 17th century about the size of the universe?

Q 31: What did some scientists try to explain by suggesting that stars repel each other?

Q 32: How does the current theory resolve the earlier contradictions?

Passage Three

Most people lie in everyday conversation when they are trying to appear likable and competent, according to a study conducted by University of Massachusetts psychologist Robert S. Feldman.

The study found that 60 percent of people lie at least once during a 10-minute conversation and told an average of two to three lies. (33) It also found that lies told by men and women differ in content, though not in quantity. Men do not lie more than women or vice versa (反之亦然), but men and women lie in different ways. Women were more likely to lie to make the person they were talking to feel good, while men lied most often to make themselves look better.

One hundred and twenty one pair of students were arranged to participate in the study. They were told that the purpose of the study was to examine how people interact when they meet someone new. Participants were asked to have a 10-minute conversation with another person. The students were then asked to watch the video of themselves and identify any inaccuracies in what they said during the conversation. They were encouraged to identify all lies, no matter how big or small.

(34) Feldman said the students who participated in the study were surprised at their own results. When they were watching themselves on videotape, people found themselves lying much more than they thought they had.

"It's very easy to lie," Feldman said. "We teach our children that honesty is the best policy, but we also tell them it's polite to pretend they like a birthday gift they've been given (35) Kids get a very mixed message regarding the practical aspects of lying, and it has an impact on how they behave as adults."

Questions 33 to 35 are based on the passage you have just heard.

Q 33: What is the finding made by Feldman about lying?

Q 34: What did the participants find when they were asked to watch the video of themselves?

Q 35: What does Feldman say about children regarding lie?

Unit 2

Section A

Directions: In this section, you will hear 8 short conversations and 2 long conversations. At the end of each conversation, one or more questions will be asked about what was said. Both the conversation and the questions will be spoken only once. After each question there will be a pause. During the pause, you must read the four choices marked A）, B）, C）and D）, and decide which is the best answer. Then mark the corresponding letter on Answer Sheet 2 with a single line through the centre.

11. A）She'd prefer to see a different type of movie than a comedy.
   B）She has already finished her research paper.
   C）She won't be able to go to a movie with the man.
   D）She'd like the man to help her with her research paper.

12. A）He prefers to work part time.
   B）He wants to change his class schedule.
   C）He's having a difficult time finding a part-time job.
   D）He doesn't want to work on campus.

13. A）They're the only tickets to the well-paid job.
   B）They don't help much in getting a good job.
   C）They play a key role in promotion.
   D）They don't make much difference as far as the pay is concerned.

14. A）The man is willing to confess his sins.
   B）The man used to smoke cigarettes while writing.
   C）The man thinks smoking is an awful habit.
   D）The man's wife allows him to drink alcohol but not to smoke.

15. A）He hadn't heard the news about his brother.
   B）He hasn't talked to his brother since he transferred.
   C）His brother doesn't want to transfer.
   D）He doesn't think his brother should transfer.

16. A) Which seminar the woman wants to sign up for.

   B) If the woman keeps money at the bank.

   C) Where the woman learned about the seminar.

   D) If the woman has taken other classes on personal finances.

17. A) He's used to cold weather.

   B) He expected the weather to be warmer over the weekend.

   C) He has never liked the weather in October.

   D) He didn't see the forecast for the weekend.

18. A) Leave the art exhibit.   C) Take the artwork down.

   B) Help the man understand the display.   D) Call the museum director.

Questions 19 to 22 are based on the conversation you have just heard.

19. A) To ask her to go canoeing.   C) To ask if he can borrow her car.

   B) To invite her to a cook out.   D) To tell her about a trip he is going to took.

20. A) A lunch.   B) A sleeping bag.   C) A canoe.   D) A tent.

21. A) Swimming.   B) Driving.   C) Sleeping outdoors.   D) Canoeing.

22. A) To find out whether she wants to go canoeing.

   B) To tell her whether his car is repaired.

   C) To find out what kind of food she is bringing.

   D) To tell her what time they are leaving.

Questions 23 to 25 are based on the conversation you have just heard.

23. A) He happened to see the position-wanted advertisement in a newspaper.

   B) He wanted to begin his career with a decent job.

   C) He believed he can get a lot of experience working there.

   D) He believed working in a public office would great benefit his future business.

24. A) Because he was not respected for lack of efficiency working there.

   B) For financial matter.

   C) Because he just could not put up with the lengthy and rigid procedures.

   D) Because he wanted to live together with his family.

25. A) Go to school for further study.   C) Resigning from the public office.

   B) Begin his own business with his wife.   D) Working for a private company.

Section B

Directions: In this section, you will hear 3 short passages. At the end of each passage, you will hear some questions. Both the passage and the questions will be spoken only once. After you hear a question, you must choose the best answer from the four choices marked A), B), C), and D). Then mark the corresponding letter on the Answer Sheet with a single line through the center.

Passage One

Questions 26 to 28 are based on the passage you have just heard.

26. A) To discuss one way it impacted jazz music.

   B) To explain why the government reduced some taxes.

   C) To describe a common theme in jazz music.

   D) To discuss the popularity of certain jazz bands.

27. A）They didn't use singers.

    B）They gave free concerts.

    C）They performed in small nightclubs.

    D）They shortened the length of their performances.

28. A）The music contained strong political messages.

    B）The music had a steady beat that people could dance to.

    C）The music included sad melodies.

    D）The music contained irregular types of rhythms.

Passage Two

Questions 29 to 31 are based on the passage you have just heard.

29. A）A museum exhibition of African baskets.

    B）Changes in basket-weaving.

    C）Differences between African and American baskets.

    D）The development of basket weaving in one town.

30. A）Their mothers taught them.

    B）They travelled to Africa.

    C）They learned in school.

    D）They taught themselves.

31. A）They sell them as an occupation.

    B）They make them as a hobby.

    C）They use them on their farms.

    D）They make and sell them to make a living.

Passage Three

Questions 32 to 35 are based on the passage you have just heard.

32. A）Factors that affect the ability to remember.

    B）The influence of childhood memories on adulthood.

    C）A proposal for future psychological research.

    D）Benefits of a busy lifestyle.

33. A）The need to exercise the memory.

    B）How the brain differs from other body tissues.

    C）The unconscious learning of a physical activity.

    D）How nerves control body movement.

34. A）Repeat it aloud.

    B）Write it down.

    C）Make a mental picture of it.

    D）Learn to record it.

35. A）Ask questions about the assigned reading.

    B）Give an example of active learning.

    C）Explain recent research on recalling childhood memories.

    D）Make an assignment for the next class session.

Section C

Directions: In this section, you will hear a passage three times. When the passage is read for the first time, you should listen carefully for its general idea. When the passage is read for the second time, you are required to fill in the blanks numbered from 36 to 43 with the exact words you have heard. For blanks numbered from 44 to 45 you are required to fill in the missing information. For these blanks, you can either use the exact words you have just heard or write down the main points in your own words. Finally, when the passage is read for the third time, you should check what you have written.

Computer scientists in the United States are working on a (36) _____ computer for young people in developing countries. The dream is for every child to own one.

The (37) _____ is led by Nicholas Negroponte, (38) _____ of the Media Lab at the Massachusetts Institute of Technology. Mister Negroponte first (39) _____ the idea of a one hundred dollar laptop computer in January. He just presented an early (40) _____ of the computer at the World Summit on the Information Society.

To save money, the computers are expected to use the free (41) _____ system Linux instead of a product like Microsoft Windows. Users without electric power will be able to turn a wind-up handle to (42) _____ the battery. A special full-color (43) _____ will have the ability to change to a black-and-white image. That way, users could see it even in bright sunlight. And the computers will be able to connect (44) _____ to each other and to the Internet.

The machines will not be able to store huge amounts of information. But they will be made to survive rough conditions. Also, the lime-green color should make them more appealing to children — and less appealing to robbers. M.I.T. has set up a non-profit organization called One Laptop per Child to develop the computer. Five companies, including Google and News Corporation, have each given two million dollars to (45) _____ the group. The plan is to sell the computers to education ministries that order at least one million of them.

答案与原文

Unit 2

答案

Section A

(11-15) CACBD (16-20) BBAAB (21-25) CDABD

Section B

(26-30) AADDA (31-35) BAADB

Section C

(36) low-cost (37) project (38) chief (39) announced
(40) version (41) operating (42) recharge (43) display
(44) wirelessly (45) finance

📖 原文

Section A

M: How about a movie tonight? That new comedy is opening in town.

W: Sounds great, but I've got to be finishing sketches on my psychology research paper.

Q: What does the woman imply?

Question 12

W: You won't have to look very hard to find a job on campus. But I don't think you'll find anything that isn't just part-time. (但我认为你可能找不到兼职之外的工作。)

M: That suits me. Anything more than that, and I'll have to change my class schedule.

Q: What does the man mean?

Question 13

M: What do you think of this new study that challenges the idea that college degrees are the only tickets to a well-paid job?

W: Well, it's true that people without a college degree can find work of some kind, but in today's high-tech society their chances of promotion are pretty limited.

Q: What does the woman think of the college degrees?

Question 14

W: Have you got any sins you want to confess? Drugs? Alcohol?

M: I prefer cigarettes, but my wife made me stop smoking. This is the first book I've ever written without smoking, and it was awful, it was just awful!

Q: What can be inferred from the conversation?

Question 15

W: I hear that your brother is planning to transfer to another university.

M: Not if I can talk him out of it. And believe me, I'm trying.

Q: What does the man imply?

Question 16

W: I'd like to enroll the free seminar you advertised in newspaper, the one on managing personal finances.

M: Okay. Now the ad did say that you have to have a saving account at our bank to be eligible. Do you have one here?

Q: What does the man want to know?

Question 17

W: Did you see the weather forecast for this weekend? I can't believe how the temperature's going to dip.

M: I know. That isn't my idea what October should be like.

Q: What does the man mean?

Question 18

M: This exhibit is a total bore! I can't believe they call this art.

W: I think I've seen enough.

Q: What will the woman probably do next?

Now you will hear two long conversations.

Conversation One

M: (19) <u>Hi Jane, now that the midterms are over, a bunch of us are getting away for the</u> <u>weekend to go canoeing. Wanna come along?</u>

W: Well, uhm, it'd be great to get away, but I've never done it before.

M: None of the others have either except for me. I went once last fall. But there'll be an instructor in each canoe the first day.

W: I don't know.

M: Oh, come on. This is our last chance to take a break before finals. The scenery is beautiful, and if it gets too hot we can dive in whenever we feel like it. The river's really calm this time of the year, no rapids to deal with.

W: That's a relief. What would I have to bring?

M: Let's see. Tom's bringing food for the Friday night cookout for everyone. And the people who run the trip have tents set up and they supply food and drinks for all day Saturday. On the way back Sunday morning we'll stop somewhere for breakfast. (20) <u>So, you have to</u> <u>bring a bathing suit and a sleeping bag.</u>

W: (21) <u>Well, I do love camping and sleeping out. Where is this place?</u>

M: Well, it's about an hour and a half to the place where we meet the trip guiders. We leave our car there and they drive us and the canoes upriver to the place where we start canoeing.

W: And who's driving us to the meeting place?

M: Well, I was hoping we could take your car. Mine's in the shop again.

W: Oh, I see. It's not me you want, it's my car.

M: Don't be silly. So what would you say?

W: Oh, why not!

M: (22) <u>Great I'll give you a call when I find out when everyone wants to leave on Friday.</u>

Questions 19 to 22 are based on the conversation you have just heard.

Q 19: What is the main reason the man calls the woman?

Q 20: What is one thing the woman has to bring?

Q 21: What does the woman say she enjoys doing?

Q 22: What does the man need to talk to the woman again?

Conversation Two

W: So you're an architect?

M: Yes.

W: Do you work for a public or private organization, or are you self-employed.

M: (25) <u>I'm working for a private design and construction company,</u> but I started with the government.

W: Oh, what made you decide to work for the government?

M: Well, (23) <u>it was really a matter of chance. I saw an advertisement for a vacant position in</u> <u>a newspaper, and I thought "Why not have a try"</u>. In fact, I had no preferences to where I work, public or private.

W: And do you still have this idea?

M: More or less, yes, although I'm now working for a private firm, I worked for the government for several years. It was alright. Of course, there're the administrative procedures one has to put with, but it's not that bad, if you don't mind the lengthy and rigid procedures. And things are not very efficient.

W: Is that why you left the public office?

M: (24) <u>Money factor, actually.</u> You see, I got married and my wife doesn't work, and we wanted to start a family right away. (25) <u>So we thought it might be better if I moved to work for a private company.</u> And this is also why it's hard for me to be self-employed because self-employed work may mean that one could now and then be unemployed at the beginning of his business.

W: Thanks.

Questions 23 to 25 are based on the conversation you have just heard.

Q 23: Why did the man begin his career in a public office?

Q 24: Why did the man give up working for the government?

Q 25: What is the man doing now?

Section B

Passage One

Ok, so in our last class we were discussing big bands swing music. You remember this was a kind of dance music with a steady rhythm. But today we deal with music played by smaller jazz bands. It's called bebop which may use all sorts of new types of rhythms; some of them are very irregular. We'll talk more about that later. (26) <u>But first I want to talk about some of the social elements that I believe contributed to the development of bebop music.</u> To do this, we have to look at when bebop arose and started becoming so popular. It was from the late 1930s through the 1940s. (26) <u>The environment for bebop music was the decline of the US economy. During the great depression the economy suffered tremendously. And fewer people had money to spend on entertainment.</u> Then during the Second World War the government imposed a new tax on public entertainment, what you might call performance tax. (27) <u>The government collected money on performances that included any types of acting, dancing or singing, but not instrumental music. So to avoid this new tax, some bebop bands stopped using singer altogether.</u> They started relying on the creativity of the instrumentalist to attract audiences. This was what bebop bands did. Now remember a lot of bands have singers. So the instrumentalists simply played in the background and had occasional solos (独奏、独唱) while the singer sang the melody to the songs, but not bebop bands. So the bands' instrumentalists had much more freedom to be creative. They experimented, playing the music faster and (28) <u>using new irregular sorts of rhythms.</u>

Questions 26 to 28 are based on the passage you have just heard.

Q 26: Why does the speaker mention the decline of the US economy during the great depression?

Q 27: How did the bebop bands avoid the performance tax?

Q 28: What does the speaker describe as a significant characteristic of bebop music?

Passage Two

Recently some researchers conducted an interesting case study in an ethic culture. The study was about the development of basket weaving by African-American women who live in the town of Mount Pleasant, South Carolina. The town is known for its high quality sweet grass baskets which are woven by these women. (30) They've been weaving the baskets for generations, handing down the skill from mother to daughter. Some of the baskets have been placed on permanent display at the Philadelphia Museum of Art.

The origin of their basket weaving dates back to the 17th century and even earlier when these women's ancestors came to the United States from the west coast of Africa. Now, it's mainly a hobby. But back in the 17th and 18th century African and American women wove the baskets for use on the rice plantations. There were two types of baskets then: Workbaskets and baskets for use in the home. The workbaskets were made out of the more delicate sweet grass. They were used for everything from fruit baskets to baby cradles.

Questions 29 to 31 are based on the passage you have just heard.

Q 29: What is the talk mainly about?

Q 30: According to the passage how did the women learn to weave basket?

Q 31: What is the main reason that the women in South Carolina now weave baskets?

Passage Three

Some of the most practical lessons coming out of research in psychology are the area of memory. People ask, why can't I remember that term from the physical charge or the library books in due? (33) Of a lot of people, memory may be weak, because they don't use it enough. It's like muscle if you don't exercise it, it won't get strong. That's why it's important to keep our mind active, to keep on learning through our life. We can do this by reading, playing memory game and seeking out. It's my guess though that the lack of stimulation isn't a problem for students like you. More likely, the life you are in is so busy and stimulating that it's itself may sometime interfere with learning. (34) Information need to be recorded from memory, in other words, learned. And for busy people like you and me, that will be the real problem. If we are distracted, or we are trying to think what we are going to do next, the incoming message just might not be getting recorded effectively. And that leads to the first tip for students who want to improve their memories. Give your full attention to the information you hope to retain. Research clearly shows the advantages of this, and also of active learning, of consciously trying to visualize a new fact, perhaps to make a mental picture, even a wild ridiculous one, so the new fact will stick in memory. (35) Let me illustrate that for you here a little more this evening.

Questions 32 to 35 are based on the passage you have just heard.

Q 32: What's the talk mainly about?

Q 33: What does the speaker illustrate with the example of muscle?

Q 34: What does the speaker suggest students do to learn information more effectively?

Q 35: What will the speaker probably do next?

Unit 3

Section A

Directions: In this section, you will hear 8 short conversations and 2 long conversations. At the end of each conversation, one or more questions will be asked about what was said. Both the conversation and the questions will be spoken only once. After each question there will be a pause. During the pause, you must read the four choices marked A), B), C) and D), and decide which is the best answer. Then mark the corresponding letter on Answer Sheet 2 with a single line through the centre.

11. A）He thinks he's very organized.
    B）He doesn't want to join the display.
    C）He doesn't think he should lead the study group.
    D）He knows someone who can lead the study group.

12. A）He doesn't know where his brother keeps his computer.
    B）The woman should buy a used computer.
    C）He doesn't know how much computers cost.
    D）His brother paid too much for the computer.

13. A）It had been too warm to wear the jacket.
    B）The jacket is too big for him.
    C）He doesn't like cold weather.
    D）He didn't buy the jacket until cooler weather arrived.

14. A）He started the semester in a bad mood.　　C）He has few responsibilities.
    B）He's not usually bad-tempered.　　D）He doesn't like the man.

15. A）He forgot to cancel the reservation.
    B）They can go to the restaurant after the woman has finished working.
    C）He has to work late tonight.
    D）They don't have a reservation at the restaurant.

16. A）Use bleach on his socks.　　C）Wash his red T-shirt again.
    B）Buy new white socks.　　D）Throw away his pink socks.

17. A）He isn't satisfied with his progress.
    B）He wants to move up more quickly than he's presently doing.
    C）He has advance quickly enough in his career.
    D）He feels frustrated as he tries to move up the ladder.

18. A）Try on a smaller sweater.
    B）Look for another style at a different store.
    C）Give the sweater away as a gift.
    D）Exchange the sweater for a bigger one.

Questions 19 to 22 are based on the conversation you have just heard.

19. A）She's unable to attend the study session.
    B）She has seen a doctor recently.
    C）She's concerned about medical care.
    D）She mentions the need for some medical tests.

20. A) To improve the study skills of university students.

B) To suggest changes in the student government.

C) To give people the opportunity to speak with a politician.

D) To discuss graduation requirements for political science majors.

21. A) Graduate school application procedures.

B) Funding for university education.

C) Winning the confidence of voters.

D) Preparing for an important test.

22. A) Tell her what to study for the history test.

B) Write a favorable letter of recommendation.

C) Advise her about how to run an election campaign.

D) Suggest a topic for a research paper.

Questions 23 to 25 are based on the conversation you have just heard.

23. A) Boston schools.   C) Teaching requirements.

B) Frontier life.   D) Immigration patterns.

24. A) She was a famous author.

B) Her family later became famous landowners.

C) She exemplifies the immigrant spirit.

D) She invented some labor-saving farm equipment.

25. A) To the library.   C) To a bookstore.

B) To the movies.   D) To a travel bureau.

Section B

Directions: In this section, you will hear 3 short passages. At the end of each passage, you will hear some questions. Both the passage and the questions will be spoken only once. After you hear a question, you must choose the best answer from the four choices marked A), B), C) , and D) . Then mark the corresponding letter on the Answer Sheet with a single line through the center.

Passage One

Questions 26 to 29 are based on the passage you have just heard.

26. A) They were drawing pictures.   C) They were making a telephone call.

B) They were watching TV.   D) They were tidying up the drawing room.

27. A) They locked the couple up in the drawing room.

B) They seriously injured the owners of the house.

C) They smashed the TV set and the telephone.

D) They took away sixteen valuable paintings.

28. A) He accused them of the theft.

B) He raised the rents.

C) He refused to prolong their land lease.

D) He forced them to abandon their traditions.

29. A) They wanted to protect the farmers' interests.

B) They wanted to extend the reservation area for birds.

C) They wanted to steal his valuable paintings.

D) They wanted to drive him away from the island.

Passage Two

Questions 30 to 32 are based on the passage you have just heard.

30. A) Through food.   C) Through insects.

     B) Through air.   D) Through body fluids.

31. A) They ran a high fever.   C) Their nervous system was damaged.

     B) They died from excessive bleeding.   D) They suffered from heart-attack.

32. A) To see what happened to the survivors of the outbreak.

     B) To study animals that can also get infected with the disease.

     C) To find out where the virus originates.

     D) To look for the plants that could cure the disease.

Passage Three

Questions 33 to 35 are based on the passage you have just heard.

33. A) To determine whether the Earth's temperature is going up.

     B) To study the behavior of some sea animals.

     C) To measure the depths of the ocean.

     D) To measure the movement of waves in the ocean.

34. A) They were frightened and distressed.

     B) They swam away when the speaker was turned on.

     C) They swam closer to "examine" the speaker when it was turned off.

     D) They didn't seem to be frightened and kept swimming near the speaker.

35. A) To attract more sea animals to the testing site.

     B) To drive dangerous sea animals away from the testing site.

     C) To help trace the sea animals being tested.

     D) To determine how sea animals communicate with each other.

Section C

Directions: In this section, you will hear a passage three times. When the passage is read for the first time, you should listen carefully for its general idea. When the passage is read for the second time, you are required to fill in the blanks numbered from 36 to 43 with the exact words you have heard. For blanks numbered from 44 to 45 you are required to fill in the missing information. For these blanks, you can either use the exact words you have just heard or write down the main points in your own words. Finally, when the passage is read for the third time, you should check what you have written.

Children who do not get enough good food in the first two years of life suffer lasting (36) _____. They may be undeveloped or (37) _____. They may suffer from poor health or limited (38) _____. In addition, poorly (39) _____ children are more likely to drop out of school and earn less money as adults.

Too little food is not the only cause of poor nutrition. Many children who live in homes with plenty of food suffer for other reasons. For example, the study says that mothers often fail to give their newly born babies their first (40) _____. It is full of nutrients that improve a baby's ability to fight (41) _____ and disease.

The study also links malnutrition to economic growth in poor countries. (42) _____ _____ nutrition in early childhood can cost developing nations up to three percent of their (43) _____. Many of these same countries have economies that are growing at a rate of two to three percent yearly. The study suggests that poor countries could possibly double their economic growth if they improved nutrition.

Africa and South Asia are affected the most by poor nutrition. The study says about half of all children in India do not get enough good food. Other parts of the world are also (44) _____ affected, including Indonesia, Uzbekistan, Yemen, Guatemala and Peru. The study recommends that developing countries change their policies to deal with malnutrition. Instead of directly providing food, the study suggests educational programs in health and nutrition for mothers with young babies. It also recommends cleaner living conditions and (45) _____ in health care.

答案与原文

Unit 3

答案

Section A

(11-15) CCABD   (16-20) ACDAC   (21-25) BBBCA

Section B

(26-30) BDCAD   (31-35) BCADC

Section C

(36) damage   (37) underweight   (38) intelligence   (39) nourished

(40) breast milk   (41) infections   (42) A lack of   (43) yearly earnings

(44) severely   (45) improvements

原文

Section A

Question 11

W: We should probably think about selecting someone to lead our study group. You know, somebody really organized.

M: Then you can count me out. （那就别指望我了。）

Q: What does the man mean?

Question 12

W: What do you think would be a reasonable price to pay for a new computer?

M: You are asking the wrong person. My brother gave me mine.

Q: What does the man imply?

Question 13

W: That's a nice-looking jacket. It fits you perfectly. I think you bought it recently?

M: Thanks. No, I've had it for a while. I've just been waiting for the weather to cool down.

Q: What does the man imply?

Question 14

M: What's wrong with Herald today? He snapped (口语：发怒) even no reason.

W: Don't worry. It's just the end of the semester pressure. He'll be his old self next week.

Q: What does the woman say about Herald?

Question 15

W: I'm sorry. I need to work late tonight. So you should probably cancel our reservation at the restaurant.

M: Oh, actually I've never got round to making one in the first place.

Q: What does the man mean?

Question 16

M: Oh! I turned all of my white sock pink! I threw a red T-shirt in by accident.

W: Have you tried running them through again with bleach (漂白粉)?

Q: What does the woman suggest the man do?

Question 17

W: Some say you're frustrated because you weren't moving up the ladder quickly enough?

M: I want to laugh when I hear that. I don't know if anybody has moved up the ladder more quickly than I have.

Q: What does the man mean?

Question 18

M: How do I look in this new sweater I bought yesterday? I was in a hurry, so I didn't have a chance to try it on.

W: Well, I really like the style, but it looks a little tight. You might want to take it back and get the next size up.

Q: What does the woman suggest the man do?

Now you will hear two long conversations.

Conversation One

W: Oh, Jack I'm glad I call you. (19) I want to tell you I have to skip the history study group discussion tonight.

M: Really? That' too bad. Aren't you feeling well?

W: Oh, it's not bad. It's going to be a public meeting down the town hall. The state Senator from this area is going to be there. (20) She has this meeting three or four times a year to speak with her supporters.

M: Is that you'd like to do with your evening, going to listen to a politician's...

W: Actually it's a class assignment. Prof Jackson, he's teaching that political science seminar I'm taking. He told all of us in the seminar to go and hear what the senator has to say tonight and also write up a report about the issues people bring.

M: Oh, like medical care, and tax and...?

W: Right, as long as I'm there, (21) <u>I think I'd like to bring up government funding for state universities.</u> The tuition keeps going on and it's getting harder and harder for a lot of students to afford it.

M: Tell me about it.

W: Anyway I want to do a really good job on this report. (22) <u>I need to get a letter of recommendation from Prof. Jackson for graduate school.</u> So I guess I'd better show up there tonight and see what's going on.

M: Yeah, but, what about the history test?

W: Well, I already put some time on that this morning. So I think by tomorrow afternoon, I'll be ready.

Questions 19 to 22 are based on the conversation you have just heard.

Q 19: Why does the man assume the woman is not feeling well?

Q 20: What is the general purpose of the meeting the woman plans to attend?

Q 21: What does the woman hope to discuss tonight?

Q 22: What does the woman hope Prof. Jackson will do for her?

Conversation Two

M: I've just finished reading a book of short stories by Hemlen Galen called *May Traveled Road*. I really enjoyed it. Have you ever read it?

W: Yes, it was a required reading in American literature course I took last year (23) <u>even though it's fiction you get a realistic picture of the hard life people had on American frontier.</u> (24) <u>I don't think I would survive the 19th century frontier life.</u>

M: (24) <u>Galen gives a vivid description of Julie Peterson, that young immigrant girl. She had to work on her family farm.</u>

W: Ah ha!

M: Well when Julie feels exhausted, and she is wishing she can escape from her hard labor, she looks over her father working in the next field. And she is inspired to continue her own work.

W: I do remember that story. Galen really captures the spirit of hard work that was so typical of immigrants and pioneers who settled in the American Midwest. It's difficult to imagine that nothing seems to discourage them for long.

M: I wonder how Galen learn so much about the Midwest. Was he from Boston?

W: He lived in Boston. In fact, he studied and taught in Boston School of Oratory, but I think he was born in Carbinlen, Wisconsin. He did grow up in Midwest.

M: No wonder his description is so good, (25) <u>I'm going to take this book back to the library now and see what other Galen's works I can find.</u>

Questions 23 to 25 are based on the conversation you have just heard.

Q 23: What does Hemlen Galen describe in May Traveled Road?

Q 24: Why does the man mention Julie Peterson?

Q 25: Where's the man going now?

Section B

Passage One

It's 8 o'clock on Tuesday, May 1st. Here is the news: Between the hours of 7:00 and 8:00 P.M. last night, five thieves broke into the country house of Lord and Lady Chest-field on an island. They entered by a window at the rear of the house and (26) surprised the owners who were watching television in the drawing room. After disconnecting the telephone and tying up Lord and Lady Chest-field, (27) the thieves escaped with 16 precious paintings. The market value of such art work has been estimated at somewhere around 4 million pounds. Lord and Lady Chest-field were not seriously harmed but have been treated for shock in the hospital.

Early this morning a woman with a Scottish accent telephoned the Times in London to say that the Chest-field Organization for Freedom claim the responsibility for the theft. This is the third time this year that this organization has claimed the responsibility for an act of this kind. (29) The organization defends all the farmers on the island. The farmers were forced to leave their lands when (28) Lord Chest-field, their landlord, refused to renew their traditional lease last year in order to extend the reservation area for birds.

Questions 26 to 29 are based on the passage you have just heard.

Q 26: What were Lord and Lady Chest-field doing when the thieves broke into their house?

Q 27: What did the five thieves do?

Q 28: What did Lord Chest-field do to the farmers?

Q 29: What's the organization's purpose in breaking into Lord Chest-field house?

Passage Two

A deadly infectious (感染性的、传染性的) outbreak swept through a small city in Zaire, Africa last spring, killing more than one hundred people. (31) The killer was a rare virus that caused most victims to bleed to death. As scientists rushed to control the outbreak, people in the U.S. wondered "Could it attack here?" "We are foolish if we think it couldn't come to our country." say doctors. The virus can be highly infectious. (30) If you come in contact with a victim's blood or other body fluids, you can get sick, too. All it takes is one infected person to start such a disease. That's what scientists believe happened in Zaire. The healthcare workers who treated the first victims there soon fell ill too. The problem was they had no protective equipment to prevent themselves from being infected. International rescue workers brought equipment to Zaire soon after the outbreak occurred. Now the disease appears to be under control. One big mystery is that no one knows where the virus comes from or where it will strike next. Some scientists say that the virus lies inactive in the cells of some kind of plant, insect or other animal. Then it somehow finds a way to infect humans. (32) Scientists are now headed into the jungles of Africa to find out where the virus lives. Once they find the virus, they also hope to find ways to come at it.

Questions 30 to 32 are based on the passage you have just heard.

Q 30: How does the disease mentioned in the passage spread?

Q 31: What happened to most of the victims stricken with this disease?

Q 32: Why are the scientists going to the African jungles?

Passage Three

A team of scientists recently began a project to measure the effects of loud noises on sea-animals. If the sounds don't harm the animals, then the researchers can go ahead with a plan to transmit sound waves through the Pacific Ocean to take earth's temperature. Sound travels faster through warm water than cold water. (33) <u>By analyzing the speed of sound through the ocean over a time, the scientists will be able to determine if our planet is warming up.</u> The experiment was nearly cancelled more than a year ago because environmental groups feared that the sound will confuse or harm the sea-animals. So, scientists are conducting tests on the animals first. The researchers lowered a loud speaker that emits low frequency sound about 1000 meters beneath the ocean. Scientists at the site transmit sound waves into the ocean. (35) <u>Radio transmitters attached to some of the sea-animals help the researches keep track of the animals' movements.</u> If sea-animals are distressed by the sounds, they would swim away from the speakers. So far, there aren't any signs that the animals are being harmed. (34) <u>Researchers at the site noticed that large numbers of sea-animals swim near the speaker whether it was turned on or off,</u> but it is still too soon to know for sure, the scientists admit. The test will continue through September. "If all goes well," they say, "we can begin measuring temperature changes on our planet."

Questions 33 to 35 are based on the passage you have just heard.

Q 33: What is the purpose of analyzing the speed of sound through the Pacific Ocean?

Q 34: What was the reaction of the sea-animals to the sound tests?

Q 35: For what purpose were radio transmitters used?

Unit 4

Section A

Directions: In this section, you will hear 8 short conversations and 2 long conversations. At the end of each conversation, one or more questions will be asked about what was said. Both the conversation and the questions will be spoken only once. After each question there will be a pause. During the pause, you must read the four choices marked A), B), C) and D), and decide which is the best answer. Then mark the corresponding letter on Answer Sheet 2 with a single line through the centre.

11. A) He'll help Tina prepare for the meeting.
    B) He feels sorry that he'll have to miss the meeting.
    C) He often works extra hours.
    D) He's afraid the meeting won't end on time.
12. A) The man will take the camera to be repaired.
    B) The woman will take a picture of the man.
    C) The woman will show the man how to use the camera.
    D) The woman will borrow the man's camera.
13. A) He'd like to apply for a replacement card.
    B) He needed to see a doctor two weeks ago.
    C) He's pleased that the woman found the card.
    D) He's glad he was finally able to get an appointment.

14. A）She doesn't understand the man's question.

   B）She doesn't have time to repeat the explanation now.

   C）She doesn't mind answering questions.

   D）She'll return soon.

15. A）The woman doesn't accept the man's apology.

   B）The woman wasn't bothered by the delay.

   C）The man didn't realize the woman was waiting.

   D）The man waited a long time for the bus.

16. A）She won't be a candidate next year.　　C）The news doesn't upset her.

   B）She doesn't believe the news.　　D）The news will disappoint Mary.

17. A）Try to find the woman's roommate.　　C）Give the woman a ride to the bookstore.

   B）Buy tickets for the film festival.　　D）Get a schedule for the woman.

18. A）She thinks it will rain today.　　C）She'll change the money for the man.

   B）Her hobby is collecting coins.　　D）She's keeping the money for an emergency.

Questions 19 to 22 are based on the conversation you have just heard.

19. A）Two different types of bones in the human body.

   B）How bones help the body move.

   C）How bones continuously repair themselves.

   D）The chemical composition of human bones.

20. A）They defend the bone against viruses.

   B）They prevent oxygen from entering the bone.

   C）They break down bone tissue.

   D）They connect the bone to muscle tissue.

21. A）They have difficulty identifying these cells.

   B）They aren't sure how these cells work.

   C）They've learned how to reproduce these cells.

   D）They've found similar cells in other species.

22. A）To learn how to prevent a bone disease.

   B）To understand differences between bone tissue and other tissue.

   C）To find out how specialized bone cells have evolved.

   D）To create artificial bone tissue.

Questions 23 to 25 are based on the conversation you have just heard.

23. A）Her car is being repaired.　　C）Parking is difficult in the city.

   B）She wants to help reduce pollution.　　D）The cost of fuel has increased.

24. A）A fuel that burns cleanly.

   B）An oil additive that helps cool engines.

   C）A material from which filters are made.

   D）An insulating material sprayed on engine parts.

25. A）The high temperatures required for its use.

   B）The high cost of materials used in its production.

   C）The lack of trained environmental engineers.

   D）The opposition of automobile manufacturers.

Section B

Directions: In this section, you will hear 3 short passages. At the end of each passage, you will hear some questions. Both the passage and the questions will be spoken only once. After you hear a question, you must choose the best answer from the four choices marked A), B) , C) , and D) . Then mark the corresponding letter on the Answer Sheet with a single line through the center.

Passage One

Questions 26 to 28 are based on the passage you have just heard.

26. A) The color of the dog.
    B) The price of the dog.
    C) Whether the dog will adapt to the environment.
    D) Whether the dog will get along with the other pets in the house.
27. A) It must be trained so it won't bite.
    B) It needs more love from its master.
    C) It demands more food and space.
    D) It must be looked after carefully.
28. A) They are less likely to run away.
    B) It's easier for their masters to train them.
    C) They are less likely to be shy with human beings.
    D) It's easier for them to form a relationship with their masters.

Passage Two

Questions 29 to 31 are based on the passage you have just heard.

29. A) They often go for walks at a leisurely pace.
    B) They usually have a specific purpose in mind.
    C) They like the seaside more than the countryside.
    D) They seldom plan their leisure activities in advance.
30. A) Their hardworking spirit.
    B) Their patience in waiting for theatre tickets.
    C) Their delight in leisure activities.
    D) Their enthusiasm for the arts.
31. A) The Polish people can now spend their leisure time in various ways.
    B) The Polish people are fond of walking leisurely in the countryside.
    C) The Polish people enjoy picking wild fruit in their leisure time.
    D) The Polish people like to spend their holidays abroad.

Passage Three

Questions 32 to 35 are based on the passage you have just heard.

32. A) They will be much bigger.
    B) They will have more seats.
    C) They will have three wheels.
    D) They will need intelligent drivers.

33. A）It doesn't need to be refueled.
    B）It will use solar energy as fuel.
    C）It will be driven by electrical power.
    D）It will be more suitable for long distance travel.
34. A）Passengers in the car may be seated facing one another.
    B）The front seats will face forward and the back seats backward.
    C）Special seats will be designed for children.
    D）More seats will be added.
35. A）Choose the right route.
    B）Refuel the car regularly.
    C）Start the engine.
    D）Tell the computer where to go.

Section C

Directions: In this section, you will hear a passage three times. When the passage is read for the first time, you should listen carefully for its general idea. When the passage is read for the second time, you are required to fill in the blanks numbered from 36 to 43 with the exact words you have heard. For blanks numbered from 44 to 45 you are required to fill in the missing information. For these blanks, you can either use the exact words you have just heard or write down the main points in your own words. Finally, when the passage is read for the third time, you should check what you have written.

Some American students get help with their (36) _____ from online companies whose teachers may be in another country. One example is Career Launcher India Limited. It provides mathematics help through online tutoring companies. The student in the United States and teacher in India talk to each other as they work out math problems. The teachers can explain ideas by drawing on the (37) _____ so the student can see how the answer (38) _____. Career Launcher also tutors students in India and the Middle East. The service costs about twenty to thirty dollars an hour.

Another online tutoring company is Tutor-dot-com. Its tutors are in North America. They provide help in math, science, (39) _____ and English to students from the fourth to the twelfth grades. (40) _____ say the company helps about three thousand students each day. Growing Stars is another company (41) _____ online tutoring. It works with children from grades three through twelve. It helps with math, English, science, physics, chemistry and biology. The company tutors are in India.

It (42) _____ American students about twenty dollars an hour. Growing Stars is (43) _____ into Canada, Britain and Australia. It gives each student a test to find out what he or she knows and does not know. Then an (44) _____ director creates a personal learning program for each student. And the company e-mails progress reports to the children's parents.

Some education experts are concerned about people in India helping American children with American English. They also have concerns about the quality of other instruction offered by such programs. The companies say their teachers are (45) _____ who know the differences between British and American English. The companies say they could not operate if students and their parents were not satisfied with the service.

答案与原文

Unit 4

答案

Section A

(11-15) BCCCB   (16-20) CDDCC   (21-25) BABDA

Section B

(26-30) CBDBD   (31-35) ACCAD

Section C

(36) schoolwork   (37) screen   (38) develops   (39) social studies

(40) Officials   (41) offering   (42) charges   (43) expanding

(44) academic   (45) professionals

原文

Section A

Question 11

W: Tina says you won't be able to make it to the meeting tomorrow evening.

M: Yeah, sorry about that. I just found out that I have to work over time.

Q: What does the man mean?

Question 12

W: Would you mind taking a picture of me in front of the fountain?

M: Not at all. But I'm not sure how this camera works.

Q: What will probably happen next?

Question 13

W: Oh my goodness. Your help services card is sitting right here in your file; it should have been sent out to you weeks ago. I hope you haven't had any need for it.

M: No, not yet. But it's nice to know I have it, so I don't need to reapply.

Q: What does the man mean?

Question 14

M: Excuse me, professor Smith. But I'm still confused. Could you go over that last point one more time?

W: Of course, that's what I'm here for.

Q: What does the woman mean?

Question 15

M: I'm sorry I made you wait. The bus was stuck in traffic and took forever to get here.

W: No harm done. I was able to catch up on some reading.

Q: What can be inferred about the conversation?

Question 16

M: I just heard the news that Mary won the election. That must be a big disappointment for you.

W: Well, actually, she probably was the best candidate this time around, and I can always run again next year.

Q: What does the woman imply?

Question 17

W: Do you have your film festival schedule with you? I'd like to find out what's playing this weekend.

M: I passed it on to my roommate, but there should be more in the bookstore. I can pick one up for you next time going there.

Q: What does the man offer to do?

Question 18

M: Gee, you have a lot of change in that jar. Are you a coin collector?

W: No, I'm just saving them for a rainy day.（储存起来以备不时之需。）

Q: What does the woman mean?

Now you will hear two long conversations.

Conversation One

W: Ok, last night you were supposed to read an article about human bones. Are there any comments about it?

M: Well, to begin with, I was surprised to find out there were so much going on in bones. I always assumed they were pretty lifeless.

W: Well, that's an assumption many people make. But the fact is bones are made of dynamic living tissue that requires continuous maintenance and repair.

M: Right. That's one of the things I found so fascinating about the way the bones repair themselves.

W: Ok. So can you tell us how the bones repair themselves?

M: Sure. See, there are two groups of different types of specialized cells in the bone that work together to do it. (20) The first group goes to an area of the bone that needs repair. This group of cells produces the chemical that actually breaks down the bone tissue, and leaves a hole in it. After that the second group of specialized cells comes and produces the new tissue that fills in the hole that was made by the first group.

W: Very good. This is a very complex process. (21) In fact, the scientists who study human bones don't completely understand it yet. They are still trying to find out how it all actually works. Specifically, because sometimes after the first group of cells leaves a hole in the bone tissue, for some reason, the second group doesn't completely fill in the hole. And this can cause real problems. It can actually lead to a disease in which the bone becomes weak and is easily broken.

M: Ok, I get it. So if the scientists can figure out what makes the specialized cells work, maybe they can find a way to make sure the second group of cells completely fills the hole in the bone tissue every time. (22) <u>That'll prevent the disease from every occurring.</u>

Questions 19 to 22 are based on the conversation you have just heard.

Q 19: What is the discussion mainly about?

Q 20: What is the function of the first group of specialized cells discussed in the talk?

Q 21: What does the professor say about scientists who study the specialized cells in human bones?

Q 22: According to the student, what is one important purpose of studying specialized cells in human bones?

Conversation Two

M: Hi Diana, mind if I sit down?

W: Not at all, Jerry. How have you been?

M: Good. But I'm surprised to see you on the city bus. Your car in the shop?

W: No. (23) <u>I've just been thinking a lot about the environment lately. So I decided the air will be a lot cleaner if we all use public transportation when we could.</u>

M: I'm sure you are right. But, the diesel bus isn't exactly pollution free.

W: True. But they'll be running a lot cleaner soon. We were just talking about that in my environmental engineering class.

M: What's the city gonna do? Install pollution filters of some sort on their buses?

W: They could, but those filters make the engines work harder and really cut down on fuel efficiency. Instead they found a way to make their engines more efficient.

M: How?

W: (24) <u>Well, there is a material called the coniine oxide. It's a really good insulator. And a thick coat of it gets sprayed on the certain part of the engine.</u>

M: An insulator?

W: Well, yeah. Actually, what it does is reflect back the heat of burning fuel. So the fuel will burn much hotter and burn up more completely.

M: So a lot less unburned fuel comes out to pollute the air, right?

W: Yeah, and the bus will need less fuel. So with the savings on fuel cost, they say this will all pay for itself in just six months.

M: Sounds like people should all go out and get some this stuff to spray their car engines.

W: (25) <u>Well, it's not really that easy. You see, normally, the materials are fine powder. To melt it so you can spray a coat of it on the engine parts; you first have to heat it over 10,000 degrees and then, well, you get the idea. It's not something you or I be able to do ourselves.</u>

Questions 23 to 25 are based on the conversation you have just heard.

Q 23: Why did the woman decide to ride the city bus?

Q 24: What is the coniine oxide?

Q 25: According to the woman, what may limit the use of the coniine oxide in cars?

Section B

Passage One

Most people have had a dog or wanted one as their companion at some time in their lives. (26) If you are thinking of buying a dog, however, you should first decide what sort of companion you need and whether the dog is likely to be happy in the surroundings you can provide. Specialist advice is available to help you choose the most suitable breed of dog. But in part, the decision depends on common sense. Most breeds were originally developed to perform specific tasks.

So, if you want a dog to protect you or your house, for example, you should choose a breed that has the right size and characteristics. You must also be ready to devote a good deal of time to training the dog when it is young and give it the exercise it needs throughout its life, unless you live in the country and can let it run freely. (27) Dogs are demanding pets. Whereas cats identify with the house and so are content if their place there is secure, a dog identifies with its master and consequently wants him to show proof of his affection. (28) The best time to buy a baby-dog is when it is between 6 and 8 weeks old so that it can transfer its affection from its mother to its master. If baby dogs have not established a relationship with the human being until they are over three months old, their strong relationship will always be with dogs. They are likely to be too shy when they are brought out into the world to become good pets.

Questions 26 to 28 are based on the passage you have just heard.

Q 26: What's mentioned as a consideration in buying a dog?

Q 27: Why does the speaker say a dog is a more demanding pet than a cat?

Q 28: Why is it advised to buy baby dogs under three months old?

Passage Two

(29) People in Poland take their pleasure seriously. They like to have an aim even when spending the time which is entirely their own. During the summer, people start work very early in the morning so that they can finish early and enjoy a leisurely afternoon. It is difficult to imagine Polish people going aimlessly for a walk in the country, though they might go to pick wild fruit, to visit a place of historical importance or to walk 20 km as a training exercise. (30) They are often admired for their immense (极大的、浓厚的) enjoyment of the arts. All parks are beautifully cared for and are for the use and enjoyment of the people. Quite ordinary people will talk with obvious delight about concerts.

There is nearly always a crowd at the door of the theatre, asking for returned tickets. (31) People in Poland now have far more leisure time and more money than ever before. It is therefore possible to spend the weekends in many new ways. Many people now have over 20 days holiday a year. This provides an opportunity for holidays in the country or at the seaside.

Questions 29 to 31 are based on the passage you have just heard.

Q 29: What is special about the Polish way of spending leisure time?

Q 30: For what does the author admire the Polish people?

Q 31: What do we learn from the passage?

Passage Three

What kind of car will we drive by the year 2010? Rather different from the type we know today. With the next decade bringing greater change than the past 50 years, people who will be designing the models of tomorrow believe that environmental problems may well accelerate the pace of the car's development. (32) **The vision is that of a machine with 3 wheels instead of 4,** (33) electrically-powered, environmentally clean and able to drive itself along intelligent roads, equipped with built-in power supplies. Future cars will pick up the fuel during long journeys from a power source built into the road, or stored in small quantities for traveling in the city. (34) Instead of today's seating arrangement two in front, two or three behind, all facing forward, the 2010 car will have an interior with adults and children in a family circle. This view of the future car based on a much more sophisticated road system. Cars will be automatically controlled by a computer. (35) All the drivers will have to do is say where to go and the computer will do the rest. It will become impossible for cars to crash into one another. The technology already exists for the car to become a true automobile.

Questions 32 to 35 are based on the passage you have just heard.

Q 32: What is the designer's vision of the cars of tomorrow?

Q 33: What else does the passage tell us about the future car?

Q 34: What is the seating arrangement for future cars?

Q 35: What is the only thing the driver of the future car has to do?

Unit 5

Section A

Directions: In this section, you will hear 8 short conversations and 2 long conversations. At the end of each conversation, one or more questions will be asked about what was said. Both the conversation and the questions will be spoken only once. After each question there will be a pause. During the pause, you must read the four choices marked A）, B）, C）and D）, and decide which is the best answer. Then mark the corresponding letter on Answer Sheet 2 with a single line through the centre.

11. A）He expects to hear from his brother.

    B）He expects a gift for the woman's birthday.

    C）The woman is wrong about when the man's birthday is.

    D）His brother is going to visit him.

12. A）Cars that drive themselves will be very expensive.

    B）The woman is planning to buy an intelligent car.

    C）The woman is working with some engineers on intelligent cars.

    D）Most people do not like driving to work.

13. A）She doesn't think it will snow.

    B）The location of the group discussion has been changed.

    C）The discussion might be cancelled.

    D）She'll probably be too tired to walk to the group discussion.

14. A) He should look professional and knowledgeable about high technology.

B) He should pay special attention to his personal appearance.

C) He should wear a business suit rather than casual dress.

D) He should make the interviewer aware of his professional qualities.

15. A) She's enjoying her coffee.

B) She's waiting for someone.

C) She's having a chat with the man.

D) She's inviting the man to sit down.

16. A) Studying Chinese culture.

B) Spending his summer vacation.

C) Visiting the Great Wall and the Summer Palace.

D) Teaching English.

17. A) Keep up with the times.

B) Spending her time on the important things.

C) Slow down the pace of her life.

D) Pay attention to her voice.

18. A) He arrived at the theater late.

B) He left his watch in the theater.

C) The production seemed much shorter than it actually was.

D) He did not enjoy the production.

Questions 19 to 22 are based on the conversation you have just heard.

19. A) Spring.　　B) Summer.　　C) Autumn.　　D) Winter.

20. A) It's too early to tell.

B) It will not arrive till later of the season.

C) It will not strike this year.

D) It's right on the way.

21. A) By name.　B) By number.　C) By location.　D) By month.

22. A) Study a weather map.　　C) Listen to a weather report.

B) Visit a weather station.　　D) Go to a storm shelter.

Questions 23 to 25 are based on the conversation you have just heard.

23. A) She doesn't want to take final exams.

B) She hasn't prepared well for his tests.

C) She has too many exams on the same day.

D) She needs to get good scores on his tests.

24. A) She should go to the Dean of Students Office.

B) She ought to talk immediately to his professors.

C) She should begin studying at once.

D) She ought to decide which tests are most important.

25. A) Psychology.　　B) Anthropology.　　C) Calculus.　　D) Chemistry.

Section B

Directions: In this section, you will hear 3 short passages. At the end of each passage, you will hear some questions. Both the passage and the questions will be spoken only once. After you hear a question, you must choose the best answer from the four choices marked A), B), C), and D). Then mark the corresponding letter on the Answer Sheet with a single line through the center.

Passage One

Questions 26 to 28 are based on the passage you have just heard.

26. A) The name of a German town.　　　　C) A kind of German sausage.
　　B) A resident of Frankfurt.　　　　　 D) A kind of German bread.
27. A) He sold fast food.　　　　　　　　C) He was a cook.
　　B) He raised dogs.　　　　　　　　　 D) He was a cartoonist.
28. A) Because the Americans found they were from Germany.
　　B) Because people thought they contained dog meat.
　　C) Because people had to get used to their taste.
　　D) Because it was too hot to eat right away.

Passage Two

Questions 29 to 31 are based on the passage you have just heard.

29. A) They give out faint cries.
　　B) They make noises to drive away insects.
　　C) They extend their water pipes.
　　D) They become elastic like rubber bands.
30. A) Quiet plants.　　　　　　　　　　C) Healthy plants.
　　B) Well-watered plants.　　　　　　　D) Thirsty plants.
31. A) They could drive the insects away.
　　B) They could keep the plants well-watered.
　　C) They could make the plants grow faster.
　　D) They could build devices to trap insects.

Passage Three

Questions 32 to 35 are based on the passage you have just heard.

32. A) To look for a different lifestyle.　　C) For adventure.
　　B) To enjoy themselves.　　　　　　　D) For education.
33. A) There are 200 vehicles for every kilometer of roadway.
　　B) It has a dense population.
　　C) There are many museums and palaces.
　　D) It has many towering buildings.
34. A) It is a city of contrasts.
　　B) It possesses many historical sites.
　　C) It is an important industrial center.
　　D) It has many big and beautiful parks.
35. A) It helps develop our personalities.
　　B) It enables us to acquire first-hand knowledge.
　　C) It makes our life more interesting.
　　D) It brings about changes to our lifestyle.

Section C

Directions: In this section, you will hear a passage three times. When the passage is read for the first time, you should listen carefully for its general idea. When the passage is read for the second time, you are required to fill in the blanks numbered from 36 to 43 with the exact words you have heard. For blanks numbered from 44 to 45 you are required to fill in the missing information. For these blanks, you can either use the exact words you have just heard or write down the main points in your own words. Finally, when the passage is read for the third time, you should check what you have written.

The International Student Exchange Program (ISEP) was started in 1979. ISEP is a group of colleges and universities around the world. They (36) _____ to provide international educational (37) _____ for their students.

Two hundred sixty schools in the United States and thirty-five other countries are members of the (38) _____. More than twenty-four thousand students have taken part.

Students can study for up to one year in the United States or any of the other countries (39) _____. Students do not have to go through the usual application (40) _____ to get into a school. And they pay only what they would have to pay for a term at their own school at home. To take part in the ISEP program, students must attend a member college or university. Each school has an ISEP (41) _____. This person helps students apply to the ISEP office in Washington, D.C.

To be accepted, students must have good (42) _____. They must also provide TOEFL scores. Students are asked to list up to ten choices of American schools they would like to attend. Officials at the ISEP office then place students in the (43) _____ offered in colleges and universities.

ISEP officials say students who want to study in a foreign country (44) _____ do so during their third or fourth year of college. Students are advised to begin preparations at least one year before they want to experience the program. Applications must be sent to Washington by February of each year. The students (45) _____ can then begin their year in the United States in September.

ISEP officials also have advice for high school students who think they would like to take part in the program during college, "Be sure to attend a college or university that offers the International Student Exchange Program."

答案与原文

Unit 5

📋✓ 答案

Section A

(11-15) AACDB (16-20) DCDBA (21-25) ACCAB

Section B

(26-30) CABAD (31-35) DDCAB

Section C

(36) <u>cooperate</u>   (37) <u>experiences</u>   (38) <u>program</u>   (39) <u>involved</u>

(40) <u>process</u>   (41) <u>coordinator</u>   (42) <u>grades</u>   (43) <u>openings</u>

(44) <u>generally</u>   (45) <u>accepted</u>

原文

Section A

Question 11

W: If I am not mistaken your birthday is coming up. Has your brother sent you something?

M: Not yet. He never forgets it though.

Q: What does the man imply?

Question 12

W: I'm tired of driving all the way to work and back everyday. If only the cars could drive themselves!

M: Well, haven't heard that some engineers are working on them? I guess you'll soon be able to buy one if only you can afford the cost.

Q: What can be inferred from the conversation?

Question 13

M: Do you think you feel energetic enough to walk to our study group discussion tonight?

W: If there is one! I guess you haven't heard the weather reports. Over a foot of snow is expected.

Q: What does the woman imply?

Question 14

M: Hi, Janet, I've got a job interview on Thursday. What clothes do you think I should wear?

W: Business suit of course. But in this competitive society, professional expertise counts for more than personal appearance.

Q: What advice did the woman give the man concerning his job interview?

Question 15

M: Excuse me, would you mind if I took this seat?

W: Actually, I'm expecting someone. We're going to have a chat over coffee here.

Q: What's the woman doing now?

Question 16

W: What's your plan for the summer vacation?

M: I'm going to travel. When I was still in college, I read all about the Great Wall and the Summer Palace. Now that I'm teaching English in China, what better chance is there for me to visit them?

Q: What is the man doing now in China?

Question 17

W: I've got so much to do but so little time to do it. I'm totally exhausted before I get to the end of the day.

M: Why not slow down a little bit. You don't have to do all the things you assume to be important.

Q: What advice did the man give the woman?

Question 18

W: So how was the drama club's new production last night? Did I miss out on anything good?

M: Hardly, I kept looking at my watch the whole time.

Q: What does the man mean?

Now you will hear two long conversations.

Conversation One

M: Is that a map? Are you going sailing or something?

W: I wish. It's a hurricane-tracking chart. It's a map of tropical oceans southeast of us. It follows the development of tropical storms, even hurricanes. They develop and move around the Atlantic in Caribbean and here on Florida coast. We got hit a lot by those in July or August, at least strong winds or heavy rains.

M: Do you think that the tropical storm is on the way?

W: Too early to tell, but we need to be prepared. The radio mentioned possible evacuation routes.

M: Really? It's that serious?

W: You'd better got to believe it. Late summer is hurricane season. The television updates locations and speeds every hour.

M: What did they say is out there now?

W: A couple of tropical depressions, two storms and two hurricanes.

M: What's the difference?

W: Wind velocity. A depression is least serious actually, and a hurricane is the most serious.

M: How serious are the winds in hurricanes?

W: They have sustained winds of 74 mile per hour and up.

M: What are the names on the map? David, Arlene, Francisco, and Gina.

W: You know weather forecasters give the hurricanes the names of people to make storms easy to identify.

M: I wonder what the status of the storm is now.

W: You shall turn on the television, and it has the best coverage. There is an update coming up in five minutes.

Questions 19 to 22 are based on the conversation you have just heard.

Q 19: In which season would Southeast American most probably get hit by hurricanes?

Q 20: Does the woman think the tropical storm is on the way?

Q 21: How do weather forecasters identify hurricanes?

Q 22: What are the man and woman going to do next?

Conversation Two

M: Hi, Janet. Have you seen the exam schedule for this term yet?

W: No, I haven't. How bad does it look?

M: Well, it all depends on the classes you're taking and whether your professors are giving final exams.

W: I know that! And that's why I'm so nervous. I think I've got tests in every class I'm taking. Would you believe that I have four exams scheduled for the same day?

M: You've got to be kidding. Isn't there some school regulation about that— you're not required to take more than three on the same day?

W: Well if there is a rule. I'm certainly going to find out about it. I'm not sure I can even handle two or three tests, much less four.

M: You really should check with the Dean of Students Office. The same thing happened to Richard last year and he was able to reschedule one of his.

W: By the way, do you want to know when our anthropology and psychology tests are?

M: Sure, why not? Anthropology is 4th period on Tuesday the 15th and psychology is 2nd period on Wednesday the 16th.

W: I'm not much worried about the psychology test, but Professor Gore said that the anthropology test was going to be on everything we covered this term. You know those anthropologists.

M: Yeah. That sounds terrible. My calculus and chemistry tests are probably going to be tough.

W: Let's get together when it's all over.

Questions 23 to 25 are based on the conversation you have just heard.

Q 23: Why is the woman upset?

Q 24: What does the man suggest to the woman?

Q 25: What exam does the woman think will be especially difficult?

Section B

Passage One

Most people know what a hot dog is. It's a sausage in a roll. But do you know why it's called a hot dog? (26) Well, the long red sausage which goes into a hot dog is called a Frankfurter. It got its name from the German town Frankfurt. The sausages were very popular, but hot frankfurters were difficult to sell in crowds. (27) One man, Harry Stevens, had the job of feeding the crowds in baseball games. He had an idea. Why not put the frankfurters in long hot bread rolls? This made them easy to sell. The "Red Hots" had a hot and attractive taste and became very popular. But in 1903, an American cartoonist drew a long German sausage dog in place of the frankfurter, so a frankfurter in a roll soon became known as a "hot dog". It was a joke, (28) but some people really thought the sausages contained dog meat. For a while, sales of hot dogs fell, but not for long.

Questions 26 to 28 are based on the passage you have just heard.

Q 26: What is a frankfurter?

Q 27: What was Harry Stevens' job?

Q 28: Why did sales of hot dogs decrease for some time?

Passage Two

(29) We all scream for water when thirsty, but do you know in very hot, dry weather, plants also make faint sounds — as if they are crying out for help?

You see, in a plant's stem there are hundreds of "water pipes" that bring water and minerals from the soil all the way up to the leaves. As the ground turns dry, it becomes harder and harder for the plants to do this.

In severe droughts, plants have to fight to pull out any water available. Scientist Robert Winter has found out that when it is really bad their water pipes snap from the tension like rubber bands. When that happens, the whole plant vibrates a little. The snapping pipes make noises ten thousand times more quiet than a whisper.

Robert knows that healthy, well-watered plants are quiet. (30) He also knows that many insects prefer attacking dry plants rather than healthy plants. How do the insects know which are healthy plants and which are not? Robert thinks that the insects may listen for the plants that cry and then they may buzz in to kill.

To test his theory, Robert is using a device that can imitate plant cries. He attaches it to a quiet, healthy plant so the plant sounds thirsty. Then he watches insects to see if they attack more often than usual.

(31) If he is right, scientists could use the insects' ability against them（利用昆虫的这一能力对付它们）. They could build traps that imitate crying plants. So when the insects buzz in to eat, they won't buzz out.

Questions 29 to 31 are based on the passage you have just heard.

Q 29: What do plants do when they are thirsty?

Q 30: What plants do many insects tend to attack?

Q 31: What could scientists do if Robert's theory proves to be true?

Passage Three

People enjoy taking trips, but what are the reasons they leave home? (32) One reason is for education. People travel because they want to broaden their horizons to learn about other people and other places. They are curious about other cultures. When people are tourists, they get a quick look at different ways of living. Even a short look at another kind of life style is an important lesson.

On a trip, a person can learn directly — by visiting museums and historic spots. (33) What does a tourist learn who sees the art museums, visits the historical palaces and other scenic spots in Paris, and shops along the River Seine? He gets a vivid picture — a real life — one of the French people. He learns about their attitudes, how they feel about business, beauty and history.

What about the tourist who goes to Hong Kong? (35) Does he get the same information that he could get from a book? He might read that Hong Kong is crowded, that there is less than 200 square meters of space for each person, (35) but seeing and feeling the lack of space will impress him much more. He might read that there are nearly 200 vehicles for every kilometer of roadway, but the sight of so many vehicles parked along the roadside will be a much more vivid lesson. (34) The tourist to Hong Kong will never forget the contrasts — the straight vertical lines of the tall modern buildings and the moving lines of boats that people live in.

Questions 32 to 35 are based on the passage you have just heard.

Q 32: Why do people leave home to travel according to the passage?

Q 33: What do we learn from the passage about Paris?

Q 34: What impression will a tourist get of Hong Kong?

Q 35: What does the passage tell us about traveling?

Unit 6

Section A

Directions: In this section, you will hear 8 short conversations and 2 long conversations. At the end of each conversation, one or more questions will be asked about what was said. Both the conversation and the questions will be spoken only once. After each question there will be a pause. During the pause, you must read the four choices marked A）, B）, C）and D）, and decide which is the best answer. Then mark the corresponding letter on Answer Sheet 2 with a single line through the centre.

11. A）The storm took a heavy toll of the lives and property of the fisherman.
    B）The speakers thanked the meteorologists for their help.
    C）The fisher man got back safe and sound.
    D）The fishing boats didn't set sail because of the bad weather.

12. A）They don't enjoy swimming.   C）They don't know how to swim.
    B）They won't go swimming in the lake today.   D）They'll swim in the lake tomorrow.

13. A）The style of sweater she's wearing is very common.
    B）The man saw Jill wearing the sweater.
    C）She wore the sweater for the first time yesterday.
    D）She usually doesn't borrow clothes from Jill.

14. A）She's planning a trip to Antarctica.
    B）She thinks attending the lecture will be helpful to her.
    C）Her geography class is required to attend the lecture.
    D）She has already finished writing her report.

15. A）The woman should join the chess club.
    B）He's not a very good chess player.
    C）The woman needs a lot of time to play chess.
    D）He's willing to teach the woman how to play chess.

16. A）Ask Alice if the man can borrow the novel.
    B）Return the novel to Alice immediately.
    C）Help the man find this own copy of the novel.
    D）Find out how much the novel costs.

17. A）He has already tasted the chocolate pudding.
    B）Chocolate is his favorite flavor.
    C）He doesn't want any chocolate pudding.
    D）There is no more chocolate pudding left.

18. A）He is a novelist.
    B）He writes instruction books for terrorists.
    C）He is full of crazy ideas.
    D）He planned a suicide attack with a Boeing 747.

Questions 19 to 22 are based on the conversation you have just heard.

19. A）Columbia.   B）Brazil.   C）United States.   D）China.

20. A）Four dollars.   B）Five dollars.   C）Six dollars.   D）Seven dollars.

21. A）By telephoning his friend.
    B）By writing his friend a letter.
    C）By checking the post office's records.
    D）By checking the signature of his friend on the return receipt.
22. A）Yes, because they are faster.
    B）No, because they cost more.
    C）Yes, because they provide very good service.
    D）No, because they don't operate outside the United States.

Questions 23 to 25 are based on the conversation you have just heard.

23. A）Four.　　　　B）Five.　　　　C）Six.　　　D）Seven.
24. A）Because he has taught himself a lot of programming.
    B）Because he has already finished the course before.
    C）Because he thinks that he is good at programming.
    D）Because it won't be of much help to his study.
25. A）Because his English is not quite good.
    B）Because all the foreign students have to take the test.
    C）Because it would be good for his future study.
    D）Because he is a first year student.

Section B

Directions: In this section, you will hear 3 short passages. At the end of each passage, you will hear some questions. Both the passage and the questions will be spoken only once. After you hear a question, you must choose the best answer from the four choices marked A）, B）, C）, and D）. Then mark the corresponding letter on the Answer Sheet with a single line through the center.

Passage One

Questions 26 to 28 are based on the passage you have just heard.

26. A）To find out whether they take music lessons in their spare time.
    B）To find out whether they can name four different musical instruments.
    C）To find out whether they enjoy playing musical instruments in school.
    D）To find out whether they differ in their preference for musical instruments.
27. A）They find them too hard to play.
    B）They think it silly to play them.
    C）They find it not challenging enough to play them.
    D）They consider it important to be different from girls.
28. A）Children who have private music tutors.　　C）Children who are between 5 and 7.
    B）Children who are 8 or older.　　D）Children who are well-educated.

Passage Two

Questions 29 to 30 are based on the passage you have just heard.

29. A）Because there weren't any professional teams in the U.S. then.
    B）Because Pele hadn't retired from the Brazilian National Team yet.

C）Because this fast-moving sport wasn't familiar to many Americans.

D）Because good professional players received low salaries.

30. A）When it has a large number of fans.

B）When it plays at home.

C）When it has many international stars playing for it.

D）When the fans cheer enthusiastically for it.

31. A）It wasn't among the top four teams.   C）It won the World Cup.

B）It didn't play as well as expected.   D）It placed fourth.

Passage Three

Questions 32 to 35 are based on the passage you have just heard.

32. A）Students from America.   C）Students from Australia.

B）Students from England.   D）Students from Japan.

33. A）Those who know how to program computers.

B）Those who get special aid from their teachers.

C）Those who are very hardworking.

D）Those who have well-educated parents.

34. A）Japanese students study much harder than Columbian students.

B）Columbian students score higher than Japanese students in maths.

C）Columbian students are more optimistic about their maths skills.

D）Japanese students have better conditions for study.

35. A）Physics.   C）Environmental science.

B）Mathematics.   D）Life science.

Section C

Directions: In this section, you will hear a passage three times. When the passage is read for the first time, you should listen carefully for its general idea. When the passage is read for the second time, you are required to fill in the blanks numbered from 36 to 43 with the exact words you have heard. For blanks numbered from 44 to 45 you are required to fill in the missing information. For these blanks, you can either use the exact words you have just heard or write down the main points in your own words. Finally, when the passage is read for the third time, you should check what you have written.

Many countries need to do more to offer education and training for people of all ages. So says a new report from the Organization for Economic (36) _____ and Development, in Paris.

The report says the number of people being educated continues to increase. But it says there is still a (37) _____ of training for adults who need it the most. These include people in (38) _____ jobs or no job at all. And the difference in (39) _____ continues to grow between those who are better educated and those who are not.

The OECD report notes great (40) _____ in school performance in some countries. For example, ninety-seven percent of South Koreans born in the nineteen seventies have completed upper (41) _____ education. This (42) _____ to thirty-two percent of those born in the nineteen forties.

In OECD countries, fifty-seven percent of the university graduates now are women. But the report says the share of women among mathematicians, computer scientists or engineers is thirty percent or less. And university-educated women in many countries earn less than similarly (43) _____ men.

The report says OECD countries spend an average of seven thousand dollars on per student per year. Switzerland and the United States spend the most on education, more than eleven thousand dollars. They also are among the countries that pay their teachers the most. But higher spending is no (44) _____ of a higher quality education. The Bush administration says its federal education law, called No Child Left Behind, is improving student performance. The OECD says the test results used in the report are not recent enough to show any possible effects. But it (45) _____ the attempt to deal with problems in schools.

答案与原文

Unit 6

答案

Section A

(11-15) CBBBD   (16-20) ACABC   (21-25) DDCAD

Section B

(26-30) DABCB   (31-35) AADCA

Section C

(36) Cooperation   (37) shortage   (38) low-skilled   (39) earnings
(40) improvement   (41) secondary   (42) compares   (43) qualified
(44) guarantee   (45) praises

原文

Section A

Question 11

M: Thanks to the weather forecast, all the fishing boats made for the harbor and reached safety before the storm struck.

W: Thanks heavens for the meteorologists. Without them, that storm would have taken a heavy toll.

Q: What do we learn from the conversation?

Question 12

W: I'm not swimming in the lake unless it warms up outside today.

M: Me neither. Unfortunately I think it's supposed to stay as cold all day.

Q: What can be inferred about the speakers?

Question 13

M: That sweater is so unusual, and yet it looks familiar. Did I just see you wearing it yesterday?

W: Well, not me, but...see, it belongs to my roommate Jill, and she is in your chemistry class.

Q: What does the woman imply?

Question 14

M: You wanna go to a lecture tonight over in the science auditorium? It's some guy who spent a year living in Antarctica.

W: No kidding! I'm doing a report on Antarctica for my geography class. Maybe I can get some good information to add to it.

Q: What does the woman mean?

Question 15

W: I'd really like to learn how to play chess, but it looks so complicated. It seems like it will take a really long time to learn.

M: Well, it takes a long time to get good at it. But we can go over the basics the afternoon if you want.

Q: What does the man imply?

Question 16

M: Do you think you can lend me that novel when you are finished with it? I've been looking all over for a copy, but apparently it sold out at all the bookstores.

W: Oh, it's not mine. It belongs to Alice. But I'll see what she says.

Q: What will the woman probably do?

Question 17

W: Umm...are you going to try some of this chocolate pudding? It's incredible.

M: Well, to be honest with you, I've never been a big fan of chocolate.

Q: What does the man imply?

Question 18

W: One of your books describes a suicide attack with a Boeing 747. Do you ever get the feeling that terrorists are using your novels as an instruction book?

M: I don't think they are the people who read my books. And they don't need me to come up with the crazy ideas.

Q: What do we learn about the man from the conversation?

Now you will hear two long conversations.

Conversation One

M: Give me a pack of first-class stamps please.

W: Here you are. That will be five dollars. Anything else?

M: Yes, I want some post cards and some foreign airmail stamps. I want to send letters to Brazil.

W: Just a moment, I'll look up the rate for airmail letters to Brazil.

M: Can you tell me how much it will cost to send a package to Columbia? Also, I want to know how long it will take.

W: Do you have the package with you? I would have to weigh it to see how much it would cost. There are several ways to send packages to foreign countries. The fastest way costs the most, of course. I'll give you an example. If you had a two-pound package and you wanted to send it the fastest way, it would cost about six dollars, and it would take a week to get there.

M: Do you insure packages?

W: Yes.

M: How?

W: All you have to do is declare the value of the package and decide how much you want to insure it for. The rates are reasonable.

M: Is there a way I can be sure that my friend in Columbia receives my package?

W: The post office rarely gets a package lost. You can, however, request a return receipt. With a return, when the delivery person gives your friend the package, your friend has to sign for it. Then we will notify you that he or she has it.

M: What about these overnight delivery services I see advertised on TV.

W: They are usually as good as the post office, but they may cost more. Also remember that they only have service with the United States.

M: Thank you, you really helped me a lot.

Questions 19 to 22 are based on the conversation you have just heard.

Q 19: Where does the man want to send his letter?

Q 20: How much does a two-pound package cost by the fastest way to Columbia?

Q 21: How can the man know that his friend has received the package?

Q 22: Will the man send the package by the overnight delivery service and why?

Conversation Two

W: Have you settled in?

M: Yes, I feel quite at home now. I haven't got used to the food yet but I'm really enjoying the life on campus.

W: Good. Now we'd better make sure you enjoy your studies. We offer a very wide range of options on the foundation course, as you know. But you can only take six courses. Do you know what you want to do yet?

M: Yes, more or less. But I'm not sure whether to do biological sciences or German.

W: Well, that's quite a difference. Let's see ... you've selected to do: Physical sciences, basic electronics, art and design, CAD ... that's computer-aided design and English.

M: Yes, five course.

W: That's quite a range. Don't you want to do maths or computer programming, for example?

M: Well, I'm interested in computers, especially in writing computer games. I'd like to produce educational software, educational games, eventually, I've taught myself a lot of programming and I was good at maths. I don't think I need either of them.

W: Then why do you choose to do art and design?

M: That will be good for my graphics. I need that to produce games ... CAD too. I've never done computer aided design before.

W: Now, right, you've got some powerful packages in the computer graphics and CAD offices ... hope you enjoy that. So, now that leaves English. It's mostly English literature.

I know English is all right. But as a first year student, you'll have to take Cambridge Proficiency Test.

M: All right.

Questions 23 to 25 are based on the conversation you have just heard.

Q 23: How many foundation courses can the student take?

Q 24: Why doesn't the student think he needs to take the computer programming course?

Q 25: Why does the man have to take the Cambridge Proficiency Test?

Section B

Passage One

(26) The piano and violin are girls' instruments. Drums and trumpets are for boys. According to psychologists, Susan Onco and Michael Balton, children have very clear ideas about which musical instruments they should play. They find that despite the best efforts of teachers these ideas have changed very little over the past decade. They interviewed 153 children aged between 9 and 11 from schools in northwest England. They asked them to identify 4 musical instruments and then to say which they would like to play most and which they would least like to play. They also asked the children for their views on whether boys or girls should not play any of the 4 instruments. The piano and the violin were both ranked more favorably by girls than by boys, while boys prefer the drums and trumpets. There was broad agreement between boys and girls on which instruments each sex should play and the reasons vary. And while (27) almost half of all boys said they avoid certain instruments because they were too difficult to play, only 15% of girls gave that as a reason. (28) Earlier studies indicated that very young school children aged between 5 and 7 showed no bias in choosing musical instruments, but their tastes become more clear between the ages of 8 and 10. One survey of 78 teachers suggested that after that age both boys and girls begin to restrict themselves to the so-called male or female instruments.

Questions 26 to 28 are based on the passage you have just heard.

Q 26: Why did Susan and Michael interview children aged between 9 and 11?

Q 27: Why do many of the boys avoid certain instruments?

Q 28: Which group of children have a bias when choosing musical instruments?

Passage Two

In the 1970s, the famous Brazilian football player Pele retired from the national team of Brazil and became a professional player for a team in New York. Football, or soccer, wasn't very popular in the United States at that time. (29) Few North Americans knew anything about this fast moving sport. There was no money to pay professional players and there was little interest in football in high schools and colleges. When Pele and other international stars began playing in various U.S. cities, people saw how interesting the game was and began to go to the matches. It is now common for important games to have fifty to sixty thousand fans. Support from the fans is important to the football. The fans cheer enthusiastically for their favorite players and teams, who respond by playing better than before. (30) In most World Cups, the home team, or the team from the host country — usually plays better than most people expect. In 1966, 1974 and 1978, the home teams of England, West Germany and Argentina all won the World Cup. The World Cup is called that because teams from every continent have played in it. However, since the Cup began, all of the winning teams have been from Europe or South America. Teams from Asia or Africa always do well but they haven't yet won. (31) <u>Mexico played surprisingly well in the 1970 Cup, which it hosted, but it wasn't among the 4 final teams.</u>

Questions 29 to 31 are based on the passage you have just heard.

Q 29: Why wasn't football a popular sport in the U.S. in the 1970s?

Q 30: When does a football team have the best chance to win the World Cup?

Q 31: How did Mexico do in the 1970 World Cup?

Passage Three

The world's smartest adolescence in mathematics and science are in Singapore, according to a global survey of educational achievement. In the 3rd International Mathematics and Science Study, a 13-year-old from Singapore achieved the best scores in standardized tests of maths and science that were administered to 287,896 students in 41 countries in 1994 and 1995. The survey suggests that science and maths education is especially strong in the Far East. (32) <u>While well behind those top scores, students from Australia earned higher marks in maths than their counterparts in England, who in turn did better than American students.</u> The study collected information on the students, teachers and homes. (33) <u>Not surprisingly, the highest-scoring students had well-educated parents or came from homes containing study-aids such as computers, dictionaries or even such elemental facilities as desks.</u> The study shows that boys generally did better than girls in science, but there was little difference between them in maths. (35) <u>Boys scored better than girls in physics and chemistry.</u> There were no sex differences in the life and environmental sciences. In addition to being tested, students in the project were asked how proficient they thought they were in maths and science. (34) <u>Students in some countries, such as Columbia and Kuwait, had an overly optimistic view of their skills. Meanwhile, some of the best students from Japan and Korea, for example, were needlessly pessimistic even though they did far better in maths than almost all of other students.</u>

Questions 32 to 35 are based on the passage you have just heard.

Q 32: Of the 4 groups of students, who scored the lowest in maths according to the survey?

Q 33: What kind of students are most likely to become top scorers?

Q 34: In what way do Columbian students differ from Japanese students?

Q 35: In which subject did boys score higher than girls?

Unit 7

Section A

Directions: In this section, you will hear 8 short conversations and 2 long conversations. At the end of each conversation, one or more questions will be asked about what was said. Both the conversation and the questions will be spoken only once. After each question there will be a pause. During the pause, you must read the four choices marked A), B), C) and D), and decide which is the best answer. Then mark the corresponding letter on Answer Sheet 2 with a single line through the centre.

11. A) He studies engineering.

    B) He has only recently become interested in philosophy.

    C) He wasn't at the lecture.

    D) He thinks Professor Warner is a good teacher.

12. A) The reports should have been completed by today.

    B) Only the first part of the report is due next Friday.

    C) Some students didn't finish their reports on time.

    D) Some students haven't started their reports yet.

13. A) Spend thirty dollars on the painting.   C) Look for a less expensive painting.

    B) Sell one of his paintings.   D) Buy the painting without the frame.

14. A) Exercise less frequently.   C) Visit him as soon as possible.

    B) Take less medicine each day.   D) Take a new kind of headache medicine.

15. A) His job starts next week.   C) His professor was mistaken about the job.

    B) He's eager to start his new job.   D) He believes the job interview went well.

16. A) Janet didn't attend.   C) The man wasn't invited.

    B) Janet's friends did a lot of work.   D) It was cancelled at the last minute.

17. A) Wear his suit.   C) Find out who's going to the party.

    B) Prepare for cold weather.   D) Dress informally.

18. A) Most of them were written near the end of the author's lifetime.

    B) Many of them aren't included in the library's collection.

    C) They were all highly praised by literary critics.

    D) Many readers like to collect them.

Questions 19 to 22 are based on the conversation you have just heard.

19. A) Because the job helps him to make big money.

    B) Because the job is interesting.

    C) Because it's her brother's first job.

    D) Because the job is steady.

20. A) It belongs to her family.

    B) She goes there for each summer vacation.

    C) Her family borrows it from their friend.

    D) Renting it is quite expensive.

21. A) When she was still a child.   C) When she studied in middle school.

    B) When she studied in college.   D) When she studied in elementary school.

22. A) Try snow-skiing.   C) Have some dessert.

    B) Meet her brother.   D) Come to the lake and visit her family.

Questions 23 to 25 are based on the conversation you have just heard.

23. A) Excited.   B) Doubtful.   C) Shocked.   D) Delighted.

24. A) It is too expensive.   C) It alters the shape of the car's surface metal.

    B) It will bring severe pollution problem.   D) It can cause electrical shocks.

25. A) anything that touches the surface of the car will get a shock because of electricity.

    B) the new type car will not shock anybody due to the small amount of electricity.

    C) the new type of car will be less polluting than getting the regular car repainted.

    D) people will frequently get their car repainted.

Section B

Directions: In this section, you will hear 3 short passages. At the end of each passage, you will hear some questions. Both the passage and the questions will be spoken only once. After you hear a question, you must choose the best answer from the four choices marked A), B), C), and D). Then mark the corresponding letter on the Answer Sheet with a single line through the center.

Passage One

Questions 26 to 28 are based on the passage you have just heard.

26. A) They invited him to a party.
    B) They asked him to make a speech.
    C) They gave a special dinner for him.
    D) They invited his wife to attend the dinner.

27. A) He was embarrassed.   C) He felt sad.
    B) He felt greatly encouraged.   D) He was deeply touched.

28. A) Sam's wife did not think that the company was fair to Sam.
    B) Sam's wife was satisfied with the gold watch.
    C) Sam did not like the gold watch.
    D) The company had some financial problems.

Passage Two

Questions 29 to 31 are based on the passage you have just heard.

29. A) The number of students they take in is limited.
    B) They receive little or no support from public taxes.
    C) They are only open to children from rich families.
    D) They have to pay more taxes.

30. A) Private schools admit more students.
    B) Private schools charge less than religious schools.
    C) Private schools run a variety of programs.
    D) Private schools allow students to enjoy more freedom.

31. A) The churches.   C) The local authorities.
    B) The program designers.   D) The state government.

Passage Three

Questions 32 to 35 are based on the passage you have just heard.

32. A) She was found stealing in a bookstore.
    B) She caught someone in the act of stealing.
    C) She admitted having stolen something.
    D) She said she was wrongly accused of stealing.

33. A) A book.   B) $ 3,000.   C) A handbag.   D) A Christmas card.

34. A) She was questioned by the police.
    B) She was shut in a small room for 20 minutes.
    C) She was insulted by the shopper around her.
    D) She was body-searched by the store manager.

35. A）They refused to apologize for having followed her through the town.

　　B）They regretted having wrongly accused her of stealing.

　　C）They still suspected that she was a thief.

　　D）They agreed to pay her ＄3,000 damages.

Section C

Directions: In this section, you will hear a passage three times. When the passage is read for the first time, you should listen carefully for its general idea. When the passage is read for the second time, you are required to fill in the blanks numbered from 36 to 43 with the exact words you have heard. For blanks numbered from 44 to 45 you are required to fill in the missing information. For these blanks, you can either use the exact words you have just heard or write down the main points in your own words. Finally, when the passage is read for the third time, you should check what you have written.

In the United States, the term "organic" has a (36) _____ meaning set by the Department of Agriculture. The department has an official label to mark products that have met the (37) _____ of its National Organic Program.

Organic products usually cost more, but their sales are growing. As a result, so is (38) _____ to label more products organic because many people believe they are (39) _____.

Now Agriculture Department officials are trying to decide whether fish can be called organic. There are rules for organic produce, organic (40) _____ products, organic meat and chicken — but nothing about fish.

Many (41) _____ of fish farms believe they could sell more fish if they could label them organic. The industry that sells wild-caught fish is already (42) _____ from farm-raised seafood. That pressure could increase if the Agriculture Department (43) _____ proposed requirements for labeling fish organic.

Earning the organic label requires controlled conditions. The question is whether fish that swim wild and free — like Alaskan salmon — could meet the proposed requirements. Yet fish farms might not all be able to meet them either. Some operations are criticized for their (44) _____ of fish and the risk of pollution to waterways. Fish farmers and the wild-caught industry also argue about the possible presence of harmful chemicals in each other's products.

In 2000, an advisory committee considered requests by fish farmers to call their products organic. The experts said farm-raised fish should be labeled organic only if they were fed almost completely organic plant food. Farmed fish often have little or no fish in their diet. But those proposed (45) _____ were not used.

答案与原文

Unit 7

答案

Section A

(11-15) ABDBC　　　　(16-20) BDBDB　　　　(21-25) ADBAC

Section B

(26-30) CDABC   (31-35) ADDBC

Section C

(36) <u>legal</u>   (37) <u>requirements</u>   (38) <u>competition</u>   (39) <u>healthier</u>

(40) <u>dairy</u>   (41) <u>operators</u>   (42) <u>under pressure</u>   (43) <u>approves</u>

(44) <u>treatment</u>   (45) <u>guidelines</u>

原文

Section A

Question 11

W: I saw you in the lecture hall yesterday on your way out to Professor Johnson's philosophy class. I was quite surprised. I couldn't imagine you are someone interested in philosophy.

M: I don't know what's so surprising. There are lots of engineering students in that class.

Q: What can be inferred about the man?

Question 12

M: Did I hear that right? Our reports are due next Friday?

W: Just the introduction, the rest will find out about today in class.

Q: What does the woman mean?

Question 13

M: This painting would go great in my room, but they want 30 dollars for it and it's probably more for the frame.

W: Then why don't you buy it separately?

Q: What does the woman suggest the man do?

Question 14

W: Dr. Smith, those stretching exercises that you recommended are really helping with my back pain. But the pills you prescribed, I think, are giving me a headache.

M: That's not unusual, let's try cutting back to just once a day, all right?

Q: What does the man suggest the woman do?

Question 15

W: Congratulations, Tom. I heard you got a job with the Wilson Company.

M: Hmm, thanks, Prof. Thompson. But it's a little too soon for congratulation; all I got so far is an interview, early next week, on Thursday.

Q: What does the man imply?

Question 16

W: I'm never going to volunteer to help Janet with the party again.

M: I know what you mean. We ended up doing most of the cleaning-up.

Q: What can be inferred about the party?

Question 17

M: I'm thinking about wearing a suit to the party tonight, what do you think?

W: Well, I haven't heard anything about dressing up. I bet a sweater would be fine.

Q: What does the woman suggest the man do?

Question 18

W: I've never seen a larger collection of this author's books than the one here in this library. It's impressive there are so many she managed to write in her lifetime.

M: Yeah, actually a lot more than even this collection was.

Q: What does the man imply about the author's books?

Now you will hear two long conversations.

Conversation One

W: Are you done with your lunch, Michael?

M: Yes I am. And I'd really like to take a look at your photos now, Ann.

W: Well, here they are. I just got them developed.

M: Who's that? Not a boyfriend, I hope.

W: I'm afraid not. That's my brother Tom. He just finished his MBA last year and now he's working for American Bank.

M: Wow that sounds like a pretty good job. Does he like it?

W: I don't know. According to him, it's not very exciting working in a bank — he's assigned to the loan department — but he's really happy to have a steady job. He jokes that by working in a loan department he's going to be able to pay back his own loans. The ones he needed for school, of course.

M: This must be your Mom and Dad. That's a beautiful cabin in the background. Does it belong to your family?

W: No way. We just go to the lake every summer and rent the cabin. But we've been going there for twenty years — so in a way it seems like it's ours.

M: Here's one of you water-skiing. I didn't know you could ski.

W: Actually, I love skiing. I first skied when I was only five-year-old and I've been doing it ever since. I can jump, slalom, trick, and even barefoot ski.

M: I've never had a chance to water-ski, but I'm pretty good at snow-ski. It sure would be fun to try water-skiing though.

W: Well, next summer you'll just have to come and visit us at the lake.

M: That would be great. Let's count on it.

W: By the way, it looks like they're getting ready to close the cafeteria. Maybe we should return our trays.

Questions 19 to 22 are based on the conversation you have just heard.

Question 19: Why does the woman's brother feel happy to have the job?

Question 20: What does the woman say about the cabin at the lake?

Question 21: When did the woman begin to learn ski?

Question 22: What does the woman invite the man to do?

Conversation Two

M: Have you heard that in another few years you may be able to buy a car that changes colors everyday to match the clothes you're wearing.

W: Oh, please be serious. Then, I suppose they will change shapes as well. If you want a big car to take all your friends camping, I suppose you'll just be able to snap your fingers and make it happen. Or if you want a sporty two-seater, you could just tell the car what you wanted, and it would do the rest for you. Is that how it will work?

M: No, I'm serious. They have found a way to alter the surface of metals so that they can reflect different colors just by passing a small amount of electricity over them.

W: Oh, I see. So anything that touches the outside of the car will get a shock. That sounds lovely.

M: It's only a tiny amount of electricity. It wouldn't be enough to shock anybody.

W: Well, it sounds pretty difficult to believe.

M: Yes, it's quite amazing. The important thing you have to remember is that the color of an object is really just an illusion created by the way light bounces off its surface. Engineers have been able to produce a car that changes colors at the touch of a button by slightly rearranging the position of the particles on the surface of the metal.

W: It sounds so amazing. But I guess it could be hardly possible.

M: It is already possible today. The only problem is that it is very expensive. To produce a car with a surface that changed colors would cost twice as much as what a regular car costs. For that much money you could just buy the car and have it repainted twenty times, so it's not very practical yet.

W: Yes, but in other ways it could be more practical. If you took your car to be painted twenty times it would use quite a bit of polluting chemicals, and it would take a long time.

M: You're right there, but how many people really get their car repainted that many times?

W: Hmm, I suppose you're right, but I sure would love to have my car match my clothes every day.

Questions 23 to 25 are based on the conversation you have just heard.

Q 23: What is the woman's reaction to the new-typed car the man describes?

Q 24: What is the problem with the new-typed car?

Q 25: Both the man and the woman agree that _____.

Section B

Passage One

Sam had worked 30 years for the same company and now he had to retire. As a sign of gratitude, the company held a dinner in his honor. "Sam," announced his boss, "It is my great honour to present this gift to you on behalf of the company." Sam walked down to the front of the table and accepted the gift with pride. It was a gold watch and on it was written "To faithful Sam for 30 years of service." Sam wept, "I am at a loss for words." At home, Sam's wife looked at the gold watch critically, "For this you worked 30 years? A cheap gold-plated watch?" "It's the thought dear," answered Sam, "The important thing is that I am not working any more." His wife held the gold watch to her ear and said, "Neither is your watch."

Questions 26 to 28 are based on the passage you have just heard.

Q 26: What did the company do to honor Sam?

Q 27: How did Sam feel when he saw what was written on the watch?

Q 28: What can we infer from the story?

Passage Two

Religious and private schools receive little or no support from public taxes in the United States. As a result, they are more expensive to attend. The religious schools in America are usually run by churches. Therefore they tend to be less expensive than private schools. When there is free education available to all children in the United States, why do people spend money on private schools? Americans offer a great variety of reasons for doing so. Some parents send their children to private schools because the classes there are usually smaller. In their opinion, the public schools in their area are not of high enough quality to meet their needs. Private schools in the United States range widely in size and quality, and they offer all kinds of programs to meet the needs of certain students.

Questions 29 to 31 are based on the passage you have just heard.

Q 29: Why is it usually expensive to attend religious or private schools?

Q 30: What is one of the reasons for people to send their children to private schools?

Q 31: Who usually runs religious schools in the United States?

Passage Three

An elderly woman yesterday made a legal claim against a department store because it had wrongly accused her of stealing a Christmas card. Mrs. Doss White, 72 years old, is claiming $3,000 damages from the store for wrongful arrest and false imprisonment. Mrs. White visited the store while doing Christmas shopping, but did not buy anything. She was followed through the town by a store manager. He had been told that a customer saw her take a card and put it in her shopping bag. He stopped her at a bookstore as she was reading a book. Mrs. White said, "This man, a total stranger, suddenly grasped my bag and asked if he could look in it." She was taken back to the store and shut in a small room in full view of shoppers for 20 minutes until the police arrived. At the police station she was body-searched and nothing was found. Her lawyer said that the department store sent an insincere apology and they insisted that she may have been stealing. The hearing continues today.

Questions 32 to 35 are based on the passage you have just heard.

Q 32: What does the story tell us about the old woman?

Q 33: What was said to have been stolen?

Q 34: What happened to Mrs. White after she was taken back to the store?

Q 35: What was now the attitude of the department store in this legal case?

Unit 8

Section A

Directions: In this section, you will hear 8 short conversations and 2 long conversations. At the end of each conversation, one or more questions will be asked about what was said. Both the conversation and the questions will be spoken only once. After each question there will be a pause. During the pause, you must read the four choices marked A）, B）, C）and D）, and decide which is the best answer. Then mark the corresponding letter on Answer Sheet 2 with a single line through the centre.

11. A. The man is a good student.

B）The man shouldn't work overtime.

C）She wishes that she had a job.

D）She doesn't want to work with the man.

12. A）She doesn't expect to meet with Kevin today.

B）She can't wait any longer for Kevin.

C）Kevin is often late.

D）Kevin has probably overslept.

13. A）The books are all required for the history course.

B）Some of the books are for courses other than history.

C）He plans to read more than just the books that are required.

D）He's worried he may not finish the required reading.

14. A）Watch a movie on television.   C）Go to the tennis court.

B）Go out to dinner with the man.   D）Play in the tournament.

15. A）She wishes she could help the man.

B）She has a bigger problem than the man has.

C）She knows a mechanic who can fix the man's car.

D）The man should buy a new car.

16. A）He wants the woman to repeat her question.

B）He agrees with the woman.

C）He wants to talk about the movie.

D）He wants to see the movie again.

17. A）He's disappointed with his interview.

B）He had to cancel his interview.

C）He doesn't want to discuss the interview now.

D）He shouldn't have applied for the job.

18. A）He felt better an hour ago.

B）His headache should be gone in an hour.

C）He forgot to take the medicine for his headache.

D）His head still hurts.

Questions 19 to 22 are based on the conversation you have just heard.

19. A）She wants to learn about Richard Sears.

B）She is helping the man with his assignment.

C）She needs to buy a filing cabinet.

D）She wants to order some textbooks.

20. A）Teachers.   B）Farmers.   C）Students.   D）Laborers.

21. A）As textbooks.   B）As fuel.   C）As newspapers.   D）As art.

22. A）Taxes on factory goods rose.   C）Shipping prices rose.

B）Some people lost their farms.   D）Some small stores were out of business.

Questions 23 to 25 are based on the conversation you have just heard.

23. A）The economy is slowing down.   C）She may not find a job after college.
    B）She may not be able to finish the college.   D）The tax is going to be raised.

24. A）It is on the verge of bankruptcy.   C）It has experienced a rapid increase in sales.
    B）It is improving steadily.   D）It is going down hill fast.

25. A）She will join the man's company.   C）She will stay in her parents' house.
    B）She will start her own business.   D）She will try to find a job.

Section B

Directions: In this section, you will hear 3 short passages. At the end of each passage, you will hear some questions. Both the passage and the questions will be spoken only once. After you hear a question, you must choose the best answer from the four choices marked A), B), C), and D). Then mark the corresponding letter on the Answer Sheet with a single line through the center.

Passage One

Questions 26 to 29 are based on the passage you have just heard.

26. A）She sat back and relaxed.   C）She entered university.
    B）She decided to retire.   D）She worked out a new English program.

27. A）8 years.   B）20 years.   C）16 years.   D）30 years.

28. A）Bring a great deal of useful experience to the university.
    B）Improve human relationships in the university.
    C）Bring a fear of aging among young students on the campus.
    D）Improve the reputation of the university.

29. A）She is learning English and Drama.
    B）She is learning how to make sound judgments.
    C）She is learning how to teach minority students.
    D）She is learning to perceive, not to judge.

Passage Two

Questions 30 to 32 are based on the passage you have just heard.

30. A）The difference between classical music and rock music.
    B）Why classical music is popular with math students.
    C）The effects of music on the results of math tests.
    D）How to improve your reasoning ability.

31. A）Because it stimulates your nerve activity.
    B）Because it keeps you calm.
    C）Because it strengthens your memory.
    D）Because it improves your problem solving strategies.

32. A）Piano music could interfere with your reasoning ability.
    B）The effects of music do not last long.
    C）The more you listen to music, the higher your test scores will be.
    D）Music, whether classical or rock, helps improve your memory.

Passage Three

Questions 33 to 35 are based on the passage you have just heard.

33. A）To drive the car automatically.
    B）To measure the driver's pulse.
    C）To prevent car accidents.
    D）To monitor the driver's health.

34. A）It sends out signals for help.
    B）It sounds an alarm to warn the driver.
    C）It takes over the driving immediately.
    D）It stops the car automatically.

35. A）It monitors the signals transmitted from the driver's brain.
    B）It can measure the driver's alcohol level in the blood.
    C）It can quicken the driver's response to emergencies.
    D）It bases its analysis on the driver's heartbeat.

Section C

Directions: In this section, you will hear a passage three times. When the passage is read for the first time, you should listen carefully for its general idea. When the passage is read for the second time, you are required to fill in the blanks numbered from 36 to 43 with the exact words you have heard. For blanks numbered from 44 to 45 you are required to fill in the missing information. For these blanks, you can either use the exact words you have just heard or write down the main points in your own words. Finally, when the passage is read for the third time, you should check what you have written.

Many college students in the United States use their summer（36）_____ to earn money in a temporary job. But more and more are working as summer interns. Some internship programs accept students in high school. Internships are usually（37）_____, and the work might not always be the most exciting. But they offer a chance to（38）_____ experience in business, public service or some other area of interest. They can also be a chance to get to know a possible future（39）_____. More importantly, internships can help students make sure their area of study is a good choice.

For most organizations, interns mean（40）_____ workers for little or no cost. They also get a chance to see if a student might make a good future（41）_____. Some interns are promised a full-time job once they finish their studies. Yet some students have no choice but to get a paying job during the summer. They have a real（42）_____ need. Interns provide free labor, but internship programs can（43）_____ costs for travel, housing and meals.

Businesses might require interns to receive college credit for their experience. These businesses are concerned about labor laws that say workers must receive something（44）_____ their work. So, if not money, then credits. Many colleges and universities resist such requirements. They say students should earn credit only for school experience. Some other schools provide the credits but（45）_____ students for them. So, for a student from a poor family, an unpaid internship just may not be possible.

答案与原文

Unit 8

答案

Section A

(11-15) BCCCB   (16-20) BADCB   (21-25) ADCBD

Section B

(26-30) CBADC   (31-35) ABCBD

Section C

(36) break   (37) unpaid   (38) gain   (39) employer
(40) extra   (41) employee   (42) financial   (43) involve
(44) in return for   (45) charge

原文

Section A

Question 11

M: My boss keeps asking me to work overtime but I always said "no" because I don't wanna jeopardize my studies, but I'm starting to waver.

W: I wouldn't give in if I were you.

Q: What does the woman mean?

Question 12

M: What's keeping Kevin? He said last night he'd meet us here by 2 o'clock and it's already 2:30.

W: It's so typical of him, isn't it? Just watch, he's going to show up in 5 minutes with some wild excuse.

Q: What does the woman mean?

Question 13

W: Wow, are all these books you've got here required for the modern European history class?

M: No, a lot of these listed are optional, but you know me, when I do something, I do it 200 percent.

Q: What does the man mean?

Question 14

M: Let's go to a movie after dinner.

W: That's tempting. However, the tennis tournament is tomorrow, and I need to get in a short practice session tonight.

Q: What will the woman probably do this evening?

Question 15

M: I just got this car and it's already falling apart. First, one of the door handles fell off and now the inside light won't go on when you open the door.

W: Hey, what's the big deal? Falling apart is when your car needs a new engine, like mine does.

Q: What does the woman imply?

Question 16

W: You didn't care for the movie, did you?

M: You can say that again.

Q: What does the man mean?

Question 17

W: How did your job interview go?

M: I don't think I came across as well as I could have.

Q: What does the man mean?

Question 18

W: Oh my, you still don't look too good. Didn't you take the pain reliever I gave you?

M: Yeah, an hour ago. Guess I've got a headache that just won't quit.

Q: What does the man mean?

Now you will hear two long conversations.

Conversation one

M: What are you doing?

W: (19) I'm ordering some filing cabinet out of a catalog.

M: What do you need them for?

W: There's so much stuff piling up in my dormitory room. If I don't do something soon, I won't be able to move in there.

M: Do you usually order from a catalog?

W: Sometimes. Why?

M: Oh, it's just in the history class today we were talking about how the catalog sales business first got started in the US. A Chicago retailer, Montgomery Ward started it in the late 1800s. (20) It was really popular among farmers. It was difficult for them to make it to the big city stores so they ordered from catalogs.

W: Was Ward the only one in the business?

M: At first, but another person named Richard Sears started his own catalog after he heard how much money Ward was making.

W: What made them so popular?

M: Farmers trusted Ward and Sears for one thing. They delivered the products the farmers paid for and even refunded the price of things the farmers weren't satisfied with. (21) The catalog became so popular that some countries school teachers even used them as textbooks.

W: Textbooks?

M: Yeah, Students practice spelling the names and adding up the prices of things in the catalogs.

W: Was everybody that exited about it?

M: That's doubtful. (22) <u>Say they drove some small store owners out of business.</u> Sears and Ward sold stuff in such large quantities. They were able to undercut the prices at some small family owned stores.

Questions 19 to 22 are based on the conversation you have just heard.

Q 19: Why was the woman reading a catalog?

Q 20: Who were the main customers of Sears and Ward's business?

Q 21: What unusual way were the catalog used?

Q 22: What was one of the negative effects of the catalog business?

Conversation Two

W: (23) <u>I'm not optimistic about finding a job after I finish college.</u>

M: Oh? Why not?

W: The economy is going down-hill fast.

M: I know. What is this would coming to? It's getting to the point where even a degree won't help you anymore.

W: That's right. And the way things are going, I'll be lucky to even move out of my parents' house.

M: I know what you mean. First they raised taxes, then they cut education, and the salaries haven't gone up in years — it's just one thing after another.

W: By the way, how's your business coming along?

M: (24) <u>Oh, it's getting there. Our sales are up only 2 percent, but it's a step in the right direction.</u>

W: I remember when you opened 10 years ago you almost went bankrupt. The company certainly has come a long way.

M: Yeah, but it's got a long way to go. Say, maybe you'd like to come work for me!

W: (25) <u>Well, I'm not sure I want to work as a clothes-hanger inspector.</u>

M: No ... I mean as a manager.

W: (25) <u>That's more like it.</u>

Questions 23 to 25 are based on the conversation you have just heard.

Q 23: What is the woman worrying about?

Q 24: What do we know about the man's business from the conversation?

Q 25: What will the woman most probably do after she graduates from the college?

Section B

Passage One

After retiring from 30 years of teaching, Ethbell Pepper could easily have decided to sit back and relax and enjoy a peaceful retirement. But that kind of life is not for Ethbell Pepper. "I just wanted to do something different. If you are going to participate in life, do it. Don't just sit down and look out of the window." She says. At 68, she decided to become one of the pioneer participants in a program at the University of California. The program offers campus housing and classes to people over sixty. She enrolled in a class called Human Relationships and Diverse Society. "I taught my minority students in my English and drama classes in high school for 20 years. But in this course, I found out a lot about other cultures I didn't know then. One of the most important lessons that I'm learning is to perceive, not to judge." Elder adults can add to the educational resources of the university by bringing with them a lot of valuable experience. Their presence on campus helps break some long believes about aging. Young students may have fears of growing older. But that kind of fear can be reduced as they see that older people can be active, healthy, and continue to contribute to society. The younger students can begin to see aging as a natural part of living.

Questions 26 to 29 are based on the passage you have just heard.

Q 26: What did Ethbell do when she was 68?

Q 27: How long did Ethbell teach minority students?

Q 28: What do elderly people do to the university?

Q 29: What's the most important lesson Ethbell is learning?

Passage Two

Do you have a tough math test coming up? Then listen to some classical piano music just before the test. You might end up with a higher score. Researchers at a university in California conducted an experiment. They asked a group of college students to listen to some piano music by a famous 18th century composer before taking a math test. They were surprised to find that the students' scores jumped 8 to 9 points. The music seems to excite nerve activities in the brain; similar to the activity that occurs when a person is figuring out a math problem. However, the scientists warn before you get too excited about applying this method to your math test, you should remember that brain exciting effects last only 10 or 15 minutes. Would rock music work as well as the piano music did? No, the scientists say. In fact, the less complex music might even interfere with the brain's reasoning ability.

Questions 30 to 32 are based on the passage you have just heard.

Q 30: What is this passage mainly about?

Q 31: Why can classical music play a positive role in problem solving?

Q 32: What is one of the findings of the research?

Passage Three

When a sleepy driver has trouble in keeping his eyes on the road and gets too close to another car, an alarm will sound to warn the driver. If nothing is done, the car will automatically come to a stop and in this way prevent an accident. This is a new device which will soon be tested in an experimental car in Japan. The computer warning system keeps track of a driver's condition by monitoring his heart beat with signals transmitted from a band round his wrist. The wrist band records the driver's pulse which measures the heart beat. Each pulse in the wrist sends a signal to the computer. By analyzing the pulse rate, the computer can determine whether a driver is drunk, sleeping or ill. Devices in other parts of the car can also tell the computer if the car is too close to another vehicle or is moving dangerously. The computer will sound the alarm when a problem arises, and will automatically stop the car if the driver ignores the warning.

Questions 33 to 35 are based on the passage you have just heard.

Q 33: Why is a computer system installed in an experimental car?

Q 34: What did the computer system do first when a problem arises?

Q 35: What is special about the new computer system?

Unit 9

Section A

Directions: In this section, you will hear 8 short conversations and 2 long conversations. At the end of each conversation, one or more questions will be asked about what was said. Both the conversation and the questions will be spoken only once. After each question there will be a pause. During the pause, you must read the four choices marked A), B), C) and D), and decide which is the best answer. Then mark the corresponding letter on Answer Sheet 2 with a single line through the centre.

11. A) She hasn't spoken to her friend for a long time.

    B) She intends to visit her friend in Texas.

    C) She sometimes travels abroad for her job.

    D) Her friend has never been to Texas before.

12. A) Meet at the bus stop.　　　C) Get off the bus at the next stop.

    B) Finish their candy bars.　　D) Meet in front of the restrooms.

13. A) He won't be able to repair the briefcase.

    B) The repair shop is closed until Tuesday.

    C) The woman should buy a smaller briefcase.

    D) The briefcase will be ready before Tuesday.

14. A) Find out how much work will be required for the class.

    B) Take another class instead of creative writing.

    C) Ask his advisor about the instructor in the Wednesday class.

    D) Sign up for the Wednesday class.

15. A) He'll take his friends to Florida.

    B) He's not sure what he'll do.

    C) He planned his trip a long time ago.

    D) He'd rather not travel during spring break.

16. A) He thinks clothing prices will decrease even further.

    B) He's going to go shopping soon.

    C) He didn't know that stores were having sales now.

    D) He wants to see what the woman bought.

17. A) She's glad the man waited for her.　　C) She wasn't very late for the meeting.

    B) She'd like to reschedule the meeting.　　D) She's sorry that she missed the meeting.

18. A) She'll play chess with the man this afternoon.

    B) She doesn't know how to play chess.

    C) She'll wear a warm jacket to the match.

    D) She'd rather not go out with the man.

Questions 19 to 22 are based on the conversation you have just heard.

19. A）All students pay the same amount per year.
   B）Students choose how many meals a week they will pay for.
   C）Students will get money back for meals they don't eat.
   D）Students would get free meals on weekends.

20. A）When they get the meal.   C）At the beginning of the year.
   B）At the beginning of each week.   D）At the end of the semester.

21. A）They can invite guests to meals at a reduced price.
   B）They receive cards that allow them to be served first.
   C）They can help decide what will be on the menu.
   D）They pay less per meal than those who eat there only part of the time.

22. A）By paying meals one at a time.   C）By ordering their meals in advance.
   B）By borrowing a student's meal card.   D）By buying a weekend meal card.

Questions 23 to 25 are based on the conversation you have just heard.

23. A）To support one of the candidates.   C）To write a newspaper article.
   B）To call on people to vote.   D）To hear more about the speakers' ideas.

24. A）He is too busy.   C）He doesn't know how to vote.
   B）He is not interested in politics.   D）He feels it doesn't make a difference.

25. A）The way government supports small business.
   B）The election process for representatives.
   C）The amount of money to support local education.
   D）The news coverage of debates.

Section B

Directions: In this section, you will hear 3 short passages. At the end of each passage, you will hear some questions. Both the passage and the questions will be spoken only once. After you hear a question, you must choose the best answer from the four choices marked A）, B）, C）, and D）. Then mark the corresponding letter on the Answer Sheet with a single line through the center.

Passage One

Questions 26 to 28 are based on the passage you have just heard.

26. A）To protect persons and property.   C）To teach and train citizens.
   B）To collect taxes.   D）To save natural resources for future use.

27. A）By selling services that make life comfortable.
   B）By selling land containing oil.
   C）By selling public lands.
   D）By selling coal and other natural products.

28. A）Environmental pollution and protection
   B）Taxes and services for the public.
   C）Police efforts to protect people.
   D）People's attitude toward taxes.

Passage Two

Questions 29 to 32 are based on the passage you have just heard.

29. A）He didn't like physics any more.

    B）His eyesight was too poor.

    C）Physics was too hard for him.

    D）He had to work to support himself.

30. A）He was not happy with the new director.

    B）He was not qualified to be an engineer.

    C）He wanted to travel.

    D）He found his job boring.

31. A）He wanted to work with his friend.

    B）He enjoyed traveling around the world.

    C）He wanted to go to Spain.

    D）He was rejected by the engineering firm.

32. A）He enjoyed teaching English.

    B）He wanted to earn more to support his family.

    C）The owner of the school promised him a good position.

    D）He could earn more as a teacher than as a travel agent.

Passage Three

Questions 33 to 35 are based on the passage you have just heard.

33. A）It can be cooked in many ways.

    B）It is delicious but inexpensive.

    C）It gives higher yields than other grain crops.

    D）It grows easily in various conditions.

34. A）Fried potatoes.

    B）Tomato juice.

    C）Sweet corn.

    D）Chocolate beans.

35. A）They led to the discovery of America.

    B）They made native American foods popular.

    C）They brought great wealth to Spain.

    D）They made native American life styles well-known.

Section C

Directions: In this section, you will hear a passage three times. When the passage is read for the first time, you should listen carefully for its general idea. When the passage is read for the second time, you are required to fill in the blanks numbered from 36 to 43 with the exact words you have heard. For blanks numbered from 44 to 45 you are required to fill in the missing information. For these blanks, you can either use the exact words you have just heard or write down the main points in your own words. Finally, when the passage is read for the third time, you should check what you have written.

A federal judge in the United States says the Terrorist Surveillance Program（36）_____ the Constitution. This is the first such ruling against the secret program（37）_____ by President Bush. The National Security Agency（38）_____ the program after the attacks on the United States on September eleventh, two thousand one.

The program lets the agency（39）_____ the international calls and e-mail of （40）_____ in the United States without the need for a court order. The Justice Department is moving quickly to（41）_____ the ruling by Judge Anna Diggs Taylor in Detroit, Michigan. Her order Thursday to stop the program will not be（42）_____ at least until she hears arguments on September seventh. The American Civil Liberties Union brought the case in January for a group including reporters, researchers and（43）_____ defense lawyers. They say the program（44）_____ their work and violates free speech and privacy rights. Judge Taylor agreed. She suggested that the president acted like a king and violated the separation of powers in the Constitution. The judge is a former civil rights worker. President Jimmy Carter appointed her to the court in nineteen seventy-nine. Administration officials say the surveillance program is carefully administered and has helped stop terrorist attacks. On Friday President Bush （45）_____ the ruling. He said those who praise it do not understand the nature of the world in which we now live.

答案与原文

Unit 9

答案

Section A

(11-15) BADDB   (16-20) BABBC   (21-25) DADDA

Section B

(26-30) ACBDA   (31-35) CBDDB

Section C

(36) violates   (37) approved   (38) established   (39) monitor

(40) individuals   (41) appeal   (42) enforced   (43) criminal

(44) interferes with   (45) condemned

原文

Section A

Question 11

M: Oh, you must be sad with your best friend taking a job in Texas. It's so far away.

W: Yeah, I'm really going to miss her. But at least I have a good reason to visit a new part of the country now.

Q: What does the woman imply?

Question 12

M: My fingers are sticky from that candy bar. Do you mind if I use the restroom to wash up before we leave?

W: Sure, I'll be over at the bus stop.

Q: What will the speakers probably do next?

Question 13

W: This string on my briefcase is broken. Do you think you could replace it sir, by next Tuesday?

M: Let's see, oh sure that won't be a problem. It won't even take that long.

Q: What does the man mean?

Question 14

M: So, my adviser wants me to take the creative writing class that meets on Wednesday, instead of the Monday class because the instructor in the class is supposed to be great. But that'd mean I'd have to spend the whole day on campus every Wednesday.

W: Well, but the instructor can make a big difference in how much you get out of the class.

Q: What does the woman imply the man should do?

Question 15

W: Have you finalized your plans for spring break yet?

M: Well, I could visit some friends in Florida, or go to my roommate's home. It's a tough choice.

Q: What does the man mean?

Question 16

W: This is such a great time to buy winter clothes. So many stores are having sales now and the price reductions are pretty substantial.

M: Yeah, It's just what I've been waiting for. There are so many things I need.

Q: What does the man imply?

Question 17

M: Where have you been? I was just about to give up on you.

W: Sorry, my bus was delayed. But I'm glad you were patient. It would have been hard for us to find another time to meet this week.

Q: What does the woman mean?

Question 18

M: It's so cold and windy. This would be a good afternoon for a chess match.

W: Yeah, I'd love to. The trouble is I'm afraid I never figured out the rules.

Q: What can be inferred about the woman?

Now you will hear two long conversations.

Conversation One

M: Hey, Linda, did you get that letter about the new options for food service next year?

W: Not yet. Are there a lot of changes?

M: There sure are. (19) <u>Instead of paying one fee to cover all the meals for the whole school year, we'll now be able to choose many meals per week we want, and can contract for just that amount.</u> (20) <u>We still have to pay for the whole year at the beginning, but we can choose to buy seven, ten, fourteen, or twenty-one meals per week.</u> They give you a card with the number of meals you get per week marked on it.

W: That's a big change, Tom ... and a complicated system.

M: Yeah, but it'll be much better for people who don't eat three meals a day, seven days a week in the cafeteria, because they won't have to pay the meals they don't eat.

W: But what's the deal for those who do eat at school all the time?

M: (21) <u>It's better for them too, because the more meals you contract for, the cheaper each one is.</u>

W: I see. It still sounds rather complicated.

M: True. It took me several hours to figure it out. I decided to go with the ten-meal plan.

W: Why's that?

M: Well, I never eat breakfast and I often go away on weekend, so the ten-meal plan gives me lunch and dinner every weekday at fairly low price. And I won't be paying for meals that I don't usually eat.

W: But what about the weekends when you are on campus?

M: (22) <u>Well, there are often guests on campus on weekends, so they allow you to buy single meals on a walk-in basis on Saturdays and Sundays.</u> The price per meal is much higher that way, but I'm away so much that it'll still be less money for me to pay single-meal prices on the weekend rather than sign up for the fourteen-meal-a-week plan.

W: Hmm. I guess I'll have to sit down and figure out my eating patterns so I can get the best deal.

Questions 19 to 22 are based on the conversation you have just heard.

Q 19: What is the main feature of the new method of paying for meals?

Q 20: When do students pay for the meals they contract for?

Q 21: How does the new plan benefit students who eat all of their meals in the cafeteria?

Q 22: How can weekend guests eat in the cafeteria?

Conversation Two

W: I'm going to leave work early today. There's a debate this evening at 6 o'clock. So I'm going to get an early dinner and head over there.

M: Who's debating about what?

W: The two candidates for the state senate are going to answer questions from reporters. *The Daily News* is sponsoring the event. Members of the audience will also have a chance to ask questions — so maybe I'll speak too.

M: Oh, so you're interested in politics. Are you supporting one of them?

W: No, (23) <u>I just learn more about the candidates so I can make an informed（明智的）decision.</u>

M: Well, I don't think I'll be voting, so I guess I won't bother with that.

W: (24) <u>Why aren't you going to vote?</u>

M: (24) <u>Oh, my one vote doesn't matter.</u>

W: Sure it does!

M: Well ... besides that ... (25) <u>I don't think any of the politicians these days represent my ideas. I'd like to see the government support guaranteed loans for people who want to start small business.</u> I've wanted to open my own bakery for years and I can't get a loan.

W: You know what? (25) <u>That's one of the issues they'll probably discuss tonight.</u> One of the candidates wants tax breaks for large companies. He says that will create more jobs. The other candidate owns a restaurant. She wants to start programs to promote small business.

M: Hmm ... maybe I should show up there myself.

Questions 23 to 25 are based on the conversation you have just heard.

Q 23: Why is the woman going to the debate?

Q 24: What reason does the man give for not voting?

Q 25: According to the woman, what is an important issue in the upcoming debate?

Section B

Passage One

We use all sorts of services without thinking how we get them. But such services cost money. We pay for them through taxes. What would happen if everyone in a city stops paying taxes? The water supply would stop. The streets might not be cleaned. There would be no police force to protect people and property.

The chief duty of every government is to protect persons and property. More than three fourths of the money spent by our government is used for this purpose. The next largest amount of public money goes to teach and train our citizens. Billions of dollars each year are spent on schools and libraries. Public money is used to pay the teachers and other public officials.

Years ago the government made money from the sale of public lands. But most of the best public lands have now been sold. The money raised was used to help pay the costs of government. There are still some public lands that contain oil, coal, gas, and other natural products. They could be sold, but we want to save them for future years. So we all must pay our share for the services that make our lives comfortable.

Questions 26 to 28 are based on the passage you have just heard.

Q 26: What's the chief duty of every government?

Q 27: How did the government raise money in the past?

Q 28: What is the passage mainly about?

Passage Two

When I was at school, my ambition was to be a pilot in the Air Force. But my eyesight wasn't good enough. So I had to give up that idea. I went to university and studied physics. I wanted to stay on there and do research, but my father died about that time. So I thought I'd better get a job and earn my living. I started working in an engineering firm.

I expected to stay in that job for a long time, but then they appointed a new managing director. I didn't get on with him, so I resigned and applied for a job with another engineering company. I would certainly have accepted the job if they had offered it to me, but on my way to the interview I met a friend who was working for a travel agency. He offered me a job in Spain and I've always liked Spain, so I took it.

I worked in the travel agency for two years and then they wanted to send me to South America. But I had just got married. So I decided to stay here. Then we had a baby and I wasn't earning enough to support the family. So I started giving English lessons at a school in the evenings.

I liked the English teaching more than working for the travel agency, and then the owner of the school offered me a full-time job as a teacher. So I resigned from the agency. Two years later, the owner of the school wanted to retire, so he asked me to take over as the director. And here I am.

Questions 29 to 32 are based on the passage you have just heard.

Q 29: Why did the man give up studying physics?

Q 30: Why did the man resign from the engineering firm?

Q 31: Why did the man take the job at the travel agency?

Q 32: Why did the man start to teach English part time?

Passage Three

Columbus sailed from Spain in September 1492, looking for gold. Native Americans greeted him, offering gifts of corn. Columbus found little gold on that trip, but he collected many plants, including corn, to bring back to Spain.

Columbus didn't know it, but the corn was much more valuable than gold. Farmers from Europe to Asia accepted it immediately. They grew it on cold mountainsides and in tropical forests.

Today it feeds millions of people all over the world.

On his second trip, Columbus brought back a few chocolate beans to make chocolate. Europeans and Asians loved this new drink, and soon they were paying a great deal of money for the beans. Chocolate beans became so valuable in Central America that they were used as cash for 200 years.

Tomatoes and potatoes took some time to become popular. Eventually, however, they became the basis of a lot of popular foods. It is hard to imagine life without fried potatoes or chocolate.

Thanks to native American cultures, many people are able to enjoy lots of tasty food.

Quetions 33 to 35 are based on the passage you have just heard.

Q 33: Why is corn feeding millions of people today?

Q 34: What did Columbus bring back on his second trip?

Q 35: What was the result of Columbus' two trips to America?

Unit 10

Section A

Directions: In this section, you will hear 8 short conversations and 2 long conversations. At the end of each conversation, one or more questions will be asked about what was said. Both the conversation and the questions will be spoken only once. After each question there will be a pause. During the pause, you must read the four choices marked A), B), C) and D), and decide which is the best answer. Then mark the corresponding letter on Answer Sheet 2 with a single line through the centre.

11. A）She originally proposed it.　　C）She's quite sure it will take place.
　　B）She doesn't think it's a good idea.　　D）Its success depends on the weather.

12. A）Not all of the advertised books were on sale.
　　B）Some of the books were still packed.
　　C）The store was too crowded for him to enter.
　　D）He had to work at the bookstore this morning.

13. A）She's not sure she wants to go to the party.
　　B）She just returned from a visit to the Andersons.
　　C）She may not be able to give the man a ride.
　　D）The party isn't on Friday.

14. A）She'll continue to use the Laundromat near the dorms.
　　B）She recently switched Laundromats.
　　C）She doesn't use the same Laundromat the man uses.
　　D）The Laundromat near the dorms isn't convenient for her.

15. A）Try to change his reservations to a different time.
　　B）Travel by train instead of by plane.
　　C）Continue trying to get a ticket.
　　D）Cancel his travel plans.

16. A）They should wait for him.　　C）He'll try to join them later.
　　B）They should go without him.　　D）They should bring him some pizza.

17. A）The jobs have already been filled.
　　B）The man should hand in his application very soon.
　　C）The man can start work today.
　　D）The man isn't qualified for any of the jobs.

18. A）She read only half of the book.
　　B）The man should choose a different book to read.
　　C）The man will enjoy the book eventually.
　　D）The main characters in the book aren't interesting.

Questions 19 to 21 are based on the conversation you have just heard.

19. A）They can't get rid of excess fat of arms.　　C）They easily make a person tired.
　　B）They damage arm muscles.　　D）They raise a person's blood pressure.

20. A）They can make a person physically fit.
　　B）They can reduce a person's blood pressure.
　　C）They can speed up metabolism.
　　D）They can slow down aging.

21. A）Wearing arms weights while you are swimming.
　　B）Jogging vigorously for a long time.
　　C）Cycling with special bicycles that require you to use both your arms and legs.
　　D）Walking slowly while swinging your arms back and forth.

Questions 22 to 25 are based on the conversation you have just heard.

22. A）He needs a new pair of glasses when using a computer.
　　B）Staring at the computer screen for hours will not hurt eyes.
　　C）He should know how to use a computer skillfully.

D）He should know how to protect his eyes when using a computer.

23. A）It helps the eyes absorb eye drops.

    B）It helps to keep the eyes moist.

    C）It helps to maintain a person's concentration.

    D）It prevents a build-up of chemicals in the eyes.

24. A）Go to an eye doctor.   C）Take more breaks and rest his eyes.

    B）Improve his computer skills.   D）Drink more coffee.

25. A）He has been working at his chemistry paper.

    B）He doesn't know how to use a computer.

    C）He doesn't want to write his chemistry paper.

    D）He needs to get an office job.

Section B

Directions: In this section, you will hear 3 short passages. At the end of each passage, you will hear some question. Both the passage and the questions will be spoken only once. After you hear a question, you must choose the best answer from the four choices marked A）, B）, C）, and D）. Then mark the corresponding letter on the Answer Sheet with a single line through the center.

Passage One

Questions 26 to 29 are based on the passage you have just heard.

26. A）A car outside the supermarket.   C）Paul's car.

    B）A car at the bottom of the hill.   D）The sports car.

27. A）Inside the car.   C）In the garage.

    B）At the foot of the hill.   D）In the supermarket.

28. A）The driver of the sports car.   C）The man standing nearby.

    B）The two girls inside the car.   D）The salesman from London.

29. A）Nobody.   C）The bus driver.

    B）The two girls.   D）Paul.

Passage Two

Questions 30 to 32 are based on the passage you have just heard.

30. A）His friend gave him the wrong key.

    B）He didn't know where the back door was.

    C）He couldn't find the key to his mailbox.

    D）It was too dark to put the key in the lock.

31. A）It was getting dark.

    B）He was afraid of being blamed by his friend.

    C）The birds might have flown away.

    D）His friend would arrive any time.

32. A）He looked silly with only one leg inside the window.

    B）He knew the policeman wouldn't believe him.

    C）The torch light made him look very foolish.

    D）He realized that he had made a mistake.

Passage Three

Questions 33 to 35 are based on the passage you have just heard.

33. A）The threat of poisonous desert animals and plants.

    B）The exhaustion of energy resources.

    C）The destruction of oil wells.

    D）The spread of the black powder from the fires.

34. A）The underground oil resources have not been affected.

    B）Most of the desert animals and plants have managed to survive.

    C）The oil lakes soon dried up and stopped evaporating.

    D）The underground water resources have not been polluted.

35. A）To restore the normal production of the oil wells.

    B）To estimate the losses caused by the fires.

    C）To remove the oil left in the desert.

    D）To use the oil left in the oil lakes.

Section C

Directions: In this section, you will hear a passage three times. When the passage is read for the first time, you should listen carefully for its general idea. When the passage is read for the second time, you are required to fill in the blanks numbered from 36 to 43 with the exact words you have heard. For blanks numbered from 44 to 45 you are required to fill in the missing information. For these blanks, you can either use the exact words you have just heard or write down the main points in your own words. Finally, when the passage is read for the third time, you should check what you have written.

Some unusual words describe how a person spends his or her time. For example, someone who likes to spend a lot of time sitting or（36）_____ down while watching television is sometimes called **a "couch potato."** A couch is a piece of（37）_____ that people sit on while watching television.

Robert Armstrong, an artist from California,（38）_____ the term couch potato in 1976. Several years later, he listed the term as a（39）_____ with the United States government. Mister Armstrong also helped write a（40）_____ book about life as a full-time television watcher. It is called the "Official Couch Potato Handbook."

Couch potatoes enjoy watching television just as **"mouse potatoes"** enjoy working on computers. A computer mouse is the（41）_____ that moves the pointer, or cursor, on a computer screen. The（42）_____ of mouse potato became popular in 1993. American writer Alice Kahn is said to have invented the（43）_____ to describe young people who spend a lot of time using computers.

Too much time inside the house using a computer or watching television can cause someone to get "cabin fever" . A cabin is a simple house usually built far away from the city. People go to a cabin to relax and enjoy quiet time. Cabin fever is not really a disease. However, people can experience（44）_____ and（45）_____ if they spend too much time inside their homes. This is especially true during the winter when it is too cold or snowy to do things outside. Often children get cabin fever if they cannot go outside to play. So do their parents. This happens when there is so much snow that schools and even offices and stores are closed.

答案与原文

Unit 10

答案

Section A

(11-15) CCCAC   (16-20) BBCDA   (21-25) CDBCA

Section B

(26-30) CDAAA   (31-35) BBDDC

Section C

(36) <u>lying</u>   (37) <u>furniture</u>   (38) <u>developed</u>
(39) <u>trademark</u>   (40) <u>funny</u>   (41) <u>device</u>
(42) <u>description</u>   (43) <u>term</u>   (44) <u>boredom</u>
(45) <u>restless</u>

原文

Section A

Question 11

M: Say, remember that proposal for an international festival next spring? Do you think there's any chance it'll ever get off the ground?

W: I don't think it's a question of whether it'll happen. It's just a matter of where it'll be held.

Q: What does the woman imply about the international festival?

Question 12

W: The bookstore on Center Street is having a sale. They're advertising discounts of up to 70% on a lot of their books.

M: Yeah. I was there when they opened this morning. It was so packed that I didn't even go inside.

Q: What does the man mean?

Question 13

M: Can you drive me to the Anderson's party Friday night?

W: It depends on if I get my car back from the shop.

Q: What does the woman imply?

Question 14

M: I've been washing my clothes in the same Laundromat you use, the one near the dorms. But I can't stand it that their prices keep going up. I think I might start going to that one over on 2nd Avenue.

W: Well, the one on 2nd might be cheaper. But for me the convenience of having a Laundromat so close to where I live is worth the extra dollars.

Q: What does the woman mean?

Question 15

M: I can't believe I can't get a plane ticket for the December holidays. I mean, it's only October.

W: Well, you know I wouldn't worry about it too much. People cancel their reservations all the time.

Q: What does the woman imply the man should do?

Question 16

W: A bunch of us are going out for pizza.

M: Count me out, but have a good time.

Q: What does the man mean?

Question 17

M: Excuse me, I heard that there were a couple of jobs available in the library. So I'd like to apply for one of them. Can I fill out the application form at home and bring it back next week?

W: Sure, but you should know that we're about to start looking at the applications, and we hope to make some job offers in a few days.

Q: What does the woman imply?

Question 18

M: I started reading that book you loaned me, but I'm having a tough time keeping up with the main characters. It's hard to remember them all.

W: Yeah, I know. The first part isn't easy. All I can say is stick with it. Once you get halfway through you won't want to put it down.

Q: What does the woman imply?

Now you will hear two long conversations.

Conversation one

W: Exercise, exercise, exercise, we hear so much about it these days that even the experts can't agree on which exercises are best. Now some doctors are strongly encouraging arm exercises.

M: Arm exercises? Is that because our arms are too fat or flabby?

W: Actually, that's not the main reason. (20) They say that arm exercises are an ideal way to become physically fit.

M: (19) But don't arm exercises raise your blood pressure?

W: (19) That they do, but the article I read mentioned some ways to compensate for that.

M: How?

W: By adding leg exercise, the arms don't do all the work. Arm exercises alone aren't enough to increase metabolism (新陈代谢) before fatigue sets in. The more of a body that is involved in the exercises, the better.

M: And in turn, I'm sure that there is a great chance of losing weight.

W: Sounds right to me.

M: So, what exercises do the experts recommend?

W: They have mentioned quite a few. (21) But some of the more popular ones are cycling with special bicycles that make you use both your arms and legs, and walking vigorously while wearing arms weights.

M: I must try that. I like to walk a lot.

Questions 19 to 21 are based on the conversation you have just heard.

Q 19： What problem will arm exercises produce?

Q 20： Why do some doctors strongly recommend arm exercises?

Q 21： Which of the following exercises are suggested?

Conversation Two

W: Hi, Tom. (25) How is your chemistry paper going?

M: (25) It's coming along, Mary. But I've been staring at the computer screen for hours and my eyes hurt.

W: Yes. Doing that can make your eyes really dry and tired. You should take a break.

M: I can't. I have to get this paper written. It's due tomorrow.

W: You know I've read about computers and eye problems recently. (22) The article says that they are usually caused by not blinking your eyes enough.

M: Blinking? I thought I just needed new glasses.

W: No. (23) When you blink, the movement of closing and opening your eyes, even though it happens really fast, helps moisten your eyes. It's the lack of moisture that causes the problem.

M: That makes sense. But what does it have to do with the computer?

W: People who use computers tend to stare at the monitor and blink less often than they normally would. That leads to dry, irritated eyes.

M: Well, that's certainly how mine feel now. They really hurt.

W: The article I read about the office workers found that the workers averaged 22 blinks a minute when relaxed. But just 7 a minute while looking at the text on a computer screen.

M: Wow. That's quite a difference.

W: They also kept their eyes open wider, which means the moisture evaporated more quickly.

M: I wonder if using some kind of eye-drops will make them feel better.

W: That might help. (24) But the best prescription is to take a break and rest your eyes.

M: Thank you so much for your helpful information.

W: You are welcome.

M: Ok, now let's go and get some coffee. I can finish this later tonight.

Questions 22 to 25 are based on the conversation you have just heard.

Q 22： What does Mary try to tell Tom?

Q 23： Why is blinking important?

Q 24： What should Tom do to improve his situation?

Q 25： What can be inferred about Tom?

Section B

Passage One

Paul, a salesman from London, was driving past a sports car parked outside a supermarket, when he saw it start to roll slowly down the hill. Inside the car were two young girls on the passenger seat — but no driver. Paul stopped quickly, jumped in front of the sports car and tried to stop it, pushing against the front of the car. Another man who was standing nearby got into the car and put on the hand-brake, saving the girls from injury.

It was at this point that Paul noticed his own car rolling slowly down the hill and going too fast for him to stop it. It crashed into a bus at the bottom of the hill and was so badly damaged that it had to be pulled away to a garage.

As if this was not bad enough, Paul now found he had no one to blame. He was so busy chasing his car that he didn't get the name of the driver of the sports car, who just came out of the supermarket and drove away without realizing what had happened.

Questions 26 to 29 are based on the passage you have just heard.

Q 26: Which car was badly damaged?

Q 27: Where was the driver of the sports car when the accident happened?

Q 28: Who did Paul think was to blame for the accident?

Q 29: Who was injured in the accident?

Passage Two

My friend, Vernon Davies kept birds. One day he phoned and told me he was going away for a week. He asked me to feed the birds for him and said that he would leave the key to his front door in my mailbox.

Unfortunately, I forgot all about the birds until the night before Vernon was going to return What was worse, it was already dark when I arrived at his house. I soon found the key Vernon gave me could not unlock either the front door or the back door. I was getting desperate. I kept thinking of what Vernon would say when he came back.

I was just going to give up when I noticed that one bedroom window was slightly open. I found a barrel and pushed it under the window. As the barrel was very heavy, I made a lot of noise.

But in the end, I managed to climb up and open the window. I actually had one leg inside the bedroom when I suddenly realized that someone was shining a torch up at me. I looked down and saw a policeman and an old lady, one of Vernon's neighbours. "What are you doing up there?" said the policeman. Feeling like a complete fool, I replied, "I was just going to feed Mr. Davies' birds."

Questions 30 to 32 are based on the passage you have just heard.

Q 30: Why couldn't the man open the door?

Q 31: Why did the man feel desperate?

Q 32: Why did the man feel like a fool?

Passage Three

When Iraqi troops blew up hundreds of Kuwaiti oil wells at the end of the Gulf War, scientists feared environmental disaster. Would black powder in the smoke from the fires circle the globe and block out the sun?

Many said "No way"; rain would wash the black powder from the atmosphere. But in America, air-sampling balloons have detected high concentrations of particles similar to those collected in Kuwait.

Now that the fires are out, scientists are turning their attention to yet another threat: The oil that didn't catch fire. It has formed huge lakes in the Kuwaiti desert. They trap insects and birds, and poison a variety of other desert animals and plants.

The only good news is that the oil lakes have not affected the underground water resources. So far, the oil has not been absorbed because of the hard sand just below the surface. Nothing, however, stops the oil from evaporating. The resulting poisonous gases are choking nearby residents.

Officials are trying to organize a quick cleanup, but they are not sure how to do it. One possibility is to burn the oil. Get those black powder detectors ready.

Questions 33 to 35 are based on the passage you have just heard.

Q 33: What were the scientists worried about soon after the Gulf War?

Q 34: What was the good news for scientists?

Q 35: What are the officials trying to do at the moment?

附录 A

全国大学英语四级考试听力试题和答案

2014年6月

Part I   Listening Comprehension (25 points)

Section A

Directions: In this section, you will hear three news reports. At the end of each news report, you will hear two or three questions. Both the news report and the questions will be spoken only once. After you hear a question, you must choose the best answer from the four choices marked A), B), C), and D). Then mark the corresponding letter on the **Answer Sheet** with a single line through the center.

News Item One

Questions 1 and 2 are based on the following news item.

1. A) 15 schools have started social studies.
   B) 15 schools have used digital textbooks.
   C) Digital textbooks are used for social studies.
   D) Students are ready to use electronic resources.

2. A) About 1 million dollars.   C) About 3 million dollars.
   B) About 2 million dollars.   D) About 4 million dollars.

News Item Two

Questions 3 and 4 are based on the following news item.

3. A) TSA agents.   C) The police.
   B) FBI agents.   D) Passengers.

4. A) The terminal was closed temporarily afterwards.
   B) There was a thorough search inside the airport.
   C) The security authorities identified the explosive.
   D) Passengers at the airport were safe and sound.

News Item Three

Questions 5 to 7 are based on the following news item.

5. A) Three.   B) Four.   C) Five.   D) Six.

6. A）It happened in a hospital in the town after 7 p.m., local time.

   B）It happened in a hospital in the town after 6 p.m., local time.

   C）It happened in a building opposite the hospital after 7 p.m.

   D）It happened in a building opposite the hospital after 6 p.m..

7. A）The shooting happened after 6 p.m.

   B）The criminal used an automatic weapon.

   C）The criminal had relation to an explosion.

   D）Two bodies were found in the hospital.

Section B

Directions: In this section, you will hear two long conversations. At the end of each conversation, you will hear four questions. Both the conversation and the questions will be spoken only once. After you hear a question, you must choose the best answer from the four choices marked A), B), C）and D). Then mark the corresponding letter on the *Answer Sheet* with a single line through the centre.

Conversation One

Questions 8 to 11 are based on the conversation you have just heard.

8. A）The woman's clothes.   C）The woman's words.

   B）The woman's behavior.   D）The woman's job.

9. A）Have a job interview.   C）Take a vacation.

   B）Go to the workplace.   D）Buy some clothes.

10. A）She is a new employee there.   C）She can't afford the high price.

    B）She doesn't work full time.   D）She needs to show the product.

11. A）She can gather information for her study.

    B）She can earn a large amount of money.

    C）She can get the chance to know people.

    D）She can buy some clothes at a lower price.

Conversation Two

Questions 12 to 15 are based on the conversation you have just heard.

12. A）He finds it rather stressful.   C）He can handle it quite well.

    B）He has to work extra hours.   D）He is thinking of quitting it.

13. A）The 6:30 one.   C）The 6:00 one.

    B）The 7:30 one.   D）The 7:00 one.

14. A）It is something difficult to get used to.

    B）The time on the train is enjoyable.

    C）It is an awful waste of time.

    D）He finds it rather unbearable.

15. A）Chatting with friends.

    B）Listening to the daily news.

    C）Reading newspapers.

    D）Planning the day's work.

Section C

Directions: In this section, you will hear 3 short passages. At the end of each passage, you will hear some questions. Both the passage and the questions will be spoken only once. After you hear a question, you must choose the best answer from the four choices marked A), B), C), and D). Then mark the corresponding letter on the *Answer Sheet* with a single line through the center.

Passage One

Questions 16 to 18 are based on the conversation you have just heard.

16. A) Read at least several chapters at one sitting.
    B) Get key information by reading just once or twice.
    C) Develop a habit of reading critically.
    D) Ignore small details while reading.
17. A) Choose one's own system of marking.
    B) Highlight details in a red color.
    C) Make as few marks as possible.
    D) Underline the key words and phrases.
18. A) By reading the textbooks carefully again.
    B) By comparing notes with their classmates.
    C) By focusing on the notes in the margins.
    D) By reviewing only the marked parts.

Passage Two

Questions 19 to 21 are based on the passage you have just heard.

19. A) The sleep a person needs varies from day to day.
    B) One can get by with a couple of hours of sleep.
    C) The amount of sleep for each person is similar.
    D) Everybody needs some sleep for survival.
20. A) It is a make-up story.   C) It is beyond cure.
    B) It is rare exception.   D) It is due to an accident.
21. A) The unique surroundings of his living place.
    B) His extraordinary physical condition.
    C) His mother's injury just before his birth.
    D) The rest he got from sitting in a rocking chair.

Passage Three

Questions 22 to 25 are based on the passage you have just heard.

22. A) She tenderly looked after her sick mother.
    B) She developed a strong interest in finance.
    C) She learned to write for financial newspapers.
    D) She invested in stocks and shares on Wall Street.
23. A) She inherited a big fortune from her father.
    B) She sold her restaurant with a substantial profit.
    C) She got 7.5 million dollars from her ex-husband.
    D) She made a wise investment in real estate.

24. A) She abused animals including her pet dog.
   B) She frequently ill-treated her employees.
   C) She was dishonest in business dealings.
   D) She was extremely mean with her money.

25. A) She carried on her family's tradition.
   B) She made huge donations to charities.
   C) She built a hospital with her mother's money.
   D) She made a bit fortune from wise investment.

2014年12月

Part Ⅰ Listening Comprehension (25 points)

Section A

Directions: In this section, you will hear three news reports. At the end of each news report, you will hear two or three questions. Both the news report and the questions will be spoken only once. After you hear a question, you must choose the best answer from the four choices marked A), B), C), and D). Then mark the corresponding letter on the *Answer Sheet* with a single line through the center.

News Item One

Questions 1 and 2 are based on the following news item.

1. A) It was proposed by a group of senators.
   B) Mr. Obama had carried out the reform.
   C) Illegal immigrants would soon be given citizenship.
   D) The reform failed to improve the current system.

2. A) Eight years.   B) Five years.   C) Thirteen years.   D) Eleven years.

News Item Two

Questions 3 and 4 are based on the following news item.

3. A) Running a plastic surgery clinic.
   B) Arranging for surgery and safaris.
   C) Providing consultancy to local people.
   D) Organizing trips to UK and America.

4. A) Local African clients helped keep her business going.
   B) Her clients were unable to pay her the money.
   C) Her business was affected by the global financial crisis.
   D) She still had as many European client as before.

News Item Three

Questions 5 to 7 are based on the following news item.

5. A) Better protection for the world's rainforest.
   B) A new network of nature reserves at sea.
   C) Better management of inshore fisheries.
   D) Measures to speed up the approvals process for offshore wind farms.

6. A）Enforce environmental laws and regulate development at sea.

   B）Decide the new powers between Westminster and itself.

   C）Regulate environmental groups in the UK.

   D）Supervise the parliament.

7. A）To determine the responsibility of the conservation groups.

   B）To open more coastal lands to the public.

   C）To turn the draft bill into law.

   D）To work together with environmental groups.

Section B

Directions: In this section, you will hear two long conversations. At the end of each conversation, you will hear four questions. Both the conversation and the questions will be spoken only once. After you hear a question, you must choose the best answer from the four choices marked A), B), C) and D). Then mark the corresponding letter on the **Answer Sheet** with a single line through the centre.

Conversation One

Questions 8 to 11 are based on the conversation you have just heard.

8. A）She finds English very dull to learn.

   B）She finds she needs to remember many things.

   C）She doesn't have a good memory.

   D）She does not know how to use her time.

9. A）Understanding helps people remember longer.

   B）Understanding helps people remember faster.

   C）Understanding leads to a complete memory.

   D）Understanding adds fun to remembering.

10. A）Find out the background information.

    B）Figure out the basic structure.

    C）Set apart the facts with opinions.

    D）Link up the similar information.

11. A）Show the things with the hands.

    B）Describe the things in words.

    C）Imagine the things in one's mind.

    D）Draw the things on the paper.

Conversation Two

Questions 12 to 15 are based on the conversation you have just heard.

12. A）In a hotel lobby.　　　　　　C）At the man's office.

    B）In a restaurant.　　　　　　D）At the woman's place.

13. A）He has just come back from a trip to Africa.

    B）He has completed an overseas market survey.

    C）He is the Managing Director of Jayal Motors.

    D）He is the chief designer of the latest bike model.

14. A) To select the right model.　　C) To convince the board members.
　　B) To cut down production costs.　D) To get a good import agent.
15. A) His determination.　　　　　C) His f lexibility.
　　B) His vision.　　　　　　　　D) His intelligence.

Section C

Directions: In this section, you will hear 3 short passages. At the end of each passage, you will hear some questions. Both the passage and the questions will be spoken only once. After you hear a question, you must choose the best answer from the four choices marked A), B), C), and D). Then mark the corresponding letter on the *Answer Sheet* with a single line through the center.

Passage One

Questions 16 to 18 are based on the conversation you have just heard.

16. A) How identical twins are born, raised and educated.
　　B) Why some identical twins keep their identities secret.
　　C) How being an identical twin influences one's identity.
　　D) Why some identical twins were separated from birth.
17. A) They grew up in different surroundings.
　　B) They both got married when they were 39.
　　C) Their second wives were named Linda.
　　D) Their first children were both daughters.
18. A) They want to know whether twins can feel each other's pain.
　　B) They want to understand how twins communicate when far apart.
　　C) They want to see what characteristics distinguish one from the other.
　　D) They want to find out the relationship between environment and biology.

Passage Two

Questions 19 to 21 are based on the passage you have just heard.

19. A) It is an inexpensive way of spending a holiday.
　　B) It is the first choice of vacationers on the Continent.
　　C) It is especially attractive to children and the young.
　　D) It is as comfortable as living in a permanent house.
20. A) It has a solid plastic frame.
　　B) It is very convenient to set up.
　　C) It consists of an inner and an outer tent.
　　D) It is sold to many Continental countries.
21. A) A groundsheet.　　　　　C) A gas stove.
　　B) A kitchen extension.　　D) A spare tent.

Passage Three

Questions 22 to 25 are based on the passage you have just heard.

22. A) It covers 179 square miles.　　C) It covers 97 square kilometers.
　　B) It is only half the size of Spain.　D) It is as big as New York City.

23. A）It imported food from foreign countries.

    B）It was cut off from the rest of the world.

    C）Its geographic features attracted many visitors.

    D）Its citizens enjoyed a peaceful, comfortable life.

24. A）The fast development of its neighboring countries.

    B）The increasing investment by developed countries.

    C）The establishing of diplomatic relations with France and Spain.

    D）The building of roads connecting it with neighboring countries.

25. A）They work on their farms.

    B）They raise domestic animals.

    C）They work in the tourist industry.

    D）They make traditional handicrafts.

2015年6月

Part Ⅰ   Listening Comprehension (25 points)

Section A

Directions: In this section, you will hear three news reports. At the end of each news report, you will hear two or three questions. Both the news report and the questions will be spoken only once. After you hear a question, you must choose the best answer from the four choices marked A), B), C), and D). Then mark the corresponding letter on the *Answer Sheet* with a single line through the center.

News Item One

Questions 1 and 2 are based on the following news item.

1. A）When the woman was killed.   C）The woman's identity.

    B）The main cause of her death.   D）Why she failed to return home.

2. A）19.   B）9.   C）22.   D）33.

News Item Two

Questions 3 and 4 are based on the following news item.

3. A）Islamist militants are still in control of the town.

    B）French forces have entered the town.

    C）French forces are going to land at the airport.

    D）Islamist militants are attacking the airport.

4. Why did the French launch the military operation?

    A）To control Kidal airport.   C）To fight against Islamist militants.

    B）To protect the town.   D）To protect the capital Bamako.

News Item Three

Questions 5 to 7 are based on the following news item.

5. A）Diver.   C）Table tennis player.

    B）Scientist.   D）Science fiction writer.

6. A）In 1960.   B）In 1968.   C）In 2001.   D）In his 20s.

7. A）Arthur C. Clarke was born in Sri Lanka.
   B）Arthur C. Clarke once worked for *Wireless World Magazine*.
   C）Arthur C. Clarke wrote over 100 books throughout his life.
   D）Arthur C. Clarke has never married in his lifetime.

Section B

Directions: In this section, you will hear two long conversations. At the end of each conversation, you will hear four questions. Both the conversation and the questions will be spoken only once. After you hear a question, you must choose the best answer from the four choices marked A), B), C) and D). Then mark the corresponding letter on the **Answer Sheet** with a single line through the centre.

Conversation One

Questions 8 to 11 are based on the conversation you have just heard.

8. A）It specializes in safety from leaks.
   B）It is headquartered in London.
   C）It has a partnership with LCP.
   D）It has a chemical processing plant.
9. A）He is Mr. Grand's friend.
   B）He is a safety inspector.
   C）He is a salesman.
   D）He is a chemist.
10. A）Director of the safety department.
    B）Mr. Grand's personal assistant.
    C）Head of the personnel department.
    D）The public relations officer.
11. A）Wait for Mr. Grand to call back.
    B）Leave a message for Mr. Grand.
    C）Provide details of their products and services.
    D）Send a comprehensive description of their work.

Conversation Two

Questions 12 to 15 are based on the conversation you have just heard.

12. A）She has just moved to a new apartment.
    B）She has been looking for a new roommate.
    C）She has been looking for a new house.
    D）She has just come back from Australia.
13. A）Making an appointment.
    B）Looking for a job.
    C）Meeting his professor.
    D）Having a meeting.
14. A）He has to deal with his e-mails.
    B）He must finish writing the letters.
    C）He needs to wait for a delivery.
    D）He must go to the post office.
15. A）This noon.
    B）Tomorrow afternoon.
    C）This evening.
    D）Tomorrow evening.

Section C

Directions: In this section, you will hear 3 short passages. At the end of each passage, you will hear some questions. Both the passage and the questions will be spoken only once. After you hear a question, you must choose the best answer from the four choices marked A), B), C), and D). Then mark the corresponding letter on the **Answer Sheet** with a single line through the center.

Passage One

Questions 16 to 18 are based on the conversation you have just heard.

16. A）There are mysterious stories behind his works.
    B）There are many misunderstandings about him.
    C）His works have no match worldwide.
    D）His personal history is little known.

17. A）He moved to Stratford-on-Avon in his childhood.
    B）He failed to go beyond grammar school.
    C）He was a member of the town council.
    D）He once worked in a well-known acting company.

18. A）Writers of his time had no means to protect their works.
    B）Possible sources of clues about him were lost in a fire.
    C）His works were adapted beyond recognition.
    D）People of his time had little interest in him.

Passage Two

Questions 19 to 21 are based on the passage you have just heard.

19. A）Theft.　　　　B）Cheating.　　　　C）Air crash.　　　　D）Road accidents.

20. A）Learn the local customs.　　　　C）Book tickets well in advance.
    B）Make hotel reservations.　　　　D）Have the right documents.

21. A）Contact your agent.　　　　C）Use official transport.
    B）Get a lift if possible.　　　　D）Have a friend meet you.

Passage Three

Questions 22 to 25 are based on the passage you have just heard.

22. A）Cut down production cost.　　　　C）Specialise in gold ornaments.
    B）Sell inexpensive products.　　　　D）Refine the taste of his goods.

23. A）At a national press conference.　　　　C）During a local sales promotion campaign.
    B）During a live television interview.　　　　D）At a meeting of top British businesspeople.

24. A）Insulted.　　　B）Puzzled.　　　　C）Distressed.　　　　D）Discouraged.

25. A）The words of some businesspeople are just rubbish.
    B）He who never learns from the past is bound to fail.
    C）There should be a limit to one's sense of humour.
    D）He is not laughed at that laughs at himself first.

2015年12月

Part Ⅰ　Listening Comprehension (25 points)

Section A

Directions: In this section, you will hear three news reports. At the end of each news report, you will hear two or three questions. Both the news report and the questions will be spoken only once. After you hear a question, you must choose the best answer from the four choices marked A),

B), C), and D). Then mark the corresponding letter on the **Answer Sheet** with a single line through the center.

News Item One

Questions 1 and 2 are based on the following news item.

1. A）He will return to the U.K. for medical treatment.
   B）He will remain in South Africa for medical treatment.
   C）He will stand trial in South Africa once proved fit.
   D）He will be extradited even if he is unfit to stand trial.
2. A）Having his wife killed.   C）Being involved in a taxi accident.
   B）Killing his wife in the U.K.   D）Hiring a crew of hit men.

News Item Two

Questions 3 and 4 are based on the following news item.

3. A）£945 million.   B）£1.07 billion.   C）£500,000.   D）£87,000.
4. A）Because the U.K. is a good film location.
   B）Because the cast usually comes from Britain.
   C）Because Hollywood emphasizes quality.
   D）Because production cost can be reduced.

News Item Three

Questions 5 to 7 are based on the following news item.

5. A）Protests against the dump are halted.
   B）Protesters agree to dismiss the gathering.
   C）They get support from the parliament.
   D）They get agreement of the mayors.
6. A）They have accepted the proposed compromise.
   B）They insist on stopping the dump completely.
   C）They've only agreed with partial of the proposal.
   D）They are still considering about the suggestion.
7. A）New dump will be put on hold.   C）Compensation will be offered.
   B）Existing site will be cleaned up.   D）Protesters arrested will be released.

Section B

Directions: In this section, you will hear two long conversations. At the end of each conversation, you will hear four questions. Both the conversation and the questions will be spoken only once. After you hear a question, you must choose the best answer from the four choices marked A), B), C）and D). Then mark the corresponding letter on the **Answer Sheet** with a single line through the centre.

Conversation One

Questions 8 to 11 are based on the conversation you have just heard.

8. A）She hurts her arm very badly.
   B）She is worried about the concert.

C）She fails to get a ticket for the concert.

D）She makes no progress in violin-playing.

9. A）She must have a good rest.   C）She can still practice playing.

    B）She will be better in another week.   D）She can't play for a long time.

10. A）He's not as good as the woman.   C）He can't get along well with others.

    B）He's not very trustworthy.   D）He may not be available.

11. A）Talk to Jim.   C）Not to worry too much.

    B）Take part in the rehearsal.   D）Let the group decide.

Conversation Two

Questions 12 to 15 are based on the conversation you have just heard.

12. A）To place an order.   C）To return some goods.

    B）To apply for a job.   D）To make a complaint.

13. A）He works on a part-time basis for the company.

    B）He has not worked in the sales department for long.

    C）He is not familiar with the exact details of the goods.

    D）He has become somewhat impatient with the woman.

14. A）It is not his responsibility.

    B）It will be free for large orders.

    C）It depends on a number of factors.

    D）It costs £ 15 more for express delivery.

15. A）Make inquiries with some other companies.

    B）Report the information to her superior.

    C）Pay a visit to the saleswoman in charge.

    D）Ring back when she comes to a decision.

Section C

Directions: In this section, you will hear 3 short passages. At the end of each passage, you will hear some questions. Both the passage and the questions will be spoken only once. After you hear a question, you must choose the best answer from the four choices marked A), B), C), and D). Then mark the corresponding letter on the ***Answer Sheet*** with a single line through the center.

Passage One

Questions 16 to 18 are based on the conversation you have just heard.

16. A）No one knows for sure when they came into being.

    B）No one knows exactly where they were first made.

    C）No one knows for what purpose they were invented.

    D）No one knows what they will look like in the future.

17. A）Measure the speed of wind.   C）Pass on secret messages.

    B）Give warnings of danger.   D）Carry ropes across rivers

18. A）To find out the strength of silk for kites.

    B）To test the effects of the lightning rod.

    C）To prove that lightning is electricity.

    D）To protect houses against lightning.

Passage Two

Questions 19 to 22 are based on the passage you have just heard.

19. A）She was born with a talent for languages.
    B）She was trained to be an interpreter.
    C）She can speak several languages.
    D）She enjoys teaching languages.

20. A）They want to learn as many foreign languages as possible.
    B）They have an intense interest in cross-cultural interactions.
    C）They acquire an immunity to culture shock.
    D）They would like to live abroad permanently.

21. A）She became an expert in horse racing.
    B）She learned to appreciate classical music.
    C）She was able to translate for a German sports judge.
    D）She got a chance to visit several European countries.

22. A）Take part in a cooking competition.
    B）Taste the beef and give her comment.
    C）Teach vocabulary for food in English.
    D）Give cooking lessons on Western food.

Passage Three

Questions 23 to 25 are based on the passage you have just heard.

23. A）He had only a third-grade education.
    B）He once threatened to kill his teacher.
    C）He often helped his mother do housework.
    D）He grew up in a poor single-parent family.

24. A）Stupid.   B）Active.   C）Brave.   D）Careless.

25. A）Watch educational TV programs only
    B）Write two book reports a week.
    C）Help with housework.
    D）Keep a diary.

答案与原文

答案

CET4 2014年6月

    (1-7) CB AC ABD   (8-15) ABDD CABC   (16-25) BAD DBC BADC

CET4 2014年12月

    (1-7) AC BD AAC   (8-15) BADC BCDA   (16-25) CAD ACB ABDC

CET4 2015年6月

    (1-7) BB BC DBC   (8-15) DCBC ABDD   (16-25) DCB ADC BDAC

CET4 2015年12月

(1-7) DA AD ABD　　　　(8-15) BBBA ACCD　　　　(16-25) ADC CBCB DAB

📰 原文

CET4 2014年6月

Listening Comprehension

Section A

News Item One

Digital textbooks are transforming the way many students learn. All the Fairfax County Public Schools have begun using online course material for their middle and high school students.

This school year, the schools shifted from hard cover to electronic textbooks for social studies in its middle and high schools. (1) The switch came after digital books were used in 15 schools last year. "Our students come to us technologically ready to use resources from a variety of different places," says Assistant Superintendent Peter Noonan. "The world is changing consistently. The online textbooks can change right along with the events that are happening." There's a significant financial benefit as well. "Usually it is between $50 and $70 to buy a textbook for each student," Noonan says, "which adds up to roughly $8 million for all of our students. We actually have purchased all of the online textbooks for our students for just under $6 million." (2)

1. What is happening to the schools in Fairfax County this school year?

2. With digital textbooks, how much have schools saved?

News Item Two

A man was arrested on suspicion of attempting to carry explosives through a security checkpoint at an airport, authorities said. Trey Scott Atwater was taken into custody Saturday morning after Transportation Security Administration agents spotted what they described as a suspicious item. (3) The item was in his carry-on during X-ray screening at a security checkpoint at the airport, an FBI spokesman said in a statement. Neither the FBI nor the TSA identified the explosives, (4) though an airport spokeswoman said the items were "wrapped in military grade wrapping" and are in the possession of the police. At no time was there any danger to the people at the airport. The airport terminal was temporarily evacuated while authorities "conducted a sweep, and deemed all clear," said a city spokeswoman. Atwater has been arrested on a federal count of attempting to get on an aircraft with an explosive.

3. Who found the suspicious item at the airport?

4. Which of the following statements is INCORRECT?

News Item Three

German police say four people have been killed in the south of the country in a shooting incident at a hospital and in an explosion. (5) A police spokesman confirmed the shooting took place in the St Elisabethen hospital in the town of Loerrach, shortly after 6 o'clock in the evening local time. (6) A woman armed with an automatic weapon opened fire in the clinic and killed one hospital worker. At least 3 patients and a police officer were injured. When police arrived at the scene, the woman turned the gun on the officers who shot back and killed her. German prosecutors said they believed the shooting was linked to an explosion at a building opposite the hospital where they found the bodies of a man and a child. (7)

    5. How many people have been killed by the criminal?

    6. When and where did the shooting happen?

    7. Which of the following about the news item is INCORRECT?

Section B

Conversation One

M: Hey, Jane, look at you in the silk blouse and grey skirt even high heels. (8) Are you going to a job interview, or something?

W: Well, no. Actually, I've already got a part-time job for my summer vacation.

M: Really? Congratulations! What kind of job is it?

W: A salesgirl at the Bay Department Store. This is my first day. (9) Do I look professional enough?

M: You look fantastic. But as far as I remember, the salesgirls at Bay wear some kind of uniform, don't they?

W: Yes. But the uniform are for the girls at cosmetics, electronics or children's toys sections. For the female clothes section, we tend to wear what we sell. You know, this is a kind of advertising. (10)

M: Oh, yes. So you are like the models. From what you wear now, I assume you will be selling professional clothes for office ladies this summer.

W: Not the whole summer. As far as I know, the part-time salesgirls will be sent to the sections where hands are needed. Even though I will be selling women's clothes, I might also be working at the sportswear, jeans or even the underwear sections.

M: I see. I'm sure you will learn a lot of things there. It will look really outstanding in your resume when you graduate and look for a real job.

W: Sure, especially for a business management major.

M: What about the pay? Is it good?

W: We have a basic monthly salary, which is not much. But we can get the commission for each piece of clothes as well. Besides, we can have discounts when buying clothes we sell. (11)

M: Sound really good. Hope you enjoy it.

W: Thanks.

Questions 8 to 11 are based on the conversation you have just heard.

8. What makes the man surprised?

9. What is the woman going to do?

10. Why doesn't the woman wear a uniform?

11. What privilege does the woman have from the part-time job?

Conversation Two

W: How are things going, Rod?

M: Not bad, Jane. I'm involved in several projects and it's a long working day. But I'm used to that so it doesn't bother me too much. (12)

W: I heard you have moved to a new house in the suburb. How do you like commuting to London every day? Don't you find it a strain?

M: It was terrible at first, especially getting up before dawn to catch that 6:30 train. (13) But it's bearable now that I'm used to it.

W: Don't you think it's an awful waste of time? I couldn't bear to spend three hours sitting in a train every day.

M: I used to feel the same as you, but now I quite enjoy it. (14)

W: How do you pass the time? Do you bring some work with you to do on the train?

M: Ah, that's a good question. In the morning, I just sit in comfort and read the papers to catch up with the news. (15) On the way home at night, I relax with a good book or chat with friends or even have a game of bridge.

W: I suppose you know lots of people on the train now.

M: Yes, I've bumped into someone I know on the platform every day. Last week I came across a couple of old school friends and we spent the entire journey in the bar.

W: It sounds like a good club.

　You never know. I may join it too.

Questions 12 to 15 are based on the conversation you have just heard.

12. What does the man say about his job?

13. Which train does the man take to work every day?

14. How does the man feel about commuting to work every day now?

15. How does the man spend his time on the morning train?

Section C

Passage One

Most American college students need to be efficient readers. This is necessary because full-time students probably have to read several hundred pages every week. They don't have time to read a chapter three or four times. They need to extract as much information as possible from the first or second reading. (16)

An extraordinarily important study skill is knowing how to mark a book. Students mark the main ideas and important details with a pen or pencil, yellow or blue or orange. Some students mark new vocabulary in a different color. Most students write questions or short notes in the margins. Marking a book is a useful skill, but it's important to do it right. Firstly, read a chapter with one pen in your hand and others next to you on the desk. Secondly, read a whole paragraph before you mark anything. Don't mark too much. Usually you will mark about 10% of a passage. Thirdly, decide on your own system for marking. (17) For example, maybe you will mark main ideas in yellow, important details in blue and new words in orange. Maybe you will put question marks in the margin when you don't understand something. When your chapter is a rainbow of markings, you don't have to read all of it again before an exam. Instead, you just need to review your marks and you can save a lot of time. (18)

Questions 16 to 18 are based on the passage you have just heard.

16. What should American college students do to cope with their heavy reading assignments?

17. What suggestion does the speaker give about marking a textbook?

18. How should students prepare for an exam according to the speaker?

Passage Two

The thought of having no sleep for 24 hours or more isn't a pleasant one for most people. The amount of sleep that each person needs varies. In general, each of us needs about 8 hours of sleep each day to keep us healthy and happy. Some people, however, can get by with just a few hours of sleep at night.

It doesn't matter when or how much a person sleeps. But everyone needs some rest to stay alive. (19) Few doctors would have thought that there might be an exception to this. (20) Sleep is, after all, a very basic need. But a man named Al Herpin turned out to be a real exception, (20) for supposedly, he never slept.

Al Herpin was 90 years old when doctors came to his home in New Jersey. They hoped to challenge the claim that he never slept. But they were surprised. Though they watched him every hour of the day, they never saw Herpin sleeping. He did not even own a bed. He never needed one.

The closest that Herpin came to resting was to sit in a rocking chair and read a half dozen newspapers. His doctors were puzzled by the strange case of permanent sleeplessness. Herpin offered the only clue to his condition. He remembered some talk about his mother having been injured several days before he had been born. (21) Herpin died at the age of 94, never, it seems, having slept at all.

Questions 19 to 21 are based on the passage you have just heard.

19. What is taken for granted by most people?
20. What do doctors think of Al Herpin's case?
21. What could have accounted for Al Herpin's sleeplessness?

Passage Three

Hetty Green was a very spoiled only child. She was born in Massachusetts USA in 1835. Her father was a millionaire businessman. Her mother was often ill, and so from the age of two her father took her with him to work and taught her about stocks and shares. At the age of six she started reading the daily financial newspapers and opened her own bank account. (22) Her father died when she was 21 and she inherited 7.5 million dollars. (23) She went to New York and invested on Wall Street. Hetty saved every penny, eating in the cheapest restaurants for 15 cents. She became one of the richest and most hated women in the world. At 33 she married Edward Green, a multi-millionaire, and had two children, Ned and Sylvia.

Hetty's meanness was well-known. (24) She always argued about prices in shops. She walked to the local grocery store to buy broken biscuits which were much cheaper, and to get a free bone for her much loved dog. Once she lost a two-cent stamp and spent the night looking for it. She never bought clothes and always wore the same long, ragged black skirt. Worst of all, when her son, Ned, fell and injured his knee, she refused to pay for a doctor and spent hours looking for free medical help. In the end Ned lost his leg. When she died in 1916 she left her children 100 million dollars. Her daughter built a hospital with her money. (25)

Questions 22 to 25 are based on the passage you have just heard.

22. What do we learn about Hetty Green as a child?
23. How did Hetty Green become rich overnight?
24. Why was Hetty Green much hated?
25. What do we learn about Hetty's daughter?

CET4 2014年12月

Listening Comprehension

Section A

News Item One

US President Barack Obama has said the time has come for a review on the US immigration system. He made his case at a high school in Las Vegas, Nevada, a day after a group of senators outlined a framework for reform. (1) The White House and senators envisage a path to citizenship for many of an estimated 11 million undocumented immigrants in the US. He noted that the current system was "out of date and badly broken". Mr. Obama's case for an immigration reform reflects a blueprint he rolled out in 2011, though that did not go far. Mr. Obama now backs the Senate plan including making illegal immigrants pay taxes and fines, and sending them to the back of the queue before they can become American citizens. His 2011 blueprint also focused on a path to permanent residency and eventual citizenship. After eight years, individuals would be allowed to become legal permanent residents and would eventually become citizens five years later, according to his 2011 blueprint. (2)

1. Which of the following is TRUE about the immigration reform?

2. According to Obama's 2011 blueprint, how long would it take for illegal immigrants to gain citizenship?

News Item Two

In a suburb in northern Johannesburg, South Africa, Lorraine Melvill ran around, trying to organize hospital visits for her clients staying in her guest house. She started her business, "Surgeon and Safari," back in 2000 and since then she has had people from all over the world come to her to facilitate their cosmetic procedures, and perhaps go on safari too. (3) "For most people in the first-world economies like the UK, and especially in America, their biggest desire is to go on African safari," she explains, "and yet their greatest want in their life was to have plastic surgery, so why not put the two together?" Like most companies, however, Surgeon and Safari was hit by the global financial crisis, particularly as a number of Melvill's clients were borrowing money to afford their procedures. (4) However, whilst the United States and euro zone economies may have languished, Melvill says that she has benefited from the growth of some African countries' economies. "There is a huge emergence of local Africans that chose to come to South Africa for elective surgery, (4) whether it be breast reduction, tummy tucks," she says.

3. What is Lorraine Melvill's business?

4. Which of the following statements is NOT true according to the news item?

News Item Three

The British government has published its long awaited *Marine Bill*, promising better protection for wildlife including a new network of nature reserves at sea. The bill also pledges better management of inshore fisheries and measures to speed up the approvals process for offshore wind farms by about a year. (5) In England, it will open a new right of public access to coastal lands. Environmental groups say UK seas are "in crisis" and need more protection than the government is offering. The draft bill creates a new agency, the Marine Management Organization, MMO, to enforce environmental laws and regulate development at sea. (6) The government has promised it will turn the draft bill into law by the end of this parliament. (7)

　　5. What is not included in the *Marine Bill*?

　　6. What is the function of the Marine Management Organization (MMO)?

　　7. What has the government promised to do by the end of this parliament?

Section B

Conversation One

　　W: Hi, Mr. White.

　　M: Hi, Margaret. Take a seat. How are your studies?

　　W: Not bad. But I find I have a lot of things to learn by heart. (8)

　　M: English is not easy to learn. Well, do you have a good memory?

　　W: I don't know. I think I'm OK.

　　M: Most people do have a good memory but many of them do not really know how to use their memories to remember the things they want to.

　　W: That's interesting.

　　M: Yes, that may seem funny, but it is true. With a better understanding of how to use your memory, you will be able to remember more things and retain them for a longer time. (9) There are three things to do to prepare your memory.

　　W: What are the three things?

　　M: First is understanding. Before you can remember something, you must have a good understanding of it. It is very difficult to remember something you don't understand completely.

　　W: Yes, I agree with this.

　　M: And the next is to associate.

　　W: What does associate mean?

　　M: "Associate" means "to go together" When you associate, you think of some way in which the things you want to remember go together. (10) It is easier to remember a set of facts if you can associate them in some way.

　　W: It is very helpful to learn this way.

　　M: The last thing is to visualize. Visualizing is seeing something in your mind. (11)

　　W: I see. To visualize means to close your eyes and try to picture the things we want to remember.

　　M: Yes, try to picture how they go together. When you visualize the facts, it will help you remember them.

　　W: That's very interesting. I haven't done this before. I'll try it next time and see how it goes.

　　Questions 8 to 11 are based on the conversation you have just heard.

　　8. What is the woman's problem in her studies?

　　9. According to the conversation, what is the relationship between understanding and remembering?

　　10. What do people do when they try to associate?

　　11. What does the man say about visualizing?

Conversation Two

M: Cheers, Shirley.

W: Cheers, Paul. What a lovely place for a business lunch! (12) I hope I can concentrate in this heat.

M: I am sure you will when I tell you about my ideas.

W: You know, I must say I was pleased to hear from you, but from what you said on the phone, everything is so sudden.

M: Well, my father-in-law, who is also the Managing Director of Jayal Motors, (13) has given me two weeks to prepare a report on the possibility of moving into the export market.

W: Ah, now, just one thing Paul. Have you really thought the whole idea through?

M: Of course I have.

W: Now the key thing in the whole operation is to get a good import agent, (14) and you say the bank will help?

M: I'm almost sure of it.

W: Preliminary studies are very good, Paul. But if the product can't sell, then there's little use in expanding the factory.

M: Yes, I realize that, Shirley. But we have a very good product. The chief designer has just completed a new improved model.

W: I know your bikes have a very good reputation here, but you have to build up a reputation and market in Africa.

M: Yes, of course. But the immediate problem is that my father-in-law wants a detailed report by next Monday. Two weeks isn't enough time to prepare a report, so I need your help.

W: OK, Paul, you've convinced me. I must say I admire your determination. (15)

Questions 12 to 15 are based on the conversation you have just heard.

12. Where does the conversation most probably take place?

13. What do we learn about the man's father-in-law?

14. What does the woman think is important in the whole operation?

15. What does the woman admire in the man?

Section C

Passage One

Scientists know how twins were born, now though, they are trying to explain how being half of the biological pair influences a twin's identity. (16) They want to know why many identical twins make similar choices even when they don't live near each other. For example, Jim Springer and Jim Louis are identical twins. They were separated when they were only 4 months old. The two Jims grew up in different families and did not meet for 39 years. (17) When they finally met, they discovered some surprising similarities between them. Both men were married twice, their first wives were named Linda, and their second wives were both named Betty. Both twins named their first sons James Allen. Scientists want to know what influences our personality. They study pairs of identical twins who grow up in different surroundings, like Jim Springer and Jim Louis. These twins help scientists understand the connection between environment and biology. (18) Researchers at the University of Minnesota studied 350 sets of identical twins who did not grow up together. They discovered many similarities in their personalities. Scientists believed that personality characteristics such as friendliness, shyness and fears are not result of environment. These characteristics are probably inherited. Scientists continue to study identical twins because they are uncertain about them and have many questions. For example, they want to know : "Can twins really communicate without speaking?" ; "Can one twin really feel another twin's pain?" Perhaps with more research, scientists will find the answers.

Questions 16 to 18 are based on the passage you have just heard.

16. What are scientists trying to explain according to the passage?

17. What do we learn about the twin Jims?

18. Why are scientists interested in studying identical twins raised in different families?

Passage Two

Today I'm going to talk about tents. Camping is still one of the cheapest ways of having a holiday. (19) And each year, over 3 million people take camping vacations, either here in Britain or aboard, mostly on the Continent. Obviously, camping can't be as comfortable as living in a permanent house, but modern tents can be very comfortable indeed, with windows, bedrooms, kitchens and sitting rooms. The most popular tent sold in Britain is the frame tent with 2 bedrooms and sleeping accommodation for 4 people. There is usually an outer tent of water-proofed fabric and a lighter inner tent or tents with a built-in ground sheet. (20) The outer tent fits over the frame work. This is made of metal poles which are fitted together. The inner tent is attached to this frame. Generally, the inner tent is about half the area of the outer tent. The other half of the outer tent is the living area. This doesn't usually have a ground sheet but you can buy one to fit, though it costs extra. The ordinary 4-bed frame tent doesn't usually have a separate kitchen area, but the larger ones often do. You can buy a kitchen extension for many tents, and it's worth buying one if you plan to stay camping in one place for more than a few days. (21)

Questions 19 to 21 are based on the passage you have just heard.

19. What does the speaker say about camping?

20. What does the passage tell us about the most popular tent sold in Britain?

21. What does the speaker suggest buying if you plan to stay camping in one place for more than a few days?

Passage Three

Andorra, one of the smallest countries in the world, is located high in the mountains between France and Spain. The country covers only 179 square miles. (22) That is less than half the size of New York City. High, rocky mountains surround Andorra. Until the 1930s, travelers had difficulty reaching the country. (23) Up until that time, people in Andorra lived in the way they had lived for centuries. Most Andorrans worked as farmers. Things did not change quickly. When roads were built from France and Spain to Andorra in the 1930s, life picked up speed. (24) Tourist began to visit the small country. These tourists brought in a lot of money to spend while visiting. Many people in Andorra found new jobs in shops or hotels. These changes helped to keep young people in Andorra. There were many more jobs than before the roads were built. Today tourists provided 80 to 90 percent of Andorra's income. More than a million people visit each year. They come to view the rough mountains. They enjoy the quiet way of life. Most people are also interested in the ancient buildings. There are many shops for tourists to browse in. Clothes, watches, wines and other items are sold at low prices in Andorra. Import fees are low, so tourists enjoy the inexpensive shopping. Most of the businesses in Andorra are owned by its citizens. There are not many foreign businesses. Some Andorrans still farm and raise sheep and cattle. But most are now involved with the tourist trade. (25)

Questions 22 to 25 are based on the passage you have just heard.

22. How big does the speaker say Andorra is?

23. What can be said about Andorra before the 1930s?

24. What event changed the situation in Andorra?

25. What do most people in Andorra do nowadays?

CET4 2015年6月

Listening Comprehension

Section A

News Item One

The family of Sarai Sierra, an American woman who went missing in Istanbul nearly two weeks ago, is in mourning after learning that Turkish police found her body Saturday. Turkish police found the woman's body near ancient stone walls in Istanbul's Sarayburnu district. Police suspected she had been killed at another location. Police told CNN's sister network CNN Turk that the body of the 33-year-old mother of two showed signs of stab wounds. However, the police chief of Istanbul, Huseyin Capkin, said Sierra died from a blow to her head. (1) Nine suspects had been detained in connection with the woman's disappearance and death. (2) Sierra's family and friends first sounded the alarm last week after she did not arrive on a return flight from Istanbul on January 22.

1. According to the passage, which were Turkish police unsure about?

2. How many people had been detained by Turkish police?

News Item Two

French forces say they have entered Kidal in the north of Mali, (3) the last major town they have yet to secure in their drive against Islamist militants. French forces now control Kidal airport after a number of aircraft, including helicopters, landed there last night. Islamist militants were reported to have already left the town and it was unclear who was in charge. France—the former colonial power in Mali—launched a military operation this month after Islamist militants appeared to be threatening the south. (4) French army spokesman confirms that "French troops were deployed overnight in Kidal". One regional security source told the Press that French aircraft had landed at Kidal and that protection helicopters are in the sky. Kidal, 930 miles north-east of the capital Bamako, was until recently under the control of the Islamist militants.

3. What is the situation now in Kidal according to the news?

4. Why did the French launch the military operation?

News Item Three

The British-born science fiction writer Arthur C. Clarke has died in his adopted home Sri Lanka at the age of 90. (5) During his career, he wrote more than 100 books which sold millions of copies worldwide. (7) By the time he was in his 20s, he'd come up with the idea explaining in great detail in *Wireless World Magazine* of communication satellites. In the 50s after the briefest of marriages, he moved to Sri Lanka where despite his disability, he would go diving and play table tennis everyday. His mind was still in overdrive, producing in 1968, his best-known work, 2001: *A Space Odyssey, featuring a super computer with psychotic tendencies*. (6)

5. What was Arthur C. Clarke?

6. When was Arthur C. Clarke's best-known work produced?

7. Which of the following is CORRECT according to news item?

Section B

Conversation One

W: Morning, this is TGC.

M: Good morning, Walter Barry here, calling from London. Could I speak to Mr. Grand, please?

W: Who's calling, please?

M: Walter Barry, from London.

W: What is it about, please?

M: Well, I understand that your company has a chemical processing plant. (8) My own company LCP, Liquid Control Products, is a leader in safety from leaks in the field of chemical processing. I'd like to speak to Mr. Grand to discuss ways in which we could help TGC protect itself from such problems and save money at the same time. (9)

W: Yes, I see. Well, Mr. Grand is not available just now.

M: Can you tell me when I could reach him?

W: He's very busy for the next few days. Then he'll be away in New York. So it's difficult to give you a time.

M: Could I speak to someone else, perhaps?

W: Who, in particular?

M: A colleague, for example?

W: You are speaking to his personal assistant. (10) I can deal with calls for Mr. Grand.

M: Yes, well, could I ring him tomorrow?

W: No, I'm sorry, he won't be free tomorrow. Listen, let me suggest something. You send us details of your products and services, together with references from other companies. (11) And then we'll contact you.

M: Yes, that's very kind of you. I have your address.

W: Very good, Mr...?

M: Barry. Walter Barry, from LCP in London.

W: Right, Mr. Barry. We look forward to hearing from you.

M: Thank you, goodbye.

W: Bye.

Questions 8 to 11 are based on the conversation you have just heard.

8. What do we learn about the woman's company?

9. What do we learn about the man?

10. What's the woman's position in her company?

11. What does the woman suggest the man do?

Conversation Two

W: Hi, Jill. How are you?

M: Hello, Pearl. I'm fine. How are you?

W: Kind of tired. I've just moved in a new flat. (12)

M: Really? What's your flat like?

W: Oh, it's a two-bedroom flat. I share it with an Australian girl. My bedroom is small. But it's nice.

M: Oh, I will go to see it some day. I have a lot to tell you, but I don't have time now. I have an appointment at the local Employment Office. I'm going to look for a job. (13) Say, why don't we meet for lunch?

W: Lunch? I really like it, but I can't. I have a noon meeting at school. Where are you going to be after lunch? What about having coffee together at 2:30?

M: Wonderful idea, but at 2:30? Wait a minute. That's no good for me. I have to mail a lot of letters and packages at the post office. (14) And then I'm going to the department of motor vehicles. I need a new driver's license. But look, how about later?

W: Fine, let me think. How about having dinner together?

M: Sorry, but that won't work. A friend is going to take me out to dinner. Then I'm going to the community centre. I take an exercise class there. Do you want to come?

W: Uh, sorry. I have to wait for a telephone call at home. It's kind of important. Well, I will be free tomorrow evening. (15)

M: Good! So will I. (15) Let's go out to eat.

W: That's fine. Shall we meet here at seven o'clock?

M: Good. I'm kind of in a hurry right now. See you tomorrow.

W: See you. Bye.

Questions 12 to 15 are based on the conversation you have just heard.

12. Why does the woman feel tired?

13. What is the man probably going to do before lunch?

14. Why can't the man meet the woman at 2:30?

15. When will they both have time to meet?

Section C

Passage One

What makes a person famous? This is a mystery that many people have carefully thought about. All kinds of myths surround the lives of well-known people. Most people are familiar with the works of William Shakespeare, one of the greatest English writers of the 16th and 17th centuries. Yet how many know Shakespeare the person, the man behind the works? (16)

After centuries of research, scholars are still trying to discover Shakespeare's personal history. (16) It is not easily found in his writings. Authors of the time could not protect their works. An acting company, for example, could change a play if they wanted to. Nowadays, writers have copyrights that protect their work.

Many myths arose about Shakespeare. (16) Some said he had no formal education. Others believed that he began his career by tending the horses of wealthy men. All of these myths are interesting, but are they true? Probably not. Shakespeare's father was a respected man in Stratford-on-Avon, a member of the town council. (17) He sent young William to grammar school.

Most people of Elizabethan times did not continue beyond grammar school; so, Shakespeare did have, at least, an average education.

Some parts of Shakespeare's life will always remain unknown. The Great London Fire of 1666 burned many important documents that could have been a source of clues. (18) We will always be left with many questions and few facts.

Questions 16 to 18 are based on the passage you have just heard.

16. What does the speaker say about William Shakespeare?

17. What do we learn about Shakespeare's father?

18. Why does the speaker say parts of Shakespeare's life will remain a mystery?

Passage Two

Wherever you go and for whatever reason, it's important to be safe. While the majority of people you will meet when traveling are sure to be friendly and welcoming, there are dangers—theft being the most common. (19)

Just as in your home country, do not expect everyone you meet to be friendly and helpful. It's important to prepare for your trip in advance and to take precautions while you are traveling. As you prepare for your trip, make sure you have the right paperwork. (20) You don't want to get to your destination only to find you have the wrong visa, or worse, that your passport isn't valid any more. Also, make sure you travel with proper medical insurance, so that if you are sick or injured during your travels, you will be able to get treatment. If you want to drive while you are abroad, make sure you have an international driver's license.

When you get to your destination, use official transport. (21) Always go to bus and taxi stands. Don't accept rides from strangers who offer you a lift. If there is no meter in the taxi, agree on a price before you get in. If you prefer to stay in cheap hotels while traveling, make sure you can lock the door of your room from the inside. Finally, remember to smile. It's the friendliest and most sincere form of communication, and is sure to be understood in any part of the world!

Questions 19 to 21 are based on the passage you have just heard.

19. What is mentioned as a most common danger when people go traveling abroad?

20. What is the most important thing to do when you prepare for your trip abroad?

21. What does the speaker suggest you do when you arrive at your destination?

Passage Three

The British are supposed to be famous for laughing at themselves, but even their sense of humour has a limit, as the British retailer Gerald Ratner found out to his cost. (25) When Ratner took over his father's chain of 130 jewelry shops in 1984, he introduced a very clear company policy. He decided that his shops should sell down market products at the lowest possible prices. (22) It was a great success. The British public loved his cheap gold earrings and his tasteless silver ornaments. By 1991, Ratner's company had 2,400 shops and it was worth over 680 million pounds. But in April of that year, Gerald Ratner made a big mistake. At a big meeting of top British business people, he suited up and explained the secret of his success, (23) "people say 'how can we sell our goods for such a low price?' I say 'Because they are absolute rubbish.'" His audience roared with laughter. But the British newspapers and the British public were not so amused. People felt insulted (24) and stayed away from Ratner's shops. Sales fell and 6 months after his speech, Ratner's share price had fallen by 42%. The following year, things got worse and Gerald Ratner was forced to resign. By the end of 1992, he lost his company, his career and his house. Even worse, 25,000 of his employees had lost their jobs. It had been a very expensive joke.

Questions 22 to 25 are based on the passage you have just heard.

22. What did Gerald Ratner decide to do when he took over his father's shops?

23. On what occasion did Gerald Ratner explain the secret of his success?

24. How did people feel when they learned of Gerald Ratner's remarks?

25. What does the story of Gerald Ratner suggest?

CET4 2015年12月

Listening Comprehension

Section A

News Item One

A British man accused of planning his wife's murder (2) by hit men while they were honeymooning in South Africa has lost a High Court appeal to block his extradition there until he is fit to stand trial.

The judges ruled that Shrien Dewani can be extradited as long as the South African government pledges to return him to the United Kinddom should he ultimately prove unfit to be tried. (1) Dewani's lawyers had argued that he should not be extradited while he was unfit to stand trial. He is being treated for post traumatic stress disorder and a depressive illness. His legal team can appeal the decision at the Supreme Court.

Dewani is accused of hiring a crew of hit men to kill his wife, Anni Dewani during a taxi ride in Cape Town in November 2010, just over two weeks after their wedding.

1. According to the court ruling, what will become of Shrien Dewani?

2. What was Dewani accused of?

News Item Two

The number of British films being made has declined in the past few years, according to new figures. In 2013, 62 British films with a budget over £ 500,000 were produced, compared with 87 in 2011, figures from the British Film Institute (BFI) showed. The number of low-budget films being shot has also fallen. The BFI said "a dip in production should not be confused with a decline in quality", adding that Hollywood studios were spending more in the U.K. The FBI's annual statistics said total investment in film-making in Britain rose from £ 945 million in 2012 to £ 1.07 billion in 2013. (3) This was thanks to Hollywood studios choosing the U.K. as the film location. The BFI said tax reliefs had helped encourage Hollywood studios to film more productions in the U.K. (4)

3. How much was the total investment in film-making in Britain in 2012?

4. Why do Hollywood studios prefer to make films in Britain?

News Item Three

Italian authorities have offered to delay the opening of a new rubbish dump in Terzigno near the city of Naples, if protests against the dump are halted. (5) But the mayors of several nearby towns where refuse is piling up have rejected the compromise. Saying they want the new dump proposal to be shelved altogether. (6)

There have been skirmishes for days between police and protesters over an existing dump which residents say is hazardous and plans to open a new one which they say is too close. Now the Italian government has moved to reduce tensions as saying the new dump would be put on hold and the existing site cleaned up. It's also offered compensation. (7) This has been politically embarrassing for the Prime Minister Silvio Berlusconi, who came to power two years ago, promising to solve Italy's waste disposal problems, especially in the south.

5. What is the prerequisite for the authorities to delay the opening of the new rubbish dump?

6. What is the attitude of the mayors of nearby towns about the proposal of the authorities?

7. Which of the measures is NOT included in the plan of the Italian government to reduce the tensions?

Section B

Conversation One

M: Susan, what happened to your arm?

W: It's my wrist, actually; I sprained it last weekend. And I am kind of upset about it because I'm supposed to play the violin in my string quartet's big concert next week. (8) We've been practicing for weeks and we've already sold a bunch of tickets.

M: Uh...I'm sorry to hear that. What are you gonna do?

W: Well, I was thinking about trying to play anyway. I mean I really don't want to let the other three group members down. Plus the doctor said my wrist should be feeling better by then. (9)

M: Oh, OK, so problem solved, right?

W: Not exactly. I'm worried I'm gonna be out of practice, like I haven't been able to play the violin since I sprained my wrist. What if I don't play well? I'd make the rest of the group sound bad.

M: Why don't you get somebody else to take your place?

W: Well, there's only one other person I know who could do it and that's Jim. He's a great violinist and I'm sure he'd say yes. The thing is he's not very reliable. (10) I mean, I'm in the orchestra with him and he's always showing up late for rehearsals.

M: Oh, so you're not sure you can depend on him.

W: Exactly, and we have less than a week left to rehearse for the concert. We'd really need him to show up on time for all our rehearsals.

M: I think you can have a conversation with him to tell him (11) the urgent situation and I am sure he will know how to do.

W: OK, I will try my best.

Questions 8 to 11 are based on the conversation you have just heard.

8. What makes the woman upset?

9. What does the doctor say about the woman's wrist?

10. What's the problem of Jim?

11. What does the man suggest the woman do?

Conversation Two

M: Hello. Yes?

W: Hello. Is that the sales department?

M: Yes, it is.

W: Oh, well, my name's Jane Kingsbury of GPF Limited. Hmm...We need some supplies for our design office. (12)

M: Uh...What sort?

W: Well, first of all, we need one complete new drawing board.

M: A DO44 or DO45?

W: Uh...I don't know. What's the difference?

M: Well, the 45 costs 15 pounds more.

W: Hmm...So what's the total price then?

M: It's 387 pounds.

W: Does that include value-added tax?

M: Oh, I'm not sure, (13) most of the prices do. Yes, I think it does.

W: Hmm...What are the boards actually made of?

M: Oh, I don't know. (13) I think it's a sort of plastic stuff these days. It's white anyway.

W: Hmm...And how long does it take to deliver?

M: Oh, I couldn't really say. It depends on how much work we've got and how many other orders there are to send out, you know. (14)

W: OK. Now we also want some drawing pens, ink and rulers and some drawing paper.

M: Oh, dear, the girl that takes orders for supplies isn't here this morning, so I can't take those orders for you. I only do the equipment, you see.

W: OK. Well, perhaps I'll ring back tomorrow. (15)

M: So do you want the drawing board then?

W: I'll have to think about it. Thanks very much. I'll let you know. (15) Goodbye.

M: Thank you. Goodbye.

Questions 12 to 15 are based on the conversation you have just heard.

12. What is the woman's purpose in making the phone call?

13. What do we learn about the man from the conversation?

14. What does the man say about delivery?

15. What does the woman say she will possibly do tomorrow?

Section C

Passage One

No one knows for sure just how old kites are. (16) In fact, they have been in use for centuries. 25 centuries ago, kites were well-known in China. These first kites were probably made of wood. They may even have been covered with silk, because silk was used a lot at that time. Early kites were built for certain uses. In ancient China, they were used to carry ropes across rivers. (17) Once across, the ropes were tied down and wooden bridges were hung from them. Legend tells of one general who flew musical kites over the enemy's camp. The enemy fled, believing the sounds to be the warning voices of angels. By the 15th century, many people flew kites in Europe. Marco Polo may have brought the kite back from his visit to China. The kite has been linked to great names and events. For instance, Benjamin Franklin used the kite to prove that lightning is electricity. (18) He flew the kite in a storm. He did this in order to draw lightning from the clouds. He tied a metal key and a strip of silk to the kite line. The silk ribbon would stop the lightning from passing through his body. Benjamin's idea was first laughed at, but later on it led to the invention of the lightning rod. With such grand history, kite flying is sure to remain an entertaining and popular sport.

Questions 16 to 18 are based on the passage you have just heard.

16. What does the speaker say about kites?

17. What did ancient Chinese use kites to do?

18. Why did Benjamin Franklin fly a kite in a storm?

Passage Two

I have learned many languages, but I have not mastered them the way a professional interpreter or translator has. (19) Still, they have opened doors for me. They have allowed me the opportunity to seek jobs in international contexts and help me get those jobs. Like many people who have lived overseas for a while, I simply got crazy about it. I can't imagine living my professional or social life without international interactions. (20) Since 1977, I have spent much more time abroad than in the United States. I like going to new places, eating new foods and experiencing new cultures. If you can speak the language, it's easier to get to know the country and its people. If I had the time and money, I would live for a year in as many countries as possible.

Beyond my career, my facility with languages has given me a few rare opportunities. Once just after I returned from my year in Vienna, I was asked to translate for a German judge at an Olympic level horse event. (21) I learned a lot about the sport. In Japan, once when I was in the studio audience of a TV cooking show, I was asked to go up on the stage and taste the beef dish that was being prepared and tell what I thought. (22) They asked, "Was it as good as American beef?" It was very exciting for me to be on Japanese TV speaking in Japanese about how delicious the beef was.

Questions 19 to 22 are based on the passage you have just heard.

19. What does the speaker say about herself?

20. What does the speaker say about many people who have lived overseas for a while?

21. How did the speaker's experience of living in Vienna benefit her?

22. What was the speaker asked to do in a Japanese studio?

Passage Three

Doctor Ben Carson grew up in a poor single parent household in Detroit. (23) His mother, who had only a third-grade education, worked two jobs cleaning bathrooms. To his classmates and even to his teachers, he was thought of as the dumbest kid in the class, (24) according to his own not so fond memories. He had a terrible temper, and once threatened to kill another child. Doctor Carson was headed down a path of self-destruction until a critical moment in his youth.

His mother, convinced that she had to do something dramatic to prevent him from leading a life of failure, laid down some rules. He could not watch television except for two programs a week, could not play with his friends after school until he finished his homework, and had to read two books a week and write book reports about them. (25)His mother's strategy worked. "of course, I didn't know she couldn't read, so there I was submitting these reports." He said. "She would put check marks on them like she had been reading them. As I began to read about scientists, economists and philosophers, I started imaging myself in their shoes." As he got in the habit of hard work, his grades began to soar. Ultimately, he received a scholarship to attend Yale University. And later, he was admitted to the University of Michigan Medical School. He is now a leading surgeon at Johns Hopkins Medical School, and he's also the author of three books.

Questions 23 to 25 are based on the passage you have just heard.

23. What do we learn about Ben Carson?

24. What did Ben Carson's classmates and teachers think about him when he was first in school?

25. What did Ben Carson's mother tell him to do when he was a school boy?

全国大学英语六级考试听力试题和答案

2014年6月

Part Ⅱ   Listening Comprehension (30 minutes)

Section A

Directions: In this section, you will hear two long conversations. At the end of each conversation, you will hear some questions. Both the conversation and the questions will be spoken only once. After you hear a question, you must choose the best answer from the four choices marked A), B), C) and D). Then mark the corresponding letter on *Answer Sheet* 1 with a single line through the centre.

Conversation One

Questions 1 to 4 are based on the conversation you have just heard.

1. A）Before she worked for the media company.
   B）When she was on holiday five years ago.
   C）After her friend recommended it to her.
   D）After she went to therapists and classes.

2. A）She was busier than before.   C）She liked to exercise at home.
   B）It was more convenient.   D）She was given a promotion.

3. A）She recommended people to take classes.
   B）She was willing to pay more for classes at home.
   C）She left her job immediately after her promotion.
   D）She regarded the business as a pastime at first.

4. A）She got bored with her job.   C）She needed the money.
   B）She saw an opportunity.   D）She was forced to leave.

Conversation Two

Questions 5 to 8 are based on the conversation you have just heard.

5. A）A good secondary education.   C）A happy childhood.
   B）A pleasant neighbourhood.   D）A year of practical training.

6. A）He ought to get good vocational training.   C）He is academically gifted.
   B）He should be sent to a private school.   D）He is good at carpentry.

7．A）Donwell School.　　　　C）Carlton Abbey.

　　B）Enderby High.　　　　　D）Enderby Comprehensive.

8．A）Put Keith in a good boarding school.

　　B）Talk with their children about their decision.

　　C）Send their children to a better private school.

　　D）Find out more about the five schools.

Section B

Directions: In this section, you will hear two passages. At the end of each passage, you will hear some questions. Both the passage and the questions will be spoken only once. After you hear a question, you must choose the best answer from the four choices marked A), B), C) and D). Then mark the corresponding letter on *Answer Sheet* 1 with a single line through the centre.

Passage One

Questions 9 to 11 are based on the passage you have just heard.

9．A）It will be brightly lit.　　　　C）It will have a large space for storage.

　　B）It will be well ventilated.　　　D）It will provide easy access to the disabled.

10．A）On the first floor.　　　　　C）Opposite to the library.

　　B）On the ground floor.　　　　D）On the same floor as the labs.

11．A）To make the building appear traditional.

　　B）To match the style of construction on the site.

　　C）To cut the construction cost to the minimum.

　　D）To embody the subcommittee's design concepts.

Passage Two

Questions 12 to 15 are based on the passage you have just heard.

12．A）Sell financial software.

　　B）Write financial software.

　　C）Train clients to use financial software.

　　D）Conduct research on financial software.

13．A）Unsuccessful.　　　　C）Tedious.

　　B）Rewarding.　　　　　D）Important.

14．A）He offered online tutorials.　　　C）He gave the trainees lecture notes.

　　B）He held group discussions.　　　D）He provided individual support.

15．A）The employees were a bit slow to follow his instruction.

　　B）The trainees' problems had to be dealt with one by one.

　　C）Nobody is able to solve all the problems in a couple of weeks.

　　D）The fault might lie in his style of presenting the information.

Section C

Directions: In this section, you will hear recordings of lectures or talks followed by some questions. The recordings will be played only once. After you hear a question, you must choose the best answer from the four choices marked A), B), C) and D). Then mark the corresponding letter on *Answer Sheet* 1 with a single line through the centre.

Lecture/Talk One

Now listen to the following recording and answer questions 16 to 19.

16. A）Abstract Expressionism.
    B）The artistic movement that immediately preceded it.
    C）The internal struggles of the individual artists.
    D）Mass-produced visual media and the design of common household objects.

17. A）Abstract Expressionism was a very personal art.
    B）Abstract Expressionism was more easily accessible to the masses than Pop Art.
    C）Abstract Expressionism reflected a direct relationship to the actual world.
    D）Abstract Expressionism was a little bit influenced by Pop Art.

18. A）To direct art from the personalities of the individual artists towards the world.
    B）To impose a unified symbolic meaning on his collection of materials.
    C）To concentrate less on the objects and more on the images he found.
    D）To set the stage for further development in Pop Art.

19. A）Because their use of objects and images found from everyday life was innovative.
    B）Because they believed that these images reflected the cultural values of contemporary society.
    C）Because they used everyday objects found on the street as the material for their art.
    D）Because they combined and repeated images from print media to make one single artwork.

Lecture/Talk Two

Now listen to the following recording and answer questions 20 to 22.

20. A）To do well at school.
    B）To have good looks.
    C）To start out wealthy.
    D）To become a head of a large corporation.

21. A）One who rises through the ranks to the top of a big company.
    B）One who is born into an affluent family.
    C）One who may be able to capitalize on good looks.
    D）One who is regarded as kind, but not very efficient.

22. A）Intrapreneurs tend to be the kids everyone thought would do well.
    B）Intrapreneurs are good organizers and get on well with people.
    C）Entrepreneurs often had early reputations as troublemakers.
    D）Far fewer entrepreneurs had both parents present throughout childhood.

Lecture/Talk Three

Now listen to the following recording and answer questions 23 to 25.

23. A）What the average is.   C）The reality of life.
    B）What happiness means.   D）Human genes.

24. A）Our genes.   C）Our optimism.
    B）Our intelligence.   D）Our daily decisions and habits.

25. A）29%.   B）19%.   C）37%.   D）31%.

2014年12月

Part Ⅱ　Listening Comprehension (30 minutes)

Section A

Directions: In this section, you will hear two long conversations. At the end of each conversation, you will hear some questions. Both the conversation and the questions will be spoken only once. After you hear a question, you must choose the best answer from the four choices marked A), B), C) and D). Then mark the corresponding letter on *Answer Sheet* 1 with a single line through the centre.

Conversation One

Questions 1 to 4 are based on the conversation you have just heard.

1. A) The American literature in the 19th century.
   B) The hard and independent life of some American young girls.
   C) The hard life people had in the old days on the American frontier.
   D) The effort cowboys took to survive the 19th century frontier life.

2. A) She tried to escape from the farm many times.
   B) She worked very hard.
   C) She had to work on the rich people's farm.
   D) She was a Spanish immigrant girl.

3. A) He knew lots of people from Midwest.
   B) He read many novels about Midwest.
   C) He lived in Midwest for his whole life.
   D) He grew up in Midwest.

4. A) Buy the book *Main Traveled Road* in a bookstore.
   B) Lend the book *Main Traveled Road* to the woman.
   C) Look for Hemlen Garlen's other works in the library.
   D) Write a book report on *Main Traveled Road*.

Conversation Two

Questions 5 to 8 are based on the conversation you have just heard.

5. A) Irresponsible.   C) Conservative.
   B) Aggressive.   D) Unsatisfactory.

6. A) Public relations.   C) Internal communication.
   B) Product design.   D) Distribution of brochures.

7. A) Placing advertisements in the trade press.
   B) Drawing sketches for advertisements.
   C) Making television commercials.
   D) Advertising in the national press.

8. A) She has the motivation to do the job.   C) She is not suitable for the position.
   B) She knows the tricks of advertising.   D) She is not so easy to get along with.

Section B

Directions: In this section, you will hear two passages. At the end of each passage, you will hear some questions. Both the passage and the questions will be spoken only once. After you hear a question, you must choose the best answer from the four choices marked A), B), C) and D). Then mark the corresponding letter on **Answer Sheet** 1 with a single line through the centre.

Passage One

Questions 9 to 12 are based on the passage you have just heard.

9. A) The cultural diversity.
   B) The cozy communal life.
   C) Impressive school buildings.
   D) Innovative academic programs.

10. A) It ensures their physical and mental health.
    B) It helps them soak up the surrounding culture.
    C) It is as important as their learning experience.
    D) It is very beneficial to their academic progress.

11. A) It has the world's best-known military academies.
    B) It offers the most challenging academic programs.
    C) It draws faculty from all around the world.
    D) It provides numerous options for students.

12. A) They are responsible merely to their Ministry of Education.
    B) They try to give students opportunities for experimentation.
    C) They strive to develop every student's academic potential.
    D) They ensure that all students get roughly equal attention.

Passage Two

Questions 13 to 15 are based on the passage you have just heard.

13. A) It is leaving Folkestone in about five minutes.
    B) It is now about halfway to the French coast.
    C) It crosses the English Channel twice a day.
    D) It will arrive at Boulogne at half past two.

14. A) Next to the duty-free shop.   C) In the front of A deck.
    B) Opposite the ship's office.   D) At the rear of B deck.

15. A) It is much more spacious than the lounge on C deck.
    B) It is for the sole use of passengers travelling with cars.
    C) It is for the use of passengers travelling with children.
    D) It is for senior passengers and people with VIP cards.

Section C

Directions: In this section, you will hear recordings of lectures or talks followed by some questions. The recordings will be played only once. After you hear a question, you must choose the best answer from the four choices marked A), B), C) and D). Then mark the corresponding letter on **Answer Sheet** 1 with a single line through the centre.

Lecture/Talk One

Now listen to the following recording and answer questions 16 to 19.

16. A）Depressed and disappointed.   C）Sad and lonely.
    B）Tired and sick.   D）Confused and frustrated.

17. A）Because they think people are usually very interested in sports.
    B）Because they are not interested in how jetlag affects business people.
    C）Because baseball teams want to know how to win more games.
    D）Because it is difficult to measure how jetlag affects other types of travelers.

18. A）All over the United States.
    B）The Eastern and Pacific time zones.
    C）The Pacific time zone only.
    D）The southern part of the country.

19. A）Tiredness.   C）Stomachaches.
    B）Difficulty in thinking clearly.   D）Headaches.

Lecture/Talk Two

Now listen to the following recording and answer questions 20 to 22.

20. A）They sell well if they look technologically sophisticated.
    B）They command higher prices if they are technologically complicated.
    C）They have to be complicated to accommodate many features.
    D）They are designed to confuse us so that we turn to the manufacturer for help.

21. A）To cater to the different needs and tastes of different tourists.
    B）To show that these hotels offer everything tourists might hope to have.
    C）To try their utmost to help the customers to select a good hotel.
    D）To spread the customers out amongst the different hotels.

22. A）Because it's no longer a joke; it's deadly serious.
    B）Because these systems are a way of improving things.
    C）Because complicated systems can prevent human errors.
    D）Because it would be easier to blame people than blame machines.

Lecture/Talk Three

Now listen to the following recording and answer questions 23 to 25.

23. A）Your circumstances.
    B）Your experience and qualifications.
    C）The sort of job you're seeking.
    D）Your family background.

24. A）By applying to recruiting agencies.
    B）By networking.
    C）By joining a professional organization.
    D）By leaving your name with a potential employer.

25. A）Employee's organizations.
    B）Expatriate groups.
    C）Professional organizations.
    D）Social clubs and societies.

2015年6月

Part Ⅱ Listening Comprehension (30 minutes)

Section A

Directions: In this section, you will hear two long conversations. At the end of each conversation, you will hear some questions. Both the conversation and the questions will be spoken only once. After you hear a question, you must choose the best answer from the four choices marked A), B), C) and D). Then mark the corresponding letter on *Answer Sheet* 1 with a single line through the centre.

Conversation One

Questions 1 to 4 are based on the conversation you have just heard.

1. A) Persuade the man to join her company.
   B) Employ the most up-to-date technology.
   C) Export bikes to foreign markets.
   D) Expand their domestic business.
2. A) The state subsidizes small and medium enterprises.
   B) The government has control over bicycle imports.
   C) They can compete with the best domestic manufacturers.
   D) They have a cost advantage and can charge higher prices.
3. A) Extra costs might eat up their profits abroad.
   B) More workers will be needed to do packaging.
   C) They might lose to foreign bike manufacturers.
   D) It is very difficult to find suitable local agents.
4. A) Report to the management.
   B) Attract foreign investments.
   C) Conduct a feasibility study.
   D) Consult financial experts.

Conversation Two

Questions 5 to 8 are based on the conversation you have just heard.

5. A) It has color.   C) It costs less money.
   B) It has a moving image.   D) It is not on the market.
6. A) He wanted to buy one from Japan.   C) He thought it was for business use.
   B) He wasn't sure about its quality.   D) He thought it was expensive.
7. A) She had never read the magazine herself.
   B) She knew who usually read the magazine.
   C) She was quite interested in the new device.
   D) She agreed with Bill at the end of the conversation.
8. A) A new type of telephone.   C) Some features of the magazine.
   B) The cost of telephones.   D) The readership of the magazine.

Section B

Directions: In this section, you will hear two passages. At the end of each passage, you will hear some questions. Both the passage and the questions will be spoken only once. After you hear a question, you must choose the best answer from the four choices marked A), B), C) and D). Then mark the corresponding letter on *Answer Sheet* 1 with a single line through the centre.

Passage One

Questions 9 to 11 are based on the passage you have just heard.

9. A) The ability to predict fashion trends.
   B) A refined taste for artistic works.
   C) Years of practical experience.
   D) Strict professional training.

10. A) Promoting all kinds of American hand-made specialties.
    B) Strengthening cooperation with foreign governments.
    C) Conducting trade in art works with dealers overseas.
    D) Purchasing handicrafts from all over the world.

11. A) She has access to fashionable things.
    B) She is doing what she enjoys doing.
    C) She can enjoy life on a modest salary.
    D) She is free to do whatever she wants.

Passage Two

Questions 12 to 15 are based on the passage you have just heard.

12. A) Join in neighborhood patrols.
    B) Get involved in his community.
    C) Voice his complaints to the city council.
    D) Make suggestions to the local authorities.

13. A) Deterioration in the quality of life.
    B) Increase of police patrols at night.
    C) Renovation of the vacant buildings.
    D) Violation of community regulations.

14. A) They may take a long time to solve.
    B) They need assistance from the city.
    C) They have to be dealt with one by one.
    D) They are too big for individual efforts.

15. A) He had got some groceries at a big discount.
    B) He had read a funny poster near his seat.
    C) He had done a small deed of kindness.
    D) He had caught the bus just in time.

Section C

Directions: In this section, you will hear recordings of lectures or talks followed by some questions. The recordings will be played only once. After you hear a question, you must choose the best answer from the four choices marked A), B), C) and D). Then mark the corresponding letter on *Answer Sheet* 1 with a single line through the centre.

Lecture/Talk One

Now listen to the following recording and answer questions 16 to 19.

16. A）The overall investment costs are low.
    B）It is common to use agents, but not distributors.
    C）All sales centers are in home markets.
    D）Management is centered on the overseas base.

17. A）The investment is not so high as export marketing.
    B）There is much more employment of home management.
    C）Production has expanded to overseas markets.
    D）Local management is not responsible for making a profit.

18. A）The business is established in all major world markets.
    B）The brand, or brand names, are international.
    C）The business has a global identity.
    D）The business has cost centers all over the world.

19. A）Export marketing.　　　C）Global marketing.
    B）International marketing.　　D）It's unknown.

Lecture/Talk Two

Now listen to the following recording and answer questions 20 to 22.

20. A）To illustrate the importance of extrinsic values.
    B）To explain Aristotle's views about the importance of teaching.
    C）To explain why people change what they value.
    D）To discuss Aristotle's views about human happiness.

21. A）Because it is so difficult for people to attain.
    B）Because it is valued for its own sake by all people.
    C）Because it is a means to a productive life.
    D）Because most people agree about what happiness is.

22. A）Fame cannot be obtained without help from other people.
    B）Fame cannot be obtained by all people.
    C）Fame does not last forever.
    D）People cannot share their fame with other people.

Lecture/Talk Three

Now listen to the following recording and answer questions 23 to 25.

23. A）They refused to recognize universal truths.
    B）They did not recognize the genius of certain authors.
    C）Their convictions were not well-defined.
    D）They were too interested in conformity.

24. A）It should guide a person's present actions.
    B）It must be examined closely.
    C）It is less important than the future.
    D）It lacks both clarity and universal truth.

25. A) It is easy for people to lose sight of their true path.

    B) Most people are not capable of deciding which path is best for them.

    C) The path a person takes can only be seen clearly after the destination has been reached.

    D) A person should establish a goal before deciding which path to take.

2015年12月

Part Ⅱ　Listening Comprehension (30 minutes)

Section A

Directions: In this section, you will hear two long conversations. At the end of each conversation, you will hear some questions. Both the conversation and the questions will be spoken only once. After you hear a question, you must choose the best answer from the four choices marked A), B), C) and D). Then mark the corresponding letter on *Answer Sheet* 1 with a single line through the centre.

Conversation One

Questions 1 to 4 are based on the conversation you have just heard.

1. A) Register when they arrive.　　　　C) Register their guests.

   B) Bring up to three guests.　　　　D) Show membership cards on arrival.

2. A) There is a charge for the use of the locker.

   B) Showers are installed in the changing rooms.

   C) Lockers are located in the changing rooms.

   D) Lockers are used to store personal belongings.

3. A) For 30 minutes only.　　　　C) Within the booked time only.

   B) For one hour only.　　　　D) Longer than the booked time.

4. A) Players can eat in the club room.

   B) Players have to leave the club by ten o'clock.

   C) The courts are closed earlier than the club room.

   D) Players can use both the club room and the courts.

Conversation Two

Questions 5 to 8 are based on the conversation you have just heard.

5. A) They have unrealistic expectations about the other half.

   B) They may not be prepared for a lifelong relationship.

   C) They form a more realistic picture of life.

   D) They try to adapt to their changing roles.

6. A) He is lucky to have visited many exotic places.

   B) He is able to forget all the troubles in his life.

   C) He is able to meet many interesting people.

   D) He is lucky to be able to do what he loves.

7. A) It is stressful.　　　　C) It is all glamour.

   B) It is full of fun.　　　　D) It is challenging.

8. A）Bothered.　　　　B）Amazed.　　　C）Puzzled.　　　D）Excited.

Section B

Directions: In this section, you will hear two passages. At the end of each passage, you will hear some questions. Both the passage and the questions will be spoken only once. After you hear a question, you must choose the best answer from the four choices marked A), B), C) and D). Then mark the corresponding letter on *Answer Sheet* 1 with a single line through the centre.

Passage One

Questions 9 to 11 are based on the passage you have just heard.

9. A）It is a platform for sharing ideas on teaching at the University of Illinois.
   B）It was mainly used by scientists and technical people to exchange text.
   C）It started off as a successful program but was unable to last long.
   D）It is a program allowing people to share information on the Web.

10. A）He visited a number of famous computer scientists.
    B）He met with an entrepreneur named Jim Clark.
    C）He sold a program developed by his friends.
    D）He invested in a leading computer business.

11. A）They had confidence in his new ideas.
    B）They trusted his computer expertise.
    C）They were very keen on new technology.
    D）They believed in his business connection.

Passage Two

Questions 12 to 15 are based on the passage you have just heard.

12. A）Prestige advertising.　　　　　　C）Word-of-mouth advertising.
    B）Institutional advertising.　　　　D）Distributing free trial products.

13. A）To sell a particular product.　　　C）To promote a specific service.
    B）To build up their reputation.　　　D）To attract high-end consumers.

14. A）By using the services of large advertising agencies.
    B）By hiring their own professional advertising staff.
    C）By buying media space in leading newspapers.
    D）By creating their own ads and commercials.

15. A）Decide on what specific means of communication to employ.
    B）Conduct a large-scale survey on customer needs.
    C）Specify the objectives of the campaign in detail.
    D）Pretest alternative ads or commercials in certain regions.

Section C

Directions: In this section, you will hear recordings of lectures or talks followed by some questions. The recordings will be played only once. After you hear a question, you must choose the best answer from the four choices marked A), B), C) and D). Then mark the corresponding letter on *Answer Sheet* 1 with a single line through the centre.

Lecture/Talk One

Now listen to the following recording and answer questions 16 to 19.

16. A）The ability to support oneself completely.

    B）The best schooling one's family can afford.

    C）Physical competence in tough situations.

    D）Emotional maturity ready for marriage.

17. A）Getting related to siblings in a hierarchical way.

    B）Building a different relationship with parents.

    C）Establishing friendships based on mutual adulthood.

    D）Starting a long process of separation from parents.

18. A）Fear of change.   C）Rising living costs.

    B）Emotional dependence.   D）Falling inflation rate.

19. A）All children separate from their parents with more or less equal success.

    B）It is natural for children to separate from their parents in their mid 20s.

    C）It's harder to establish emotional independence than financial independence.

    D）When a child leaves home, families usually handle it well and with ease.

Lecture/Talk Two

Now listen to the following recording and answer questions 20 to 22.

20. A）Organisms of single cells.   C）Multi-cellular organisms.

    B）Humanoid creatures.   D）Bizarre or perhaps dangerous animals.

21. A）About 130,000 years.   C）Five or so million years.

    B）Some 30,000 years.   D）No one knows.

22. A）Floods.   C）Comet or meteor strikes.

    B）Continental drift.   D）Extreme temperatures.

Lecture/Talk Three

Now listen to the following recording and answer questions 23 to 25.

23. A）To lose water.   C）To increase profits.

    B）To improve color.   D）To lengthen storage life.

24. A）The quality of other ingredients is affected.

    B）High salt intake is linked to hypertension.

    C）Salt drives food prices beyond reasonable levels.

    D）Salt retains too much water in the food.

25. A）On pavements under repair.   C）In the cosmetics industry.

    B）On roads in icy weather.   D）In treating medical abnormalities.

答案与原文

答案

CET6 2014年6月

(1-8) DACB AACD   (9-15) CAB CADD   (16-25) DAAB CAD ADC

CET6 2014年12月

    (1-8) CBDC DACC   (9-15) BCDA ACB   (16-25) BDBC ADD DBA

CET6 2015年6月

    (1-8) CBAC CCBA   (9-15) ADB BADC   (16-25) ACBC DBA DCC

CET6 2015年12月

    (1-8) CADB ADCB   (9-15) DBA CBAD   (16-25) ABCB CAD CBB

原文

CET6 2014年6月

Listening Comprehension

Section A

Conversation One

M: So, Miss Parkinson, you organize fitness training and beauty treatments for working women?

W: That's right, Mr. Cruise.

M: Could you tell me how you first got the idea for the business?

W: Certainly. (1)I suppose it all started about 5 years ago. I was on holiday and had a very bad skin accident. I found that the only thing that helped the pain was massage and gentle exercise, like yoga or stretching exercises. So I used to go to therapists and classes after work.

M: Where did you work at that time?

W: In the training department of a media company.

M: I see.

W: But then I got a promotion to training manager. (2)That meant I worked longer hours and it is difficult to get to classes. I asked some of my teachers if they would come to my house instead. And most of them agreed. (3)It was more expensive but I thought it was worth it. Lots of my friends loved the idea, too. (3)So I recommended people to them. That's when I began to realize that maybe I could make a business out of it.

M: (3) Did you give up your job then?

W: (3) No, not immediately. The idea was too scary. I had a good job with a good salary, and starting my own business seemed a bit risky. (3)So I just did it as a hobby really.

M: So why did you leave your job in the end?

W: (4)Well, the decision was made for me really. My company decided to relocate to a different town. They offered me the choice of relocating with them or quite a large sum of money if I preferred to leave. I know an opportunity when I see it. So I took the money!

M: Good for you.

Questions 1 to 4 are based on the conversation you have just heard.

1. When did Miss Parkinson become interested in her own business?

2. Why did she ask her teachers to teach her at home?

3. Which of the following is NOT true according to the conversation?

4. Why did she finally leave her job?

Conversation Two

W: Well, before we decide we're going to live in Enderby, we really ought to have a look at the schools.(5)We want the children to have a good secondary education, so we'd better see what's available.

M: They gave me some information at the district office and I took notes. It appears there are five secondary schools in Enderby, three state schools and two private.

W: I don't know if we want private schools, do we?

M: I don't think so, but we'll look at them anyway. There are Saint Mary's. That's a catholic school for girls. And Carlton Abbey. That's a very old boys' boarding school, founded in 1672.

W: Are all the state schools co-educational?

M: Yes, it seems so.

W: I think little Keith is very good with his hands.(6)We're to send him to a school with good vocational training—carpentry, electronics, that sort of thing.

M: In that case, we are best off at Enderby Comprehensive. I gather they have excellent workshops and instructors. But it says here that Donwell also has good facilities. Enderby High has a few, but they are mostly academic. No vocational training at all at Carlton Abbey or Saint Mary's.

W: What are the schools like academically? How many children go on to university every year?

M: Well, Enderby High is very good. (7)And Carton Abbey even better. 70% percent of their pupils go on to university. Donwell isn't so good,only 8%. And Enderby Comprehensive and Saint Mary's not much more, about 10%.

W: Well, it seems like there is a broad selection of schools.(8)But we have to find out more than statistics before we can decide.

Questions 5 to 8 are based on the conversation you have just heard.

5. What do the speakers want their children to have?

6. What do the speakers say about little Keith?

7. What school has the highest percentage of pupils who go on to university?

8. What are the speakers going to do next?

Section B

Passage One

Good morning, ladies and gentlemen! As instructed in our previous meeting, the subcommittee on building development has now drawn up a brief to submit to the firm's architect. In short, the building would consist of two floors. (9)There would be a storage area in the basement to be used by the research center as well as by other departments. We are, as you know, short of storage base, so the availability of a large basement would be a considerable advantage. The ground floor would be occupied by laboratories. Altogether there would be six labs. In addition, there would be six offices for the technicians, plus a general secretarial office and a reception area. (10)The first floor would be occupied by the offices of Research and Development staff. There would be a suite of offices for the Research and Development director as well as a general office for secretarial staff. It's proposed to have a staff room with a small kitchen. This would serve both floors. There would also be a library for research documents and reference material. In addition, there would be a resource room in which audio visual equipment and other equipment of that sort could be stored. Finally, there would be a seminar room with closed circuit television. This room would also be used to present displays and demonstrations to visitors to the center. (11)The building would be of brick construction so as to conform to the general style of construction on the site. There would be a pitched roof. Wall and ceiling spaces would be insulated to conform to new building regulations.

Questions 9 to 11 are based on the passage you have just heard.

9. What is said about the planned basement of the new building?

10. Where would be the Research and Development director's office?

11. Why would the building be of brick construction?

Passage Two

Huang Yi works for a company that sells financial software to small and medium-size businesses.(12)His job is to show customers how to use the new software. He spends two weeks with each client, demonstrating the features and functions of the software. The first few months in the job were difficult. He often left the client feeling that even after two weeks, he hadn't been able to show the employees everything they needed to know. It's not that they weren't interested; they obviously appreciated his instruction and showed a desire to learn. (13)Huang couldn't figure it out that the software was difficult for them to understand, or if he was not doing a good job of teaching. During the next few months, Huang started to see some patterns. He would get to a new client site and spend the first week going over the software with the employees. He usually did this in shifts, with different groups of employees listening to his lecture. (14)Then he would spend the next week installing the program and helping individuals troubleshoot. Huang realized that during the week of troubleshooting and answering questions, he ended up addressing the same issues over and over. He was annoyed, because most of the individuals with whom he worked seem to have retained very little information from the first week. They asked very basic questions and often needed prompting from beginning to end. At first, he wondered if these people were just a little slow, (15)but then he began to get the distinct feeling that part of the problem might be his style of presenting information.

Questions 12 to 15 are based on the passage you have just heard.

12. What does Huang Yi do in his company?

13. What did Huang Yi think of his work?

14. What did Huang Yi do in addition to lecturing?

15. What did Huang Yi realize in the end?

Section C

Lecture/Talk One

This lecture will concentrate on Pop Art in the United States.(16)Pop artists were inspired by mass-produced visual media, such as television, magazines, comic books, billboards, and the design of common household objects, and used these things as the starting point for their art.

Pop Art differed from earlier art movements. To understand Pop Art, it is helpful to know a little bit about the artistic movement that immediately preceded it. This movement was called Abstract Expressionism. Jackson Pollock is an example of an Abstract Expressionist. If we look at Pollock's painting entitled *Autumn Rhythm*, we see a dense field of overlapping lines that swirl and move all over the surface of the canvas.

This painting refers to the process of making the painting more than it refers to anything in the actual world. Pollock believed that his intuitive approach to making paintings could show his inner self. He said, "Painting is a state of being…and self discovery. Every good artist paints what he is."

(17)Abstract Expressionism was a highly personal art. It reflected the internal struggles of the individual artists. Pop Artists were not at all interested in this internal search. Instead, Pop Artists believed that art should have a more direct relationship to things in their world.

The economic growth that began in the United States after World War Ⅱ gained speed in the 1960s. At the same time, television became a primary source of information and entertainment for the American people. In the late 1940s, about 10 thousand Americans owned televisions; by 1957 over 40 million Americans owned them.

Artists of the 1940s and early 1950s used painting and sculpture to understand their own personal states of being.By comparison, the Pop Artists responded to the intense visual stimulation that the growing consumer culture created.

(18)Robert Rauschenberg was one of the first Pop artists. He wanted to move art away from the personalities of the individual artists and direct it towards the world. The intuitive swirling forms of a Pollock painting said nothing to Rauschenberg about the rapidly changing world that he was experiencing.

By the late 1950s, Robert Rauschenberg was using everyday objects, which he found on the street, as the material for his art. He wanted to have his art reflect the world he lived in.

Rauschenberg didn't try to impose a unified symbolic meaning on his collection of materials. Instead he wanted the work to reflect the randomness of the things you might see if you were to walk around a densely populated area.

By the early 1960s Robert Rauschenberg was concentrating less on the objects and more on the images he found. He was fascinated by how a single photograph could be distributed through a magazine or newspaper across the country virtually immediately. He thought that these printed photographs could comment on the speed at which information was being given to people living in the TV age.

Rauschenberg's use of found objects and images from everyday life was innovative and it set the stage for further development in Pop Art.

Pop artists were interested in visual communication (19)because they believed that these images reflected the cultural values of contemporary society.

16. By which of following were Pop artists inspired?

17. Which of the following statements is true about Abstract Expressionsim?

18. What was the goal of the Pop artist Robert Rauschenberg?

19. Why were Pop artists interested in visual communication?

Lecture/Talk Two

We live in a society increasingly obsessed with material success. But is such success open to all? Do we all have the potential to be millionaires? And can success be taught? What can we learn from those who do make it to the top?

Becoming a millionaire is a surprisingly haphazard affair. (20)The most certain route to riches is to start out wealthy. Over half the people in the most recent *Sunday Times* survey of the richest 200 people in the country inherited money. 25% of those who head large corporations were born into affluent families.

If you're not born wealthy, you may be able to capitalize on another advantage—good looks. "Good looks make early life easier. Teachers and other children will expect you to be kinder, cleverer, and to do better than plainer peers," explains Dr. Raymond Burr of Portsmouth University, expert on the effects of facial appearance. Being tall is also an advantage. Other qualities being equal, employers are more likely to select taller and more attractive people.However, unless you want to work with children, it can be a handicap having too pretty a baby face. You're likely to be regarded as kind, but not very efficient. You may fare better by taking to crime. Juries are far more likely to acquit you.

In a new book, *Business Elites*, Professor Cooper compares a number of successful entrepreneurs with people Cooper calls "intrapreneurs" . (21)He defines intrapreneurs as those who rise through the ranks to the top of large corporations. Cooper found major differences between the two groups. "Intrapreneurs tended to be the kids everyone thought would do well. Over half went to university. They're good organizers, and get on well with people." But the entrepreneurs often had early reputations as troublemakers. "They probably left school early, had several business disasters, and are of awkward personalities. They're also intuitive and very determined." (22)The most dramatic difference between entrepreneurs and corporation highfliers was that only 5% of Cooper's entrepreneurs had both parents present throughout childhood, compared with 91% of the intrapreneurs. In some cases, the parent had died. In others, they had been absent for long periods. "Coping with disaster early in life appears to give people vital resilience later on," suggests Cooper.

But even if you're born poor and ugly to parents who refuse to absent themselves from you, there's still plenty you can do to influence your chance of success. A range of courses and self-help manuals are available to help you forge your way to the top. "Successful people," says Breen, an organizational consultant, "are the ones who, when something doesn't work, try something else. Unsuccessful people keep on doing the same thing, only harder."

20. According to the passage, what's the most certain route to riches?

21. What's the definition of an "intrapreneur" given by Professor Cooper?

22. What's the most dramatic difference between entrepreneurs and intrapreneurs?

Lecture/Talk Three

Some people think if you are happy, you are blind to reality. But when we research it, happiness actually raises every single business and educational outcome for the brain. How did we miss this? Why do we have these societal misconceptions about happiness? Because we assumed you were average. (23) When we study people, scientists are often interested in what the average is. If we study what is merely average, we will remain merely average. Many people think happiness is genetic. That's only half the story, because the average person does not fight their genes. When we stop studying the average and begin researching positive outliers, people who are above average for a positive dimension like optimism or intelligence, a widely different picture emerges. (24) Our daily decisions and habits have a huge impact upon both our levels of happiness and success. Scientifically, happiness is a choice. It is a choice about where your brain will devote its finite resources as you process the world. If you scan for the negative first, your brain has no resources left over to see the things you are grateful for or the meaning embedded in your work. But if you scan the world for the positive, you start to reap an amazing advantage.

Now that there is research validity to these claims, the working world is starting to take notice. In January, I wrote the cover story for the *Harvard Business Review* magazine on "Happiness Leads to Profits". Based on my article called "Positive Intelligence" and my research in *The Happiness Advantage*, I outlined our researched conclusion: The single greatest advantage in the modern economy is a happy and engaged workforce. (25)A decade of research in the business world proves that happiness raises nearly every business and educational outcome: Raising sales by 37%, productivity by 31%, and accuracy on tasks by 19%, as well as a myriad of health and quality-of-life improvements. Given the unprecedented level of unhappiness at companies and the direct link between happiness and business outcomes, the question is not whether happiness should matter to companies. Given this research, it clearly should. The first question is: What can I do in my own life to reap the advantage of happiness? Training your brain to be positive at work is just liking training your muscles at the gym. Sounding simple, right? Well, think about how easy it is to make yourself go to the gym. The key with any new resolution is to make it a habit. New research on neuro-plasticity, the ability of the brain to change even as an adult, reveals that moderate actions can rewire the brain as you create "life habits."

23. When we study people, what are scientists often interested in?

24. What has a huge impact upon both our levels of happiness and success?

25. By what percentage does happiness raise sales according to a 10-year-long study?

CET6 2014年12月

Listening Comprehension

Section A

Conversation One

M: I've just finished reading a book of short stories by Hemlen Garlen called *Main Traveled Road*. I really enjoy it. Have you ever read it?

W: Yes, we were required to read it in American literature course I took last year. It's really a great book. (1) Even though it's fiction, you get a realistic picture of the hard life people had back then on American frontier. I don't think I would have survived the 19th century frontier life.

M: Me neither. Remember that story among the car roads. (2) Garlen gives a vivid description of Julie Peterson, that young Norwegian immigrant girl, who had to work on her family's farm.

W: Yeah, the story does impress me deeply.

M: Well, (2) when Julie feels exhausted, she wishes she could escape from her hard labor, but when she sees her father working in the next field, she is inspired to continue her own work. She works so hard.

W: So you can see Garlen really captures the spirit of hard work that was so typical of immigrants and pioneers who settled in the American Midwest. It's difficult to imagine that nothing seems to discourage them for long.

M: I wonder how Garlen learned so much about the Midwest. Wasn't he from Boston?

W: Yes, he lived in Boston. (3) In fact, he studied and taught in Boston School of Oritory, but I think he was born in Lawcarbinlen, Wisconsin. He did grow up in Midwest.

M: No wonder his description is so vivid. (4) I'm going to take this book back to the library now and see what other Garlen's works I can find.

W: It seems that you get really interested in Garlen and his works.

M: Yeah. (4) Would you like to go to the library with me?

W: Yes, let's go.

Questions 1 to 4 are based on the conversation you have just heard.

1. What does the woman learn from *Main Traveled Road*?

2. What do we learn about Julie Peterson from the conversation?

3. Why did the writer Hemlen Garlen learn so much about the Midwest?

4. What's the man going to do after the conversation?

Conversation Two

M: Ah, how do you do, Ms.Winsmore?

W: How do you do?

M: Do sit down.

W: Thank you.

M: I am glad you're interested in our job. Now, let me explain it. We plan to increase our advertising considerably. At present, an advertising agency handles our account, (5) but we haven't been too pleased with the results lately. We may give our account to another agency.

W: What would my work entail?

M: You'd be responsible to me for all advertising, and (6) to Mr.Grant for public relations. You'd brief the agency, whoever it is, on the kind of advertising campaign we want. You'd also be responsible for getting our leaflets, brochures and catalogs designed.

W: I presume you advertise in the national press as well as the trade press.

M: Yes, we do.

W: Have you thought about advertising on television?

M: We don't think it is a suitable medium for us, and it is much too expensive.

W: I can just imagine a scene of a typist sitting on an old-fashioned typing chair, her back aching, exhausted. Then we show her in one of your chairs, her back properly supported, feeling full of energy, typing twice as quickly.

M: Before you get carried away with your little scene, Ms.Winsmore, I regret to have to tell you again that we are not planning to go into television.

W: That's a shame! (7) I've been doing a lot of television work lately and it interests me enormously.

M: (8) Then I really don't think that this is quite the right job for you here, Ms.Winsmore.

Questions 5 to 8 are based on the conversation you have just heard.

5. What does the man think of their present advertising agency?

6. What would the woman be responsible for to Mr.Grant?

7. What is the woman most interested in doing?

8. What does the man think of the woman applicant?

228

Section B

Passage One

Many foreign students are attracted not only to the academic programs at a particular U.S. college, but also to the larger community, which affords the chance to soak up the surrounding culture. (9) Few foreign universities put much emphasis on the cozy communal life that characterizes American campuses, from clubs and sports teams to student publications and drama societies. "The campus and the American university have become identical in people's minds," says Brown University president Vartan Gregorian. "(10) In America, it is assumed that a student's daily life is as important as his learning experience."

Foreign students also come in search of choices. (11) America's menu of options— research universities, state institutions, private liberal-arts schools, community colleges, religious institutions, military academies—is unrivaled. "In Europe," says history professor Jonathan Steinberg, who has taught at both Harvard and Cambridge, "there is one system, and that is it." While students overseas usually must demonstrate expertise in a specific field, whether law or philosophy or chemistry, most American universities insist that students sample natural and social sciences, languages and literature, before choosing a field of concentration.

Such opposing philosophies grow out of different traditions and power structures. (12) In Europe and Japan, universities are answerable only to a ministry of education, which sets academic standards and distributes money.

While centralization ensures that all students are equipped with roughly the same resources and perform roughly at the same level, it also discourages experimentation. "When they make mistakes, they make big ones," says Robert Rosenzweig, president of the Association of American Universities. "They set a system in wrong directions, and it's like steering a supertanker."

Questions 9 to 12 are based on the passage you've just heard.

9. What does the speaker say characterizes American campuses?

10. What does Brown University president Vartan Gregorian say about students' daily life?

11. In what way is the United States unrivaled according to the speaker?

12. What does the speaker say about universities in Europe and Japan?

Passage Two

Hello, ladies and gentlemen, welcome aboard your Sea-link ferry from Folkestone to Boulogne and wish you a pleasant trip with us. (13) We are due to leave Folkestone in about five minutes, and a journey to Boulogne will take approximately two hours. We are getting good reports of the weather in the Channel and in France, so we should have a calm crossing. Sun and temperatures of 30℃ are reported on the French coast. For your convenience on the journey, we'd like to point out that there are a number of facilities available on board. (14) There's a snack bar serving sandwiches and hot and cold refreshments situated in the front of A deck. There is also a restaurant serving hot meals situated on B deck. If you need to change money or cash travelers' checks, we have a bank on board. You can find a bank on C deck between the ship's office and the duty free shop. Toilets are situated on B deck at the rear of the ship and on A deck next to the snack bar. For the children, there's a games room on C deck next to the duty free shop. Here, children can find a variety of electronic games. (15) Passengers are reminded that the lounge on B deck is for the sole use of passengers traveling with cars and that there is another lounge on C deck at the front of the ship for passengers traveling without cars. Finally, ladies and gentlemen, we'd like to wish you a pleasant journey and hope that you'll travel with us again in the near future.

Questions 13 to 15 are based on the passage you've just heard.

13. What does the speaker say about the Sea-link ferry?

14. Where is the snack bar situated?

15. What does the speaker say about the lounge on B deck?

Section C

Lecture/Talk One

With thousands of people traveling everyday as a part of their jobs, there is a great concern about the effect of jetlag on business travelers. In the world of international business, many men and women have trouble performing their jobs (16)because they feel tired and sick from all their traveling.

Business people are not the only professionals who suffer from jetlag. Professional sports players also find that jetlag affects their performance. I have recently read a health report and it looks at the problem of jetlag in professional baseball. You see, researchers have wondered about how a jetlag affects the job performance of people who travel for a living. (17)The problem is that it is very difficult to measure exactly how jetlag affects most travelers, how we can measure the performance of, say, an executive who travels to another country to make a business deal. This is where the idea of looking at baseball comes in. So, by looking at whether baseball teams win or lose games, researchers believe that we can see how jetlag affects performance in sports, business, and other jobs.

In the study, doctors looked at baseball records from 2001 to 2004. (18)They studied the performance of 19 teams from the eastern and pacific time zones. Looking at the results of the 2 games immediately after a team traveled from one coast to the other, the study shows that changing time zones may hurt the performance of west coast baseball teams traveling east for a game, but not the east coast teams traveling west. The reason, the researchers think, is that people traveling east suffer more from the symptoms of a jetlag.

An example of this effect can be seen in the best of the 7 big championship series played in 2003 between the San Francisco Giants and the Atlanta Braves. The games are played in the home cities of each team. So, in 2003, the Atlanta Braves and San Francisco Giants played the first 2 games in Atlanta, the next 3 games in San Francisco, and the last 2 games in Atlanta. In this contest, Atlanta won 4 of the 7 games, and was the winner of the series. Researchers believe that San Francisco Giants lost because they played more games away from home and therefore, had more jetlag.

We know from past studies that the symptoms of a jetlag are stronger when a person travels east. This is because when we travel east, our day becomes shorter, and a shorter day is more difficult to adjust to. So the players from San Francisco were at a disadvantage when they traveled east for a game in Atlanta.(19)The researchers think that the San Francisco team had more of the symptoms caused by jetlag problems such as headaches, tiredness and difficulty in thinking clearly. All of these symptoms could result in poor performance by baseball players.

16. How do business people often feel from all their traveling?

17. According to the report, why did researchers study jetlag in baseball?

18. Where are these teams in the study from?

19. Which of the following is NOT mentioned as a symptom of jetlag?

Lecture/Talk Two

Why do manufacturers of gadgets and machines make them so complicated? And why do people want to buy such complicated things? (20) Coming back to your point that we seem to want to buy these things, the evidence is they're designed to confuse us so that we appear to want them. That's a fairly subtle point. Let's say there's a tourist company. You want to go to Costa Del Sol and some hotel. You want a swimming pool. You want to be near a beach, whatever. Whatever your criteria are. You've got kids and you want children's facilities, so on...If you look in any travel brochure about the hotels and resorts, they tell you different things about each hotel. And pretty soon you discover you don't know how to make a decision, and you make a random decision. That's deliberate. Because if you choose the best hotel, everybody would go to that hotel. So what the travel companies do is they tell you this hotel's got a swimming pool. This hotel's got, you know, access to the beach. This hotel's got children's facilities, and so on. (21) Basically, the point of that is to spread the customers out amongst different hotels that they have on offer.

That sort of thing goes on with video recorders. The purpose isn't to give you features you want. The purpose is to get you into the shop, confuse you so that you can be sold a product on the basis that it is a pound cheaper than a competitor's, or that it is made by a brand name that rings a bell, or that, you know, it is at the front of the shop. And those are all things they know how to control. (20) So as you look at it, you know why they're making confusing gadgets. Well, because they sell. And they sell, because confusing people is an easy way of controlling them. I once hoped that safety critical systems would be a way of improving things. We can all laugh about a video recorder, you know, at worst, you record the wrong program or whatever. You know, it's just irritating, and we certainly laugh about it. But that sort of gadget is also available in, for instance, airplane cockpits. Have you seen an airplane cockpit? You know, they're covered in knobs, buttons and things. Or a nuclear power station. You name it. In a safety critical environment, they have gone overboard in gadgets that are rather similar to video recorders. And it's then no longer a joke. It's deadly serious. I've worked with some of these interfaces, and in airplanes. (22)And although it doesn't help me to say this, my cynical view is they're designed not to be easy to use. They are designed so that when the plane crashes, the manufacturers can say it was the pilot's fault. If the user's killed himself, so much easier to blame the user himself. Then it's not the machine's problem.

20. According to the speaker, why are the gadgets and machines made so complicated?

21. Why do travel companies tell you different things about different hotels?

22. Why are the safety critical systems made so complicated, according to the speaker?

Lecture/Talk Three

Today I'm going to talk about where to look for a job in Australia. (23) Your method of job hunting obviously depends on your circumstances, experience and qualifications, and the sort of job you're seeking.

Firstly, you may obtain copies of Australian daily newspapers, all of which contain "positions vacant" sections, including job advertisements dedicated to particular industries or professions on certain days. Most local and national newspapers are available in the reading rooms of local libraries in Australia, so you don't usually need to buy them. Jobs are also advertised in industry and trade newspapers and magazines. Australian newspapers are available in some countries from international news agencies, as well as in Australian embassies and consulates.

(24) By networking, you may get together with like-minded people to discuss business, and it is a popular way of making business and professional contacts in Australia. It can be particularly successful for executives, managers and professionals when job hunting.

You may apply to international and national recruiting agencies acting for Australian companies. Agencies mainly recruit executives and key managerial and technical staff, and some have offices overseas, for example, in the UK.

You may place an advertisement in the "situations wanted" section of a national newspaper in Australia or a local newspaper in the area where you wish to work. If you're a member of a recognized profession or trade, you could place an advertisement in a newspaper or magazine dedicated to your profession or a particular industry.

One effective way is to ask acquaintances, friends and relatives working in Australia whether they know of an employer looking for someone with your experience and qualifications. (25) If you're already in Australia, contact or join expatriate groups, professional organizations, social clubs and societies, particularly local ones.

The most effective way, according to my experience, is to apply in person to Australia companies. Always obtain a job offer in writing and a contract; steer clear of an employer who won't provide them. An official job entitles you to accident insurance, official protection from exploitation, redundancy payments, state pension, superannuation and unemployment benefit, among other things. Your best chance of obtaining some jobs (particularly temporary jobs) in Australia is to apply in person, when success is often simply a matter of being in the right place at the right time. When looking for a job for which no special qualifications or experience are required, it isn't necessarily what you know, but who you know.

Many companies don't advertise but rely on attracting workers by word of mouth and their own vacancy boards. Always leave your name and address with a prospective employer and a telephone number where you can be contacted, particularly if a job may become vacant at short notice. Advertise the fact that you're looking for a job with acquaintances, friends and relatives, and anyone you come into contact with who may be able to help.

23. Which of the following is NOT the factor related to a successful job hunting?

24. Which of the following methods is particularly successful for executives and professionals in job hunting?

25. Which of the following organizations is NOT mentioned as helpful for a job hunting in the talk?

CET6 2015年6月

Listening Comprehension

Section A

Conversation One

W: Jack, sit down and listen. This is important. We'll have to tackle the problems of exporting step by step. And the first move is to get an up-to-date picture of where we stand now.

M: Why don't we just concentrate on expanding here at home?

W: Of course, we should hold on to our position here. But you must admit the market here is limited.

M: (2) Yes, but it's safe. The government keeps out foreigners with import controls. So I must admit I feel sure we could hold our own against foreign bikes.

W: I agree. (1) That's why I am suggesting exporting, because I feel we can compete with the best of them.

M: What you are really saying is that we'd make more profit by selling bikes abroad, where we have a cost advantage and can charge higher prices.

W: Exactly.

M: (3) But, wait a minute. Packaging, shipping, financing, etc. will push up our cost and we could end up no better off, maybe worse off.

W: OK. Now there are extra costs involved, but if we do it right, they can be built into the price of the bike and we can still be competitive.

M: How sure are you about our chances of success in the foreign market?

W: Well, that's the sticky one. (4) It's going to need a lot of research. I'm hoping to get your help. Well, come on, Jack. Is it worth it, or not?

M: There will be a lot of problems.

W: Nothing we can't handle.

M: Um...I'm not that hopeful. (4) But, yes, I think we should go ahead with a feasibility study.

W: Marvelous, Jack. I was hoping you would be on my side.

Questions 1 to 4 are based on the conversation you have just heard.

1. What does the woman intend to do?
2. Why does the man think it's safe to focus on the home market?
3. What is the man's concern about selling bikes abroad?
4. What do the speakers agree to do?

Conversation Two

W: What are you reading, Bill?

M: It's this week's *New Scientist*, why?

W: I was just wondering. It looks interesting. (7)But I've never actually read it myself. It's for real scientists—or can ordinary people like me understand it?

M: Oh, it's for anyone really. It usually has articles and stories about current affairs, about science as well as papers about new development and research. I am reading about a new telephone that allows you to see the person you are speaking to as well as hear him.

W: Oh. I've heard about it. Is it on the market yet? Can I buy one?

M: (5) No, not this one. But the company has made other models to try out on business. This one is special because of its color, and the image is moving.

W: (7) Oh, that's interesting.

M: You see the first video phones—that's what they called—were made in Japan. But they can only show a still black-and-white image. So this video phone is much better than that. Mind you I'm not sure I want one. Would you?

W: (6) Well, no. I don't think I would. I bet it costs a lot of money. Does it say how much it costs?

M: (5) Yes, the early black-and-white ones cost several hundred pounds, but the one the story is about costs several thousand pounds.

W: Hmm. (6) Why does anybody want one, do you think?

M: (6) Business organizations that need to frequently contact overseas organizations would want it. It's like a face-to-face conversation. So maybe a lot of overseas travel can be avoided.

W: (7) Yes, I suppose so.

Question 5 to 8 are based on the conversation you have just heard.

5. Which of the following details is not true about the new device?

6. Why didn't Bill want one of them?

7. Which of the following statements is INCORRECT about the woman?

8. What is the conversation mainly about?

Section B

Passage One

Karen Smith is a buyer for a department store in New York. Department store buyers purchase the goods that their stores sell. (9) They not only have to know what is fashionable at the moment, but also have to guess what will become fashionable next season or next year.

Most buyers work for just one department in a store, but the goods that Karen finds may be displayed and sold in several different sections of the store. (10) Her job involves buying handicrafts from all over the world.

Last year, she made a trip to Morocco, and returned with rugs, pots, dishes, and pans. The year before, she visited Mexico, and brought back hand-made table cloths, mirrors with frames of tin, and paper flowers. The paper flowers are bright and colorful, so they were used to decorate the whole store. This year, Karen is traveling in Malaysia, Thailand, and Indonesia. Many of the countries that Karen visits have government offices that promote handicrafts. They officials are glad to cooperate with her, by showing her the products that are available.

Karen especially likes to visit markets in small towns and villages whenever she can arrange for it. She's always looking for interesting and unusual items. (11) Karen thinks she has the best job she could have found. She loves all the traveling that she has to do, because she often visits markets and small out-of-the-way places. She sees much more of the country she visits than an ordinary tourist would. As soon as she gets back to New York from one trip, Karen begins to plan another.

Questions 9 to 11 are based on the passage you have just heard.

9. What is said to make a good department store buyer?

10. What does Karen's job involve?

11. Why does Karen think she has got the best job?

Passage Two

(12) Mark felt that it was time for him to take part in his community, so he went to the neighborhood meeting after work. (13) The area city council woman was leading a discussion about how the quality of life was on the decline. The neighborhood faced many problems. Mark looked at the charts taped to the walls. There were charts for parking problems, crime, and for

problems in vacant buildings. Mark read from the charts, "Police patrols cut back, illegal parking up 20%". People were supposed to suggest solutions to the council woman. It was too much for Mark. (14) "The problems are too big", he thought. He turned to the man next to him and said, "I think this is a waste of my time. Nothing I can do would make a difference here."

As he neared the bus stop on his way home, Mark saw a woman carrying a grocery bag, and a baby. As Mark got closer, her other child, a little boy, suddenly darted into the street. The woman tried to reach for him, but as she moved, her bag shifted, and groceries started to fall out. Mark ran to take the boy's arm and led him back to his mother. "You gotta stay with mom," he said. Then he picked up the stray groceries while and the woman smiled in relief. "Thanks," she said, "You've got great timing." "Just being neighborly." Mark said. As he rode home, he glanced at the poster near his seat in the bus. (15) Small acts of kindness add up. Mark smiled and thought, "Maybe that's a good place to start."

Questions 12 to 15 are based on the passage you have just heard.

12. What did Mark think he should start doing?

13. What was being discussed when Mark arrived at the neighborhood meeting?

14. What did mark think of the community's problems?

15. Why did Mark smile on his ride home?

Section C

Lecture/Talk One

Good morning, everyone. I'm going to give a brief summary of the transition from export marketing to global marketing. Basically, there are three phases in this transition. These are: export marketing, international marketing, and global marketing.

Let's describe the first phase, which is export marketing. Export marketing has four main characteristics. Firstly, with export marketing there is home-based production and home-based management. Secondly, there is direct selling to the export markets. Next, (16) it's common to use agents and distributors. Finally, it's possible that there are sales centers in overseas markets. Overall, the investment costs are low with export marketing because almost everything, especially production and management, is still centered on the home base.

Now let's look at the second phase, international marketing. Here I also identify four main characteristics. (17) The first is that production has expanded to overseas markets. This is very important. Next, there is local management. This means you have local cost centers, individually responsible for making a profit. Finally, there is much more local employment of staff and management. (19) Altogether, this means there is more investment, so investment with international marketing is high.

Now we come to the third phase, which is global marketing, with at least four main characteristics.(18) Most important is that the brand name, or brand names, are international, like IBM or Coca-Cola. Secondly, the business is established in all major world markets. This means, and this is the third point, that the business has a global identity. Next, the business has cost centers in all major markets. The fourth and final point is that the production is often complex, with parts made and transported all over the world between various centers. An example here is a laptop, where perhaps the chips, the circuit board, the case, the screen, the packaging, the documentation, are all made in different locations around the world. Maybe Taiwan, Hong Kong, Singapore, Japan,

Brazil and Italy. (19) The result is that the global marketing phase involves very high levels of investment.

This is a good summary of the stages between export marketing and global marketing. Does anyone have any questions or need clarification on any point?

16. Which of the following is true with the phase of export marketing?

17. What do we know about the phase of international marketing?

18. What is the most important characteristic of global marketing?

19. Which of the following involves the highest levels of investment among all these phases?

Lecture/Talk Two

OK.(20) Another ancient Greek philosopher we need to discuss is Aristotle—Aristotle's ethical theory. What Aristotle's ethical theory is all about is this: He's trying to show you how to be happy—what true happiness is.

Now, why is he interested in human happiness? It's not just because it's something that all people want to aim for. It's more than that. But to get there we need to first make a very important distinction. Let me introduce a couple of technical terms: Extrinsic value and intrinsic value.

To understand Aristotle's interest in happiness, you need to understand this distinction.

Some things we aim for and value, not for themselves but for what they bring about in addition to themselves. If I value something as a means to something else, then it has what we will call "extrinsic value". Other things we desire and hold to be valuable for themselves alone. If we value something not as a means to something else, but for its own sake, let us say that it has "intrinsic value".

So how does all this relate to human happiness? Well, Aristotle asks: Is there something that all human beings value...and value only intrinsically, for its own sake and only for its own sake? (21)If you could find such a thing, that would be the universal final good, or truly the ultimate purpose or goal for all human beings. Aristotle thought the answer was yes. What is it? Happiness. Everyone will agree, he argues, that happiness is the ultimate end to be valued for itself and really only for itself. For what other purpose is there in being happy? What does it yield? The attainment of happiness becomes the ultimate or highest good for Aristotle.

The next question that Aristotle raises is: what is happiness? We all want it; we all desire it; we all seek it. It's the goal we have in life. But what is it? How do we find it? Here he notes, with some frustration, people disagree.

But he does give us a couple of criteria, or features, to keep in mind as we look for what true human happiness is. True human happiness should be, as he puts it, complete. Complete in that it's all we require. Well, true human happiness...if you had that, what else do you need? Nothing.

(22) And, second, true happiness should be something that I can obtain on my own. I shouldn't have to rely on other people for it. Many people value fame and seek fame. Fame for them becomes the goal. But, according to Aristotle, this won't work either, because fame depends altogether too much on other people. I can't get it on my own, without help from other people.

In the end, Aristotle says that true happiness is the exercise of reason—a life of intellectual contemplation...of thinking. So let's see how he comes to that.

20. What is the main purpose of the lecture?

21. Why is happiness central to Aristotle's theory?

22. According to the professor, why does Aristotle think that fame cannot provide true happiness?

Lecture/Talk Three

All right, so let me close today's class with some thoughts to keep in mind while you are reading one of Ralph Waldo Emerson's best-known essays "Self-Reliance".

Knowing something about Emerson's philosophies will help you when you read "Self-Reliance". And basically, one of the main beliefs that he had was about truth. Not that it's something that we can be taught, Emerson says it's found within ourselves. It's a bit abstract but it's very into...uh...into each person believing his or her own thought, believing in yourself, the thought or conviction that's true for you.

But actually, he ties that in with a sort of "universal truth" —something that everyone knows but doesn't realize they know. Most of us are in touch with ourselves in a way, so we just aren't capable of recognizing profound truth. It takes geniuses, people like, say, Shakespeare, who're unique because when they have a glimpse of this truth, this universal truth, they pay attention to it and express it and don't just dismiss it like most people do.

So Emerson is really into each individual believing in and trusting him or herself. You'll see that he writes about, well, first, conformity. (23)He criticizes that people of his time for abandoning their own minds and their own wills for the sake of conformity and consistency. They try to fit in with the rest of the world even though it's at odds with their beliefs and their identities. Therefore, it's best to be a non-conformist—to do your own thing, not worrying about what other people think. That's an important point. He really drives this argument home throughout the essay.

Now, we already said that Emerson really emphasizes non-conformity, right? Well, he takes this a step further. Not conforming also means, uh, not conforming with yourself or your past. (24) What does that mean? Well, if you've always been a certain way or done a certain thing, but it's not working for you any more, or you're not content, Emerson says that it'd be foolish to be consistent even with our own past. "Focus on the future," he says, "That's what matters more. Inconsistency is good."

(25) He talks about a ship's voyage and this is one of the most famous bits of the essay— how the best voyage is made up of zigzag lines. Up close, it seems a little all over the place, but from farther away, the true path shows and in the end it justifies all the turns along the way. So, don't worry if you are not sure where you're headed or what your long-term goals are. Stay true to yourself and it'll make sense in the end.

23. On what basis did Emerson criticize the people of his time?

24. What does Emerson say about the past?

25. What point does the professor make when he mentions a ship's path?

CET6 2015年12月

Listening Comprehension

Section A

Conversation One

M: Right, this is the tennis club reception area. As a member, you don't have to register when you arrive. (1) But you must remember to register your guests. And you must be able to produce your membership card if a club official asks to see it.

W: How many guests can I bring with me?

M: You can bring up to 3 at any one time.

W: Hum, that's good.

M: Yes. Well, we want to attract people to our club. (2) Now, here are the changing rooms with showers and lockers for your clothes and things. Obviously, you don't have to leave your clothes in the lockers. But we strongly advise you to. It's much safer.

W: How much do the lockers cost?

M: (2) Forty cents. But you get the coin back when you take your things out. Right, and the tennis courts are round here to the left.

W: Hum. And we can play for an hour at a time?

M: (3) You can book the courts for thirty minutes or an hour. But you can carry on playing until the next players arrive.

W: Of course. What about cafe or bar?

M: Yes, we have a club room which serves food and drink behind the reception. (4) The club room is open until 11 o'clock p.m.. But all players must leave the courts by 10 o'clock p.m..

W: Hum. That seems very good. Thank you very much for showing us around.

M: Pleasure.

Questions 1 to 4 are based on the conversation you have just heard.

1. What are members of the club required to do?

2. Which of the following details about the changing rooms is NOT correct?

3. According to the club's rules, how long can members play for?

4. Which of the following details is NOT correct?

Conversation Two

W: Charles, among other things, you are regarded as one of the America's great masters of the blues. A musical idiom does essentially about loss, particularly the loss of romantic love. Why does love die?

M: (5) People often get into love affairs because they have unrealistic expectations about somebody. Then when the person doesn't turn out to be who they thought he or she was, they start thinking maybe I can change him or her. That kind of thinking is a mistake. Because when the dust settles, people are going to be pretty much what they are. It's a rare thing for anybody to be able to change who they really are. This creates a lot of problems.

W: At 62, you continue to spend a large percentage of your life touring. What appeals to you about life on the road?

M: Music, (6) I don't especially love life on the road, but I figure if you are lucky enough to be able to do what you truly love doing, you've got the ultimate in life.

W: What's the most widely-held misconception about the life of a famous musician?

M: (7) People think it's all glamour. Actually we have the same troubles they do. Playing music doesn't mean life treats you any better.

W: How do you feel about being recognized everywhere you go?

M: You'd think I'd be used to it by now. (8) But I still find it fascinating. You go to a little town in Japan, where nobody speaks English, yet they know you on side and they all know your music. I'm still amazed by the love people express for me and by music.

Questions 5 to 8 are based on the conversation you have just heard.

5. What does the man say about most people when they get into love affairs?

6. What does the man say about himself as a singer on the road most of his life?

7. What do most people think of the life of a famous musician?

8. How does the man feel whenever he is recognized by his fans?

Section B

Passage One

In early 1994, when Mark Andreessen was just 23 years old, he arrived in Silicon Valley with an idea that would change the world. As a student at the University of Illinois, (9) he and his friends had developed a program called Mosaic, which allowed people to share information on the worldwide web.

Before Mosaic, the web had been used mainly by scientists and other technical people, who were happy just to send and receive text. But with Mosaic, Andreessen and his friends had developed a program, which could send images over the web as well. Mosaic was an overnight success. It was put on the university's network at the beginning of 1993. And by the end of the year, it had over a million users. Soon after, Andreessen went to seek his fortune in Silicon Valley. (10) Once he got there, he started to have meetings with a man called Jim Clark, who was one of the Valley's most famous entrepreneurs.

In 1994, nobody was making any real money from the Internet, which was still very slow and hard to use. But Andreessen had seen an opportunity that would make him and Clark rich within two years. He suggested they should create a new computer program that would do the same job as Mosaic but would be much easier to use. Clark listened carefully to Andreessen, whose ideas and enthusiasm impressed him greatly. (11) Eventually, Clark agreed to invest three million dollars of his own money in the project, and to raise an extra fifteen million from venture capitalists, who were always keen to listen to Clark's new ideas.

Questions 9 to 11 are based on the passage you have just heard.

9. What do we learn about Mosaic?

10. What did Andreessen do upon arriving in Silicon Valley?

11. Why were venture capitalists willing to join in Clark's investment?

Passage Two

Advertising informs consumers about the existence and benefits of products and services and attempts to persuade them to buy them. (12) The best form of advertising is probably word-of-mouth advertising which occurs when people tell their friends about the benefits of products or services that they have purchased.

Yet virtually no providers of goods or services rely on this alone, but use paid advertising instead. (13) Indeed many organizations also use institutional or prestige advertising which is designed to build up their reputation rather than to sell particular products. Although large companies could easily set up their own advertising departments, write their own advertisements and buy media space themselves, (14) they tend to use the services of large advertising agencies. These are likely to have more resources and more knowledge about all aspects of advertising and advertising media than a single company. It is also easier for a dissatisfied company to give its account to another agency than it would be to fire its own advertising staff. The client company generally gives the advertising agency an agreed budget, a statement of the objectives of the advertising campaign known as a brief and an overall advertising strategy concerning the message to be communicated to the target customers. The agency creates advertisements and develops a media plan, specifying which media will be used and in which proportions. (15) Agencies often produce alternative ads or commercials that pretested in newspapers, television stations etc. in different parts of the country,before a final choice is made prior to a national campaign.

Questions 12 to 15 are based on the passage you have just heard.

12. What is probably the best form of advertising according to the speaker?

13. What does the speaker say is the purpose of many organizations using prestige advertising?

14. How do large companies generally handle their advertising?

15. What would advertising agencies often do before a national campaign?

Section C

Lecture/Talk One

I'm going to speak about two of the major developmental tasks of young adulthood, and by developmental tasks I mean life changes that a person must accomplish as he or she grows and develops. The young adult is in his or her early to mid-twenties, and, at least in Western culture, this is the time for the achievement of independence from their parents.(16) Ideally, what's considered *optimal* (最佳的) at this point is for the young adult to be capable of supporting him/herself completely, well, that includes financially, emotionally and socially.

(17) OK, so we could say that one of the major tasks for young adults is the development of a new and different type of relationship with parents. The old relationship, in which the child related to his parents in a hierarchical way, that is, solely as parents, well, this relationship changes in the young adult years, and a new kind of relationship is established, one based on mutual adulthood. This is the sort of culmination of a long process of separation that starts in early childhood, and ideally in young adulthood the child physically separates and goes his or her own way in the world. Uh, interestingly enough, this life change seems to be happening later in life, in the later part of the twentieth century, partly because it depends on the child's ability to become financially independent, and in today's world, there is so much competition for jobs. (18) Uh, the cost of living continues to rise. Well, the result is that it's often very difficult for young adults to survive without financial assistance from their parents, and so sometimes that means that they simply stay at home and live with their parents well into their twenties.

So, as I said, it can be difficult for young-adult children to establish financial independence from their parents. And then, establishing emotional independence can also be a difficult process, and not all children separate from their parents with equal success. Some children may never be successful at this. They may be forever in the role of child, and parent forever in the role of parent.

Of course, separation is the natural thing for adult children to do at this point, to leave their parents and start their own lives. But, even though it's natural, this is still a crisis point in a family. When a child leaves, some families don't handle it well. (19) Change is a frightening thing for many people, but there is no escaping it.

Uh, we all have to learn how to change throughout our lives.

16. Ideally, what should a person achieve in one's mid 20s?

17. What is one of the major developmental tasks for young adults?

18. What account in part for the fact that this life change is happening later in young adults?

19. Which can we conclude from this talk?

Lecture/Talk Two

When I tell people what my particular branch of science is, I often get funny looks. In a way, I understand because *astrobiology* (占星生物学) is the study of life on other planets. Well, obviously, life has not been discovered on other planets, which would appear to make astrobiology a science without a subject! However, everything we know about life on our own planet suggests we have to try to understand if there are any universal requirements for life to evolve, as well as the processes involved in evolution. Consequently, scientists are deeply interested in the beginnings of life on Earth. Once we know more about what happened on home ground, as it were, we will be in a better position to understand any life forms we may once find on other planets.

When most people think of *extra-terrestrial* (外星球的) life, they conjure up images of so-called "higher" life forms: They imagine *humanoid* (有人的特点的)creatures or bizarre and probably dangerous animals of some kind. But if we consider the whole history of life on Earth, a very different picture emerges. For billions of years the only forms of life on the planet were organisms consisting of single cells.(20) It was only about 550 million years ago, during the geological period we call the *Cambrian* (寒武纪), that the seas suddenly became filled with a whole array of multi-cellular life.

So how do humans fit into this time frame? Well, human-like creature first appear in the fossil record about five or so million years ago: In geological terms, this is just a blink of an eye compared to the long history of life on Earth. (21) And *Homo sapiens*(智人), our own species, has only been around for about 130,000 years. The point is if we do find life on other planets, it will almost certainly be relatively simple, of the sort that populated the Earth for most of its existence so far.

And of course, we must be prepared for these life forms to look very different from life on Earth. (22) We must not forget that many modern life forms came about as a result of chance, their fate shaped by floods, continental drift and comet or meteor strikes. It is interesting to reflect that if a giant asteroid had not hit the Earth and wiped out the dinosaurs, they might still be ruling the planet and we might never have evolved.

20. During the period of the Cambrian, with what life forms did the seas suddenly become filled?

21. For how long has Homo sapiens, our own species, been existing on Earth?

22. Many modern life forms came about as a result of a series of chance factors. Which of the following is NOT one of these factors mentioned in the talk?

Lecture/Talk Three

We tend to take salt for granted, but from a historical perspective, it is hard to imagine how our civilization could have developed without it. The use of salt to preserve food allowed people to settle down; they no longer needed to go hunting for food every day. Soon salt came to be worth literally its weight in gold, which seems curious when salt we put on our table is so cheap.

Actually, most of the salt in the modern western diet doesn't come from a salt cellar: It is added to a very wide range of processed food in the factory, as can be seen from looking at the list of ingredients on the packaging, though we're seldom told just how much has been added. (23) Interestingly enough, the function of salt in the manufacture of food is not related purely to taste or preservation: The food industry likes adding salt to food because of its water retention properties, which means that a fair proportion of the weight of processed food is quite simply water.

(23) This may sound like a relatively harmless trick to increase profits, but in fact, the presence of all this salt is potentially harmful. (24) In many people, high salt intake is linked to high blood pressure, or hypertension, which in turn can cause heart attacks and strokes. Therefore, anyone suffering from hypertension should keep their salt intake low, and doctors estimate that cutting down on salt would benefit about a third of the population.

So should governments be doing more to limit salt consumption, for example by forcing food manufacturers to cut down on the salt used in processed foods? Predictably, the food companies are opposed to the idea. (25)The salt manufacturers also object, although the amount of salt used in foods accounts for less of their output than the salt used for application to roads during city spells, at least in this country.

Industry representatives point out that only those suffering from medical abnormalities would be harmed by consuming too much salt. However, that description applies to more and more of us these days, and salt may be part of the reason why.

23. Apart from for the purpose of taste or preservation, why does the food industry like to add salt to food?

24. In what way is the presence of this salt in processed foods potentially harmful to people?

25. Where is a greater amount of salt used than in processing food in this country according to the talk?